# A Guide to
# Late Anglo-Saxon England

## From Ælfred to Eadgar II

Donald Henson

Anglo-Saxon Books

First published 1998 by
Anglo-Saxon Books
Rprinted 2002 & 2013


Anglo-Saxon Books
Hereward, Black Bank Business Centre
Little Downham, Ely, Cambridgeshire CB6 2UA England


Printed and bound by
Lightning Source
Australia, England, USA

ISBN 9781898281214

# Contents

Foreword ............................................................................................7

Introduction ........................................................................................9

The Birth of a New State ....................................................................11
    The Origins of the English ............................................................11
    The Kingdom of England ..............................................................15
    The British Isles ...........................................................................16

A Description of Late Anglo-Saxon England ......................................19
    Physical Geography ......................................................................19
    Human Geography .......................................................................22
    Government and Politics ...............................................................29
    The Church in England .................................................................32
    English Society .............................................................................39
    Language and Literature ...............................................................41
    Personal Names ...........................................................................44
    Effects of the Norman Conquest ..................................................48

Sources of Evidence ...........................................................................53
    Historical Sources ........................................................................53
    Archaeology ................................................................................54
    Dating Methods and Dates ...........................................................55

Kings and Events ...............................................................................57
    Introduction ................................................................................57
    Summary of the Period 871-1074 .................................................59
    Ælfred .........................................................................................63
    Eadward I ....................................................................................68
    Æþelstan .....................................................................................73
    Eadmund I ..................................................................................76
    Eadred ........................................................................................78
    Eadwig .......................................................................................80
    Eadgar I ......................................................................................82
    Eadward II ..................................................................................86

# Kings and Events (continued)

Æþelred .................................................................. 87
Swegn .................................................................... 94
Eadmund II ........................................................... 95
Cnut ..................................................................... 97
Harold I ................................................................ 101
Harðacnut ............................................................. 103
Eadward III ........................................................... 105
Harold II ............................................................... 110
Eadgar II ............................................................... 112

# Appendices

1: The Officials of the King's Household ....................... 119
2: The Aldermen and Earls ....................................... 123
3: Bishops ............................................................. 133
4: Sheriffs ............................................................. 143
5: The Unification of England .................................... 149
6: The Danish Conquest of England ............................ 151
7: The Norman Conquest of England ........................... 153

# Family Trees

1: Simplified Family Tree of the Kings of England 871–1100
   and Their Heirs .................................................. 156
2: The Descendants of King Ælfred to 1066 .................. 157
3: The Family of Swegn of Denmark ........................... 158

# Maps

1: The Geography of England .................................... 161
2: The Shires of England .......................................... 162
3: The Church in England ......................................... 163
4: The Unification of England .................................... 164
5: The Danish Conquest 1009-1016 ............................ 165
6: The Norman Conquest 1066-1071 ........................... 166

# Bibliography

Primary Sources and Medieval Works .......................... 169
Modern Works ....................................................... 175

# Index

Index .................................................................. 187

# List of Tables

1: The Early Kingdoms of the English............................................................13
2: Early Overlords of the English..................................................................14
3: Daylight Hours on the First Day of Each Month....................................21
4: The Shires of England ...............................................................................24
5: The Major Boroughs of England...............................................................26
6: England's Bishoprics.................................................................................35
7: Monasteries................................................................................................37
8: Pronunciation of Old English Vowels .....................................................44
9: A Summary of Kings from Ælfred to Eadgar II.....................................57
10: Kings' Bynames.......................................................................................58

# Foreword

This book is the result of both frustration and obsession. The frustration comes from the near invisibility of England's early history in the popular consciousness. Ask any member of the public what they know of early medieval history and they are likely to reply that they have seen Celtic art in the shops run by *Past Times*, they have bought their children books about the Vikings and can name one date – 1066 and the Norman Conquest. Lists of England's Kings sold to tourists or to children on wooden rulers in countless museum shops all give the impression that William I of Normandy was the first King of England. People may have heard of Cnut, Ethelred the 'Unready' and Alfred the Great but most people would be totally unable to place them in history or name any of their achievements. Does this matter? I would say that it does, for two reasons. Firstly, any people should be aware of their own past and the origins of their own country. The people of England have a right to know who created England, when it was created and how. Secondly, academic scholarship has determined much about the early history of England which has yet to penetrate into the public domain. Scholarship should never be divorced from its public. Knowledge belongs to everyone and misunderstood knowledge can be harmful. How can universities recruit scholars of the future to investigate 10th century English history when the school curriculum says that medieval English history begins in 1066? The obsession of mine is for the energies of Kings, clergy, nobles and countless ordinary people who shaped the landscape and gave rise to the towns and villages in which we still live, who designed and created the glorious Winchester style of art, and who wrote in their own language so that we can read and understand styles of English that were in use over 1,000 years ago and be moved by the verse they left behind, or astonished at the power of the prose in the hands of skilled masters like Ælfred, Ælfric or Wulfstan. If this book enhances a little the knowledge of those already with some interest in the period then I will be pleased. If it stimulates a desire to know more among those for whom the period was previously unknown then I will be delighted.

The book uses three printed Old English characters that will be unfamiliar to the general reader – *æ* which can be read as *a*; *þ* and *ð* which can both be read as *th*. More detailed explanation of how to pronounce the English of the time is given in the text below. As sole author of the book, I take full responsibility for any inaccuracies or faults within it. Studying late Anglo-Saxon England has been a pastime for me for many years. However, it is not my profession and all that I have written below has depended on already published works by those whose business is the study of early medieval England. All who are interested in the period are in their debt and a list of their works is given in the bibliography.

# Introduction

When did the Kingdom of England begin and how was it formed? The academic answer to these questions is fairly straightforward (Stafford 1989, Campbell 1995). England was the creation of the royal house of Wessex, Alfred the Great and his descendants. It was created by a process of conquest and administrative unification that gave the Kings of England one of the most powerful government machines in Europe. This process belonged largely to the first half of the tenth century. Unfortunately, these academic answers are not the same as the popular answers, nor even the answers given to English schoolchildren. The date of 1066 has a mesmeric hold on popular imagination and on many writers of popular works on English history. The man or woman in the street is most likely to say that England was created by the French speaking Dukes of Normandy as a result of the conquest of 1066. A trawl of the shelves of any large bookshop will reveal many short histories of England, or of its Kings and Queens. Many begin their story in 1066, with little or no reference to earlier events (Best 1995, Fraser 1995, Horton 1995, Lobel et al 1995). Those that do begin earlier may make only passing reference to the period before 1066 before picking up the story in much greater detail with William I (Delderfield 1995, Fry 1990, Hibbert 1992). For instance, Hibbert (1992) has 14 pages covering the 616 years from 450 to 1066, with 16 pages devoted to the 88 years of Norman rule from 1066 to 1154. A rare exception is Weir (1996) who treats the Kings from Egbert of Wessex to Harold II with the same attention to detail as later Kings. Even in the field of coinage where the continuity between late Anglo-Saxon and Norman coinage is widely recognised and acknowledged, the *Standard Catalogue of English and United Kingdom Coins* begins in 1066 (Lobel et al 1995) and so cannot therefore really live up to its title. Much more disturbing is the teaching of history in England's schools. The English National Curriculum in history for 11 to 14 year-olds begins with medieval Britain. This is highly praiseworthy, except that the medieval period is deemed to begin in 1066. While it is true that a number of academic works dealing with medieval England begin in 1066, many do not and the continuity of English history across the 1066 barrier is now accepted. To divorce medieval England from its origins before 1066 is unsound and even perverse. Any university history department would surely treat this with derision (Hinton 1990, Loyn 1991). Finally, a relatively recent development is to term the period of the $9^{th}$ to $11^{th}$ centuries the Viking Age (e.g. Richards 1991). Although the Viking invasions and settlement were important, it is worth stressing that the Kingdom of that period was an English state, using English cultural norms, language and ethnic identity based on a shared sense of history reaching back to Bede and beyond. Hence, I prefer to use the term Late Anglo-Saxon as more accurate, if less popularly appealing (the Vikings, like the Normans, seem to have more 'advertising potential' than the Anglo-Saxons, an interesting topic in itself).

Why should this unwillingness to include the Anglo-Saxon kingdom of England within the nation's popular history exist? Is it due to there being poor sources compared with later periods? Sources for English history are indeed commoner for later periods, but the explosion in quantity of trustworthy source material really begins in the mid 12$^{th}$ century, not in 1066. Sources for the period are certainly adequate for reconstructing the history of the time in some detail. Perhaps, one reason is that 1066 is such an obvious <u>date</u>. It was a dramatic year of momentous events, with unique artefacts (the Bayeux Tapestry) and a readily understandable story. A <u>process</u> of unification cannot compare with such dramatic potential. However, the events of the 200 years before 1066 are crucial to our understanding of medieval England, and they have enough drama to satisfy any inquisitive mind.

This book is not a comprehensive history of the period; there are a number of those already (e.g. Stafford 1989, Loyn 1991). Nor is it written for the academic. It is for those with little specialist knowledge of the period and who may be curious about England's early history. As such, the Norse rulers of York and East Anglia lie outside its remit, although they were contemporary with the earlier Kings of England. Inevitably, it is a summary, bringing together information that would otherwise have to be laboriously sought in a major academic reference library, or in popular textbooks of varying reliability. The introductory sections are meant only to give the broad outlines of various aspects of the period. Greater detail can be had by using the references given in the bibliography. They set the scene for the events outlined under each reign. The bulk of the book aims to set out clearly and accurately the Kings, their families, and the main features of their reigns and events. Dividing history according to King's reigns is justified when they played such an important role at the apex of government, Church and society. However, it can obscure movements occurring over a longer timescale, and the links between reigns can be just as important. The creation of a unified English cultural style of art, language and literature in the mid-late 10$^{th}$ century is a good example of this. The appendices provide detailed amplification of selected events and features for those who want to follow up selected topics in greater detail.

# The Birth of a New State

## The Origins of the English

This book is about the Kings of England and the events of the 200 years before the Norman Conquest. However, the English have a history going back long before this. It is worth summarising that history in order that we can better appreciate the achievements of the $9^{th}$, $10^{th}$ and $11^{th}$ centuries. We can make a distinction between the Kingdom of England and the nation of the English. The Kingdom was a single state obeying one ruler and acting as a cohesive political and social unit. The nation of the English is a cultural entity covering those peoples who chose to identify themselves as English, sharing a common language, literary heritage, religion and mythical past (as revealed in Bede). This shared nationhood cut across political divisions. It does not matter whether there was any reality behind such a shared consciousness. The belief that it existed was a powerful force for cultural expression and political strategy.

Historical and archaeological evidence needs to be combined to inform us about early English history. The two are sometimes in conflict because early historical records often embody racial myths used to justify the then present. Modern historians now treat the earliest records with a great deal of caution. In the process, they may be too apt to dismiss works that were never intended to be historical records, or documents that record true history (albeit inaccurately and poorly remembered). The further back we travel in time, the less sure our ground and the more we exercise our opinions on what is true and what is myth.

What is certain is that at the end of Roman rule in Britain in 410, the whole island was in the hands of rulers sharing a Celtic culture and belonged to two broad linguistic groups; mostly Britons, with Picts in the far north. Two new cultural groupings (nations) arrived during this period; the Irish and the English. Irish settlers can be documented in historical records, place names and inscriptions in the south-west, parts of Wales and in Argyll. In Wales and the west, they would eventually be absorbed into the local cultures but in Argyll they established a Kingdom that would last and take over the rest of northern Britain during the next 500 years. The early name applied to the Irish by writers in Britain was *Scotti* and the Kingdom they created inevitably became known as Scotland. A similar process happened in the south of Britain to create England.

## The Earliest Settlers

The native rulers of Britain continued the late Roman practice of employing mercenary troops from the Germanic areas of Europe. Such troops had been stationed in Britain in the 4th century (Higham 1992, Whittock 1986). The early 5th century (c430) saw the hiring of troops from the North Sea coast opposite Britain. These troops were assigned lands for their support. For some, the taking of British lands to support themselves and their families became more important than defending those who had invited them across the sea. The earliest area to fall under their control was Kent. By the late 5th and early 6th centuries they were settling also in East Anglia, Essex, Sussex and the east Midlands (Morris 1973). A dynasty was also active in Hampshire that may have been a native British ruling family relying on English support, or a result of intermarriage between Briton and Saxon. The historical records name them as English but there is little archaeological evidence of Saxon settlement in Wessex until later, and their early names are as much Celtic as Germanic (Higham 1995). This family would become the royal house of Wessex and were the ancestors of King Ælfred and the Kings of England. Their own traditions associate them with Hampshire but the earliest evidence of settlement and the dynasty come from the upper Thames.

The English came from what is now Denmark, Schleswig-Holstein, Lower Saxony and the Netherlands. This area was a mixture of different tribal units grouped into four main 'peoples'; Jutes, Angles, Saxons and Frisians. The speech of these early settlers would be the dialects of north-west Germanic that would on the continent later become Frisian, Norse and Low German. In Britain, the new 'peoples' developed their own characteristic speech patterns and new dialects emerged. A language identifiable as English, and separate from its continental cousins, arose gradually after the settlement in Britain. Archaeological evidence of their continental origins comes from pottery and metalwork, surviving best in cemeteries. In some cases, a person buried with Anglian or Saxon grave goods may have been a native Briton adopting English culture. For instance, the 7th century English cemetery at Wasperton in Warwickshire began life as a late Roman cemetery in the 4th century (Esmonde Cleary 1989).

Most English settlement would have taken place in the east of Britain, from the Channel coast and Thames Valley northwards to the River Trent, and in the East Riding and north-east coast. In these areas, English newcomers may have swamped the native British population but, further east, there would have been greater numbers of Britons relative to English. In much of the north, the south-west and Welsh marches, population was probably British with a ruling English land-owning class. A Celtic language was still spoken the West Riding in the late 7th century (Colgrave 1927).

## The Formation of Kingdoms

British resistance to English expansion was successful until the mid 6th century. There followed a crucial period of about 3 generations from the 570s to the 650s when the whole of lowland Britain fell under English rule. It was at this time that the English achieved political cohesion in the form of various Kingdoms based around royal families asserting Angle, Saxon or Jutish racial origins. The new dynasties in Britain liked to claim distinguished ancestry, sometimes reaching back to the continent. In the case of Mercia, this was from the royal house of Angeln (in modern Schleswig), and included the distinguished Offa of the 4th century. Five of the Kingdoms had British names, or names derived from British sources; Beornice, Cent, Dere, Lindisse and Magonsæte. The rest were the names of peoples which became the accepted designations of the Kingdoms by the 8th century. For instance, Merce was the people of the marches (borders) and is better translated as Mercians rather than Mercia. The West Saxons had earlier been known as the Gewisse. The Kingdoms are listed in Table 1. The personal names given are those of the traditional founders of the Kingdom with traditional dates given in the historical sources, which cannot be relied upon for accuracy. The modern names Bernicia and Deira are only used by scholars. 'Maund' and 'Wych' (also 'Which' and 'Wyche') are found in modern place names but are not used as names of regions. The core areas are those given in the sources or determined by archaeological evidence. There is also evidence for under-Kings and Kings of small regions, for example, King Arwald of the Isle of Wight and Friþuwald of Surrey.

### Table 1 – The Early Kingdoms Of The English

| Name | Modern name | Founders | Race | Core area |
|---|---|---|---|---|
| Beornice | *Bernicia* | Ida 547 | Angle | Bamburgh |
| Dere | *Deira* | Ælle 560 | Angle | East Riding |
| Lindisse | Lindsey | ? | Angle | North Lincolnshire |
| Merce | Mercia | Crioda 570? | Angle | Leicester, Northampton |
| Magonsæte | 'Maund' | Merewealh c650 | Angle | Lugg Valley, Herefordshire |
| Hwicce | 'Wych' | Eanfrið c650 | Angle | Cotswolds |
| East Engle | East Anglia | Wuffa 571 | Angle | Norfolk, Suffolk |
| East Seaxe | Essex | Eorcenwine c520 | Saxon | Essex |
| Cent | Kent | Hengest 457, Oisc 488 | Jutish | Kent |
| Suð Seaxe | Sussex | Ælle 491 | Saxon | Sussex |
| West Seaxe | Wessex | Cerdic 519 | Saxon | Hampshire, Middle Thames |

The take over of most of lowland Britain was the work of three Kingdoms; Northumbria, Mercia and Wessex. Northumbria was the amalgamation of Bernicia and Deira. The conquest was complete by the 650s with the British restricted to three areas in the west of Britain; the Kingdom of Cornwall in modern Cornwall and Devon, various Kingdoms in modern Wales and the Kingdom of Strathclyde in west lowland Scotland. The English now ruled from Edinburgh to the English Channel. Relations between the various Anglo-Saxon Kingdoms were governed by the struggle for dominance between the main royal families. Looking back from the 8th century, certain of the early Kings were regarded as especially powerful in the period of settlement and conquest (England's heroic age?), Hengest of Kent, Ælle of Sussex, Ceawlin of Wessex, Æþelfrið of Bernicia, Æþelberht of Kent and Rædwald of East Anglia. The period after the conquest of lowland Britain saw the introduction of Christianity and the consolidation of power in the hands of three royal families who exercised a loose supremacy over other Kingdoms. The chief of these Kings were:

### Table 2 – Early Overlords of the English

| | |
|---|---|
| Eadwine | Northumbria 617–33 |
| Penda | Mercia 626–54 |
| Oswiu | Northumbria 641–70 |
| Wulfhere | Mercia 657–75 |
| Ecgfrið | Northumbria 670–85 |
| Æþelred | Mercia 675–704 |
| Ine | Wessex 688–726 |
| Æþelbald | Mercia 716–57 |
| Offa | Mercia 757–96 |
| Coenwulf | Mercia 796–821 |
| Ecgberht | Wessex 802–39 |
| Æþelwulf | Wessex 839–58 |

The concept of an English monarchy was clearly being expressed by Kings like Offa and by the late 8th century, the number of English Kingdoms had been reduced to 7 by the absorption of Lindsey, 'Maund' and 'Wych' into Mercia, with several others being clearly subordinate to more powerful neighbours. In 825, Wessex annexed the three smallest of these, Sussex, Kent and Essex, leaving four to face the onslaught of the Viking invasions in the 860s. The gradual reduction in the number of Kingdoms and the supremacy at times of one over the others were pointers on the way to unity. It was the Viking invasions that were the catalyst for the formation of a Kingdom of England and we cannot know for certain that a single Kingdom of England would have arisen and if so in what form but for their intervention.

# The Kingdom of England

It is not easy to decide who was the first King of England. The modern consensus seems to be that it was Æþelstan (Dumville 1992, Fryde et al 1986). However, the unification of those parts of Britain that we now call England was a gradual process. If England is taken to be the modern state from the Tweed and Solway down to Kent and Cornwall, then the first King of England is Henry II from 1157, when the modern northern boundary was created. This boundary is largely a historical accident. As late as 1334, Edward Balliol allowed England to incorporate the ancient English speaking lowlands of Scotland in return for support against David Bruce, an annexation stillborn by Edward's defeat. It is worth noting that England is not the Kingdom of English speaking peoples. The northernmost part of the English speaking area now lies in southern Scotland and modern England includes parts of Britain that were not traditionally English speaking; Cornwall, parts of the Welsh marches and perhaps Cumbria. England was therefore a political unit, the area owing allegiance to a King identifying himself as King of the English.

Æþelstan was the first King to use the title King of the English as his normal description. He was also the first King to rule all the Kingdoms historically thought of as English. However, even those who take Æþelstan as the first King of England accept that the policies of the royal house were set out by Ælfred and consistently carried out by his successors (Dumville 1992). It was King Ælfred, his son Eadward I, daughter Æþelflæd and grandson Æþelstan who created England. Ælfred and Eadward I preferred the title King of the Anglo-Saxons. Their rule was over those English who were not subject to Danish occupation after the Viking conquests.

At Ælfred's accession, there were four Anglo-Saxon Kingdoms:
a.  Wessex – south of the Thames, with Essex to the north
b.  Mercia – between the Thames and Humber
c.  East Anglia – Norfolk and Suffolk
d.  Northumbria – between the Humber and the Forth

By 879, Northumbria and East Anglia had been taken over by the Vikings and Mercia had been partitioned, the Vikings taking the east, with the west left as a self-governing province under the lordship of Ælfred of Wessex. Ælfred was left as the only surviving Anglo-Saxon King. Judging by his royal title, he seems to have adopted a position as leader of all the English. This is how he is described in an entry in the Chronicle (version A), written in 924, which refers to him as King over all the English race except that part which was under Danish rule. His son Eadward I and daughter Æþelflæd of Mercia undertook the conquest of the Viking lands south of the Humber between 912 and 918. In 918 Eadward also took over direct rule of English Mercia. Ælfred's grandson Æþelstan completed the process by annexing Viking ruled Northumbria in 927. The Viking dynasty of Dublin regained

Northumbria on Æþelstan's death in 939 but was driven out by Eadmund I in 944. Northumbria was again independent from 947 but was finally annexed in 954. The northernmost part of Northumbria was the area of Lothian, which was annexed by the Scots sometime between 954 and 962. This annexation was confirmed by Eadgar I in 973. It may have been reoccupied by the English for a time before finally being ceded in 1018. The area of Strathclyde south of the Solway would later become Cumberland and Westmorland but was not finally annexed by England until the 12th century. Indeed, the whole northern border with Scotland remained in doubt for some time, being finally fixed as late as 1157. With Wales, the precise border fluctuated until the Act of Union in 1536.

## The British Isles

**Cornwall** No Kingdom is isolated from its neighbours. England was only one of the states in the island of Britain. To its west lay a number of Celtic British Kingdoms. To the English, they were all described as Welsh. Cornwall was at the end of the south-west peninsula and was still an independent Kingdom at the end of the 9th century. Its history is poorly known as no documentary materials have survived from its religious houses of this date. Later medieval Welsh chronicles record the death of King Dungarth in 876, and an early tenth century stone bears the name of a King Ricatus. There is no evidence for its independence continuing beyond the reign of King Æþelstan who moved the episcopal see for Cornwall to St Germans and fixed the boundary of Cornwall at the Tamar. This may have happened in 928 when charters show him to have been at Exeter.

**Wales** North of the Severn estuary lay Glywysing, which covered the coastal plain and valleys of the south-east. From about 950, it was divided into two separate Kingdoms of Morgannwg and Gwent. The rest of Wales had been subject to Rhodri Mawr of Gwynedd and for the rest of the period it would be divided into two main Kingdoms, ruled by his descendants. Gwynedd covered the north and Deheubarth the south-west. The multiplicity of the descendants of Rhodri would lead to much strife between competing branches of the family for power in both Gwynedd and Deheubarth. At times, one ruler would succeed in uniting the whole territory but was never able to pass on an undivided inheritance to his successor. A strong, united Wales was a threat to the English border regions and was not usually encouraged. Relations between the Welsh Kingdoms and England would vary from open hostility to alliance and acceptance of English lordship. Welsh Kings would sometimes be drawn into English politics and by the middle of the 11th century a united Wales under Gruffydd ap Llewelyn was a potent ally of Earl Ælfgar of Mercia in his quarrels with Earl Harold of Wessex. However, English policy towards Wales was marked by a lack of interest in conquest, unlike after 1066. Having a divided and subordinate set of Welsh Kingdoms was enough.

**Scotland**  To the north of England was the growing power of Scotland. This Kingdom had recently been strengthened by the fusion of Pictish Alba with Irish Dalriada. Henceforth, there was one Kingdom north of the Forth with its Irish-descended dynasty capable of withstanding threats from both England and Vikings alike. Scotland expanded southwards by taking over the English speaking area of Lothian and by taking over the British speaking Kingdom of Strathclyde (Welsh and Cornish are the two surviving British languages). This Kingdom covered the area from Dumbarton southwards to Westmorland. Its native dynasty survived to 889. After this it became a subordinate Kingdom granted to members of the Scottish royal family, some of whom would in turn succeed to Scotland itself. One branch of the family provided several Kings for Strathclyde and almost succeeded in establishing a new Strathclyde dynasty. Its last King died in 1018 and from then onwards Strathclyde's fate was to be slow merger into a wider Scotland. It was King Mælcolm of Scotland who married Margareta, the sister of England's last Anglo-Saxon King to found an Anglo-Scottish dynasty that would last to the end of the 13th century.

**The Vikings**  The advent of the Vikings in the 9th century provided an added dimension to British politics. In the far north, they created the earldom of Orkney (including the Shetlands and Caithness) which existed in an ill-defined relationship to the Kingdom of Norway. The Hebrides and Isle of Man were likewise taken over and were subordinate to either Orkney or Dublin. By the 11th century, Man was a Kingdom of its own. Dublin was one of a number of towns established by the Vikings in the coastal areas of Ireland and exercising sovereignty over the Irish Sea. It was the Kings of Dublin who sought to rule at York in opposition to Kings Æþelstan, Eadmund and Eadred. They eventually settled down to being part of Irish politics and merging their identity into that of Ireland. Viking settlement in England was concentrated in Yorkshire, eastern Mercia and East Anglia, and their contribution to language, social practices and settlement was immense, even if their political control was soon ended as part of the creation of an English state.

A vital part of the enhancement of England's royal house's power was to claim dominion over the whole of Britain. Ælfred was overlord of the Welsh Kings, his son Eadward I of both Welsh and Scots. Æþelstan claimed to be ruler of all Albion and King of the whole of Britain. This was a grandiose claim that reflected an overlordship backed up by treaty and by military action. These decidedly imperial pretensions reached their peak under Eadgar I with the subordination of British rulers symbolised by their gathering at Chester in 973.

# A Description of Late Anglo-Saxon England

## Physical Geography (Map 1)

**Landscape** England is, and was, a very heterogeneous country. There are many ways of describing this variety. It was partly a matter of climate, soil and landscape, partly a matter of legal system and social custom. It was also partly a matter of race and language. The climate of the time was warmer than it is now, and this would allow crops to be grown in places that would later be marginal. It would also allow a build up of population without putting undue stress on the available resources and technology. The environment was the given physical framework within which law, society and language operated. One common distinction is between the lowlands of the south and east, and the uplands of the north and west. The uplands are centred on the three areas of land over 800 feet: the Pennines, Wales and the marches, the south-west. These have several features in common; colder and wetter climates, steeper slopes and rougher terrain, and more acidic soils. They· are therefore less well-suited to arable farming and less able to support dense populations. However, they do have advantages; hard stone for building and for milling, metal ores such as tin and lead and plenty of grazing for animals. Major sources of copper and salt are also to be found in the west. The warmer, dryer lowland regions are not uniform and contain large areas of low-lying wetland, good for producing reeds, wildfowling, fishing and water meadows but not for arable. These would also be difficult areas to travel across. Major roads obviously skirt the edges of these low-lying regions. The different soils of England would allow different types of farming, such as arable in many areas, and sheep farming on the chalk and limestone downs, and sandy heaths. Woodlands wcrc more extensive than now and offered a variety of important resources, as well as potentially new land for colonisation. The extensive coastline would offer fishing and salt production. The coastline on Map 1 is that of the twentieth century. Some parts of that coastline have seen major changes since late Anglo-Saxon times. In places, land has been added (e.g. Kent, Sussex and Lincolnshire) but in others it has been lost (e.g. Yorkshire East Riding). The rivers were an important feature as they allowed merchants and raiders to penetrate far inland. Most important boroughs were sited along, or at the end of, these rivers. Another feature of the boroughs is that they were often sited on the edges between the calcareous and clay soils as though positioned to take advantage of easy access to different farming areas. This would make easier their role as markets bringing together different types of farming produce for exchange.

**Using the Land**  Detailed analyses (Darby 1977) of the Domesday survey can yield information on the economic geography of England, and allow us to refine this picture of regional variety. Most modern writers would agree that the population of England was between 1½ and 2 million in 1066–86. The densest areas of settlement were in East Anglia, Lincolnshire, Kent and Sussex. Large parts of the country depended on arable farming to support their population, in particular four main areas: East Anglia, the middle Severn to upper Thames (Hereford-Gloucester-Oxford), the Sussex coast and south-west of the Fens (Huntingdon-Cambridge). Other areas must have had other means of supporting their people. South-eastern Mercia (Oxford to Cambridge) and parts of Lincolnshire had concentrations of meadow and may have been dairy farming areas. Other areas were probably pasturelands: Lindsey, Kent, the Wessex downs, Cornwall, the southern Pennines and parts of East Anglia. Many of these may have been sheep farming regions. Livestock were only recorded in parts of the Domesday survey but show sheep to have been especially common, mainly on marshland, sandy heaths or chalk downlands. Later evidence suggests that sheep were also common in the Cotswolds. Wool was the basis of England's later medieval wealth and was subject to price regulation in the laws of Eadgar I, over 100 years before the Domesday survey was made. The main areas of woodland seem to have been on the heavier clay soils. Woodland was densest in the Essex-Chiltern area, the Weald, Wiltshire-Somerset-Dorset, west Mercia and the edges of the Pennines.

Income from land seems to have been highest where farming was most specialised, in areas of probable sheep farming, dairying or more intensive arable. Whether the bulk of the population shared in this wealth would depend on the nature of landholding and population densities. The eastern part of England was an area of many smallholders, only loosely attached to their lord's manor. This was especially so in East Anglia, Lincoln, Northampton, Nottingham, Leicester. The south and west were areas of larger peasant holdings but more strongly subject to the manor. Areas where most people were relatively better off were probably Gloucester-Hereford-Worcester, Hampshire-Sussex, and Bedford-Huntingdon-Hertford.

**Craft and Industry**  Some industries, like pottery, were concentrated in the boroughs but others took place in the countryside. A highly important industry was salt making, found in Worcestershire and Cheshire, and along the coast. Lead production was concentrated in Derbyshire with lesser supplies from places like the Mendips. Tin was probably exploited in Devon and Cornwall, while Devon and west Mercia may have produced copper. Iron production was more widespread. Building stone was becoming important during the period and there were major quarries at Quarr on the Isle of Wight, Box in Somerset, Taynton in Gloucestershire and Barnack in Northamptonshire.

**Travel**  A seldom considered environmental factor is the length of the day. The hours of daylight vary throughout the year and for a society without extensive means of lighting this would have been a severe constraint on travel, military campaigning and daily life. For instance, at London, the longest days are from 18th–25th June at 16 hours and 40 minutes, while the shortest days are 15th–28th December at 7 hours 50 minutes. The Hastings campaign of 1066 could take advantage of over 11 hours of daylight, but the surviving English and invading Normans would only have 8 hours in which to campaign by December. The time between sunrise and sunset at London for the first day of each month is given in Table 3.

### Table 3 – Daylight Hours on the First day of Each Month

| January | 8 hrs |
|---|---|
| February | 9 hrs 10 mins |
| March | 10 hrs 50 mins |
| April | 13 hrs |
| May | 14 hrs 50 mins |
| June | 16 hrs 20 mins |
| July | 16 hrs 30 mins |
| August | 15 hrs 20 mins |
| September | 13 hrs 30 mins |
| October | 11 hrs 40 mins |
| November | 9 hrs 40 mins |
| December | 8 hrs 10 mins |

One obvious effect of this would be on travel. Transport of goods and people would be either by river or road. It is not really known how far the rivers were navigable in late Anglo-Saxon England but it is notable that most large towns were sited well inland along major rivers. Information about rates of travel is scarce. Ælfred's campaign against the Vikings in 878 is well documented. He went 25 miles from Athelney to Egbert's Stone, 12 miles in a day to Iley Oak, then 6 miles to fight the Vikings at Edington and pursue them a further 12 miles to Chippenham. Æþelstan's campaign of 934 can be traced in charters at Winchester on 28th May and at Nottingham on 7th June. If he went directly from Winchester to Nottingham that would be 120 miles in 10 days. A Viking force of 1001 landed at the Exe and struck 10 miles inland to attack Pinhoe the same day. An ordinary travelling day of 12 miles would seem reasonable, perhaps double that by forced marching. Harold II's journey south from York to London after the Battle of Stamford Bridge must have taken at the longest 11 days to cover 195 miles, around 18 miles a day. A rate of over 20 miles a day is more likely as he would probably give his forces much needed rest by not setting off directly after the battle. On horseback, perhaps 40 miles a day might be covered. A fast courier of Richard III in 1483 covered the 195 miles from London to York in 5 days. The importance of roads (Hill 1981) was such that four major national highways may have been under special royal protection (12th century evidence is backed up by one earlier reference): Watling Street connecting Canterbury and London to the Welsh marches, Ermine Street connecting London to Lincoln and the north, the Foss Way connecting Exeter to Lincoln, and the Icknield Way connecting East Anglia to the south-west. An important part of the road network was the bridges and the obligation to maintain these was a charge on land that King's seldom gave away.

## Human Geography (Map 2)

**Shires and Regions**  The shires of England were not all created at the same time. In central Wessex, the shires reflect the ancient divisions of that Kingdom. Smaller Kingdoms annexed in the 9th century became shires of their own, Kent and Sussex. It is known that Kent had two Aldermen under Ælfred and may not have formed a single shire until later. Cornwall was incorporated by Æþelstan who fixed its boundary at the Tamar. Until then western Cornwall had been under independent Kings. In East Anglia, Norfolk and Suffolk may well have been ancient divisions of that Kingdom. In Mercia, the shires were districts owing maintenance and military service to the boroughs created by Eadward I, Æþelflæd and the Vikings. One shire that may have since disappeared was Winchcombe, now in Gloucestershire. Another missing shire is Stamford. This was one of the Viking Five Boroughs and may have included Kesteven and Rutland, which itself was a special creation to provide a dower for the King's wives. Holland may have been its own shire as part of East Anglia (Hart 1973 has suggested that Lincolnshire was not created until 1075). North of the Humber and Mersey, there were no shires in the southern sense. The Ribble-Mersey area was treated as a separate part of Chester, York was the Kingdom incorporated finally in 954. Its divisions, the Ridings, were perhaps the nearest thing to a southern shire. However, the term shire was used in the north to refer to a smaller unit, a district dependant on originally royal manors. The area north of the Tees was governed by the Alderman at Bamburgh. Cumbria was only occasionally part of England until 1157. It was not until the 12th century that the north was divided into shires on the southern model. The boundaries shown on Map 2 are those of the ancient counties before local government reforms of 1888 and after. They are close to the 11th century boundaries but are not identical. The Domesday survey shows many minor changes to have been made to shire boundaries since then. For instance, the northern part of the Forest of Dean was part of Hereford not Gloucester. The names of shires were not always fixed. Wiltshire was named after the borough of Wilton but could also be called Wilset, in imitation of Dorset and Somerset.

Boundaries with Scotland and Wales are uncertain. The Welsh boundary is shown as that which defined the area under English rule in 1066 according to the Domesday Survey. The boundary in Cumbria is assumed to follow later ward boundaries and should be regarded as approximate.

Various parts of England had different legal and financial practices, as follows:

## Wessex

Followed West Saxon legal practices, divided its shires into districts known as hundreds and rated land according to the hide – Berkshire, Cornwall, Devon, Dorset, Kent, Somerset, Southampton, Surrey, Sussex, Wilton

## Mercia

Followed Mercian legal practices but also divided into hundreds and used the hide – Chester, Gloucester, Hereford, Oxford, Shrewsbury, Stafford, Warwick, Worcester

## Danelaw

a. south-east Mercia: followed Danish legal practice but used the hundred and hide – Bedford, Buckingham, Cambridge, Essex, Hertford, Huntingdon, Middlesex, Northampton
b. the Five Boroughs: rated their land by the ploughland and divided into wapentakes – Derby, Leicester, Lincoln, Nottingham
c. East Anglia: rated by the ploughland but divided into hundreds – Norfolk, Suffolk

## Northumbria

Used various systems of organisation and assessment, partly Danish in origin, partly English, partly Celtic – Bamburgh (Northumberland), Cumbria, York

The historic heartland of England, where the Kings had most of their estates, their burial places, the monasteries with royal associations and where they spent most of their time was central Wessex (Berkshire, Dorset, Somerset, Southampton, Wilton) along with Gloucester, London and Oxford. The nearest thing to a capital city was Winchester, the main site of the chancery and treasury, while London was the undoubted mercantile capital. Coronations were held at the traditional West Saxon site of Kingston upon Thames until 1016 when Cnut was crowned in London (the first King to be crowned at Westminster was Harold II). Winchester (cathedral and New Minster) and Glastonbury were the favoured burial places for most Kings.

**Population** Information about the shires as listed in the Domesday survey is given in Table 4. Populations are for rural and urban populations combined. They are very approximate, based on Domesday Book following Nash 1988, and data corrected for the recorded amounts of waste in 1086 (waste townships count as one, and partially waste as a half, so ten waste and ten partially waste townships out of 100 would equal 15% waste in all). Most of the waste was probably due to Willem I's suppression of revolts in 1068–70, although this is disputed. Figures in *italics* are for waste in 1070 and were probably due to Duke Willem's invasion in 1066. The figure for Northampton was most likely due to the revolt against Earl

Tostig in 1065, the rebels attacking Tostig's lands in the area. As the Domesday Book records only heads of households, assumptions have to be made about the average size of households to arrive at a total population figure. Those adopted here are those of Nash 1988. In all, England contained at least 1,600,000 people in 1066, nearly 10% of whom (150,000) lived in the boroughs. Allowing for under-reporting of certain categories of persons and areas, the true figure was probably between 1¾ and 2 million. Not all townships (parishes) were recorded in the Domesday survey and the figures given for these should be seen as minimum numbers. Hides and population are given in rounded figures. The equivalent of the hide in York and the Five Boroughs was the ploughland, and in Kent the sulung. Hidage assessments were changed during the late Anglo-Saxon period and those shown are for 1066.

## Table 4 — The Shires of England

| Shires | Townships | %Waste | Population | Hides | Hundreds |
|---|---|---|---|---|---|
| **Wessex** | | | | | |
| Berkshire | 189 | | 31,000 | 2,500 | 22 |
| Cornwall | 332 | | 24,000 | 160 | 7 |
| Devon | 980 | | 87,000 | 1,100 | ?30 |
| Dorset | 314 | | 39,000 | 2,300 | 39 |
| Kent | 347 | *6.5* | 73,000 | 1,200 | 63 |
| Somerset | 622 | | 63,000 | 2,900 | ?34 |
| Southampton | 454 | *c4.0* | 56,000 | 2,600 | ?44 |
| Surrey | 144 | *9.7* | 22,000 | 1,800 | 14 |
| Sussex | 336 | *12.8* | 55,000 | 3,500 | 59 |
| Wilton | 344 | | 47,000 | 4,100 | ?39 |
| **Mercia** | | | | | |
| Chester | 366 | 14.5 | 19,000 | 510 | 15 |
| Gloucester | 379 | | 42,000 | 2,400 | 39 |
| Hereford | 311 | 12.5 | 23,000 | 1,300 | 16 |
| Oxford | 250 | | 39,000 | 2,400 | 14 |
| Shrewsbury | 459 | 9.5 | 26,000 | 1,200 | 14 |
| Stafford | 342 | 19.0 | 20,000 | 510 | 5 |
| Warwick | 247 | 2.4 | 34,000 | 1,300 | 10 |
| Worcester | 275 | 2.9 | 23,000 | 1,200 | 10 |
| **East Anglia** | | | | | |
| Norfolk | 730 | | 149,000 | 2,400 | 34 |
| Suffolk | 639 | | 108,000 | 2,400 | 24 |

| Shires | Townships | %Waste | Population | Hides | Hundreds |
|---|---|---|---|---|---|
| **Southern Danelaw** | | | | | |
| Bedford | 141 | *c10.0* | 20,000 | 1,200 | 12 |
| Buckingham | 206 | *6.8* | 27,000 | 2,100 | 18 |
| Cambridge | 142 | | 25,000 | 1,200 | 16 |
| Essex | 444 | | 68,000 | 2,700 | 20 |
| Hertford | 171 | *15.8* | 30,000 | 1,100 | 9 |
| Huntingdon | 85 | 3.0 | 16,000 | 750 | 4 |
| Middlesex | 62 | *16.9* | 26,000 | 870 | 6 |
| Northampton | 354 | *(16.5)* | 45,000 | 1,400 | 29 |
| **Five Boroughs** | | | | | |
| Derby | 346 | 17.1 | 20,000 | 680 | 6 |
| Leicester | 292 | 5.7 | 39,000 | 2,500 | 4 |
| Lincoln: Holland | 35 | 4.3 | | 280 | 3 |
| Lincoln: Kesteven | 231 | 2.4 | {139,000} | 1,940 | 11 |
| Lincoln: Lindsey | 498 | 4.6 | | 1,980 | 19 |
| Nottingham | 297 | 11.6 | 37,000 | 570 | 8 |
| Rutland | 16 | | 2,000 | 40 | 2 |
| **Northumbria** | | | | | |
| Northumberland | ? | | ? | ? | ? |
| York: Amounderness | 183 | | | 540 | ?9 |
| York: East Riding | 448 | | | 3,200 | 18 |
| York: North Riding | 641 | {33.7 | +71,000} | 3,300 | 7 |
| York: West Riding | 765 | | | 3,300 | 11 |

**Boroughs** There were regional contrasts also in the boroughs (Table 5). The north was undeveloped in this respect. Eastern England was a land of a few large and medium sized boroughs as was western Mercia, although without any really large boroughs. Wessex was mostly a land of many small boroughs. The boroughs were not large, averaging only 1,700 people. Only London was of any size with perhaps 15,000 people. The other large boroughs with between 5,000 and 10,000 people were York, Winchester, Norwich, Lincoln, Oxford and Thetford. The term borough covered many types of settlement. Market rights, minting rights, having tenements for rent were among the features that could be found in a borough. However, a group of more important boroughs can be identified. These were towns with urban landholdings of several lords and could be thought of as 'county towns' (most were listed separately in the Domesday survey of 1086). In the 11th century, they were liable for taxation separately from the shires. There were also some large towns on royal or private land (in *italics* in Table 5). They would also have a mint, a borough court and burgage tenure (tenements for rent). Lesser boroughs in private hands might also have some of these features.

The Domesday survey is the only source for estimating the population of the boroughs. Table 5 lists the major boroughs by shire. The figures for population must be regarded as rough approximations and may be on the low side. From 973 to 1066 there were 24 regular coin issues and the number issued from the town's mints (column four: **Coin**) can give an indication of the borough's importance. The next column (**Mon**) gives the number of moneyers at work in 1066 as stated in the Domesday Book or calculated from the surviving coins of the period. It shows that some boroughs were no longer active as mints (e.g. Watchet) and were probably in decline by then. New finds of coins are likely to revise both sets of figures upwards. Boroughs given in brackets are not listed as such in the Domesday survey but were mints.

## Table 5 — The Major Boroughs of England

|  | **Boroughs** | **People** | **Coin** | **Mon** | **Ownership** |
|---|---|---|---|---|---|
| *Wessex* | | | | | |
| Berkshire | Wallingford | 2,000 | 22 | 4 | |
| Cornwall | *Bodmin ecclesiastical* | 500 | - | – | |
|  | (Launceston) | 50 | 2 | ?1 | ? |
| Devon | Exeter | 2,500 | 24 | 5 | |
|  | *Barnstaple* | 500 | 15 | ?1 | royal |
|  | *Lydford* | 500 | 16 | – | royal |
|  | *Totnes* | 500 | 10 | – | royal |
| Dorset | Bridport | 500 | 11 | 1 | |
|  | Dorchester | 1,000 | 15 | 2 | |
|  | Shaftesbury | 1,500 | 20 | 4 | |
|  | Wareham | 1,500 | 18 | 2 | |
| Kent | Canterbury | 2,000 | 24 | 6 | |
|  | Dover | 2,000 | 23 | 3 | |
|  | Rochester | 500 | 18 | 2 | |
|  | *Romney* | 700 | 18 | 1 | episcopal |
|  | *Sandwich* | 1,500 | 7 | 2 | episcopal |
| Somerset | Bath | 1,000 | 22 | 3 | |
|  | *Ilchester* | 500 | 21 | 1 | royal |
|  | *Taunton* | 300 | 12 | 2 | episcopal |
|  | (Watchet) | ? | 15 | – | |
| Southampton | Southampton | 1,000 | 7 | – | |
|  | Winchester | 8,000 | 24 | 7 | |
| Surrey | Guildford | 750 | 16 | 1 | |
|  | Southwark | 200 | 18 | 2 | |

|  | Boroughs | People | Coin | Mon | Ownership |
|---|---|---|---|---|---|
| **Wessex (continued)** | | | | | |
| Sussex | Chichester | 1,000 | 24 | 2 | |
|  | Hastings | 1,000 | 21 | 3 | |
| Sussex (continued) | Lewes | 1,500 | 24 | 3 | |
|  | *Steyning* | 500 | 15 | 1 | monastic |
| Wilton | Cricklade | 500 | 20 | 1 | |
|  | Marlborough | ? | – | – | |
|  | Malmesbury | 500 | 23 | 1 | |
|  | Wilton | 500 | 23 | 5 | |
|  | (Salisbury) | ? | 15 | 2 | episcopal |
|  | (Bedwyn) | 150 | 6 | 1 | |
| **Mercia** | | | | | |
| Chester | Chester | 2,500 | 24 | 7 | |
| Gloucester | Gloucester | 2,000 | 24 | 7 | |
|  | Winchcombe | 500 | 14 | 1 | |
|  | *Bristol* | 500 | 17 | 3 | royal |
| Hereford | Hereford | 500 | 21 | 7 | |
| Oxford | Oxford | 5,000 | 24 | 7 | |
| Shrewsbury | Shrewsbury | 1,500 | 24 | 4 | |
| Stafford | Stafford | 800 | 11 | 2 | |
|  | Tamworth | 200 | 16 | 2 | |
| Warwick | Warwick | 1,250 | 22 | 3 | |
| Worcester | Worcester | 750 | 23 | 5 | |
|  | (Droitwich) | | 1 | 3 | |
| **East Anglia** | | | | | |
| Norfolk | Norwich | 6,500 | 24 | 7 | |
|  | Thetford | 5,000 | 24 | 7 | |
|  | Yarmouth | 400 | – | – | |
| Suffolk | Ipswich | 2,500 | 24 | 3 | |
|  | *Bury St Edmunds* | 1,500 | 5 | 1 | monastic |
|  | *Dunwich* | 3,000 | – | – | secular lord |
|  | (Sudbury) | 700 | 7 | 1 | |
| **Southern Danelaw** | | | | | |
| Bedford | Bedford | 1,500 | 23 | 2 | |
| Buckingham | Buckingham | 1,500 | 13 | ?1 | |
|  | (Aylesbury) | | 6 | ?1 | |
| Cambridge | Cambridge | 2,250 | 23 | 5 | |

| | Boroughs | People | Coin | Mon | Ownership |
|---|---|---|---|---|---|
| *Southern Danelaw (continued)* | | | | | |
| Essex | Colchester | 2,000 | 21 | 4 | |
| Hertford | Hertford | ? | 20 | 2 | |
| | *Maldon* | 1,000 | 19 | 1 | royal |
| Huntingdon | Huntingdon | 1,200 | 22 | 2 | |
| Middlesex | London | ?15,000 | 24 | 14 | |
| Northampton | Northampton | 1,500 | 24 | 3 | |
| *Five Boroughs* | | | | | |
| Derby | Derby | 1000 | 21 | 3 | |
| Leicester | Leicester | 1500 | 23 | 2 | |
| Lincoln: Holland | none | | | | |
| Lincoln: Kesteven | Grantham | 500 | – | – | |
| | Stamford | 2,500 | 24 | 4 | |
| Lincoln: Lindsey | Lincoln | 6000 | 24 | 11 | |
| | Torksey | 1,000 | 5 | – | |
| Nottingham | Nottingham | 1000 | 19 | 2 | |
| Rutland | | none | | | |
| *Northumbria* | | | | | |
| Northumberland | Durham | ? | – | – | |
| York: Amounderness | none | | | | |
| York: East Riding | none | | | | |
| York: North Riding | York | 8,500 | 24 | 13 | |
| York: West Riding | none | | | | |

**Language** Human geography concerns people and their individual customs as much as institutional differences. Language was one of the most basic regional characteristics. However, we cannot put precise boundaries to the four main dialect areas: West Saxon, Kentish, Mercian and Northumbrian. The differences between the four were many, for instance West Saxon *heo mæg hyran* (she can hear) would be *hia meg heran* in Kentish, *heo mæg heran* in Mercian and *hio mæg hera* in Northumbrian. It is clear that the Viking influence on eastern Mercia, East Anglia and Northumbria was profound. The pronunciation and vocabulary of English in this area was different to that elsewhere. For instance, the hard *k/sk* sounds of the Vikings were *ch/sh* in Wessex and western Mercia. Hence we have in Modern English both skirt and shirt, kirk and church. Many of the words introduced by the Vikings remained foreign to the English living in the south and west. A man from Northampton might have said his *leg* while a man from Gloucester was saying his *shank*. As late as the 15th century a man from Sheffield could not buy *eggis* from a southern market, he had to ask for *eyren* instead.

# Government and Politics

**The King** The government of England had two main dimensions, the central and the local (Loyn 1984). Central government was based on the King, and his family and household. Although it was less well developed than it would become in the 12th century, the English monarchy was one of the most powerful in Europe and had created a sophisticated government machine. The King took an oath at his coronation to protect the Church, punish wrongdoers and promote justice. Additional duties were to comfort the poor, defend the realm and ensure the well being of the three orders of society: the clergy, the warrior aristocracy and the commoners whose work supported the others. The power of the Kings came from various sources. The King was probably the largest single landowner in the Kingdom, drawing rents and services, along with a personal following from his lands. Under Eadward III, the family of Godwine and his sons together had lands that exceeded those of the King in extent. However, this was exceptional and Godwine's sons were Eadward's brothers-in-law. Anyway, the unity of the family was broken by the northern revolt of 1065. The King also had an army of officials whom he appointed to carry out the functions of government. Of these, the local Sheriffs were perhaps the most important, carrying the King's will into every shire. Royal control over the Church was also important and although Bishops and Abbots were in theory freely elected, their appointments were in fact under royal control. Any government needs military forces to enforce its authority and the King had both his own household troops and the right to summon the national army for service. Military punishments of districts for various offences are recorded under Eadgar I and Harðacnut. The basis of social and economic action was the law, a body of traditional custom and declared provisions. Kings both declared and created laws throughout the period and acted as the enforcers of these. Judging cases under the law was a royal prerogative through the public courts (although sometimes delegated to private individuals), with the royal court itself able to act as a primary court and court of appeal. However, Kings were not omnipotent and had to rule with the support of the aristocracy and Church. Forfeiting the support of either could make a King's position difficult, as Eadwig and Æþelred found.

**The King's Family and the Succession** Central government however was more than the King alone. There were times when there was no King, between reigns, or when the King was under age. Neither situation created governmental crisis (as opposed to political crisis) and the administration continued without break. The core of this administration at the centre was the King's household and his family. The King's wife or mother (Stafford 1981) played an important role. It would seem that the eldest surviving wife of a King took precedence over other royal wives. Hence, the King's mother would take precedence over his wife and be responsible for the upbringing of the King's children. During this period, there were four Queens who were particularly dominant: *Eadgyfu*, Eadward I's third wife; *Ælfþryð*, Eadgar I's third wife; *Ymme*, Æþelred's second wife; and *Eadgyð*, wife of Eadward III. Such dominance arose from their position as mothers of Kings and/or from their own family connections. Some Kings married more than once and this could create political tensions. Relations between Kings' sons and their stepmothers were not always good as the reign of Eadward II showed. What helped to foment political instability was the indeterminate nature of the succession (Williams 1978). The King's eldest son would normally expect to succeed. Eadward I succeeded his father Ælfred but at least one son of Ælfred's elder brother was still living. It is unclear whether Eadward's son, born before Eadward was King, was intended for the succession or the eldest son of his second wife, Ælfward. As Ælfward died just 2 weeks after his father the issue was never put to the test. At the death of Eadmund I, his eldest son was under age and the King's brother Eadred succeeded instead. The conquest of Cnut upset this pattern and the succession tended to go according to the most powerful candidate with a legitimate claim, or according to the dead King's stated wish (so long as this was accepted by the nobility). This remained the case until the 13th century. The succession of a new King often culminated in his coronation. However, some Kings are not known to have been crowned and this did not impair their title as King nor their power. Nor was their title any the less between succession and sometimes quite late coronations, e.g. Eadward III waited 9 months before coronation. Church writers were keen to stress that coronation increased a King's status and that a crowned King could not be overthrown. Such theory was of little use to Æþelred in 1013, yet it is notable that he was recalled as soon as possible after the death of Swegn.

**The Household**  The King's household (Appendix 1) consisted of various departments (Larson 1904). His religious and clerical needs were provided for by the chapel. The chaplains organised religious services but also acted as a secretariat and were probably under one head chaplain. It may be that this official was termed the chancellor, although there is no firm evidence for this until after the Norman Conquest. The last head of the writing office under Eadward III was given the rank of Bishop, and monastic tradition after the Norman Conquest held that some earlier Bishops had been chancellor before their appointment. The military section of the household was under the command of a number of stallers, or constables. This official first appears under Cnut and the name of the office itself is Norse. However, Kings must have had military retainers before this, along with the need to organise transport and hunting. The other household heads of department were the steward, chamberlain and butler. The steward, or seneschal, would be responsible for the household itself and organising its provisioning, while the butler had charge of the cellar. The chamberlain was in charge of the King's private chambers and seems to have acted as treasurer in charge of the King's finances. These three offices were held either jointly or in rotation by probably three people at any one time. Ælfred is said to have organised the household into three shifts, each being in post for one month. This arrangement was presumably modified over time but there are still traces of multiple officeholders after 1100 In the 10<sup>th</sup> century the holders of these posts were powerful men, usually members of the great aristocratic families and major landowners in their own right. In the 11<sup>th</sup> century, the greatest officers of the household were the stallers who ranked among the highest nobility in terms of wealth. In the writs of the time, stallers can be seen acting for the King in shires where there was no Sheriff and they were obviously important executive agents of the crown. Certainly the King's household troops were used for such tasks as tax collection. There does not seem to have been a separate judicial department at this date although the known complexity of the administration is evidence of a strong systematic organisation at the centre.

The King's chief councillors were the great magnates of the realm; the Aldermen or Earls, Bishops and Abbots, along with the larger landowners (Oleson 1955). These were the people who would be gathered in periodic assemblies to participate in the taking of major decisions and whose advice, if unanimous, the King would do well not to ignore. Their presence at the centre of government served to bind the centre to the localities, which helped weld England into one state during this period.

**Local Government** Below the centre, the most important sphere of politics and government was the shire, covering about 50,000 people on average. Each had a court that met twice a year under the joint chairmanship of the Alderman and Bishop. It was here that decisions by the King were communicated to the localities by means of written messages called writs. The shire court would also act as a judicial assembly and general purpose meeting of the freemen and gentry of the shire. The Aldermen (Appendix 2) were royal officials appointed to cover groups of shires and whose main function was to lead the military forces of their district. From the reign of Cnut, they adopted the Danish term of Earl. Earldoms did not have fixed boundaries, nor were they hereditary, although there was a strong tendency for the sons of an Earl to be made Earls also. The financial, military and judicial head of the shire itself was the Sheriff (Appendix 4). It was he who supervised the collection of royal finances, managed the royal estates, kept law and order, led the military force of the shire for its own defence and supervised the work of lower courts. Most shires were divided into smaller districts called hundreds, or wapentakes in the northern Danelaw or Yorkshire. These averaged around 2,000 people, had a court that met every 4 weeks and were the backbone of the judicial and administrative life of the country. Some shires had larger units between the shire and hundred, e.g. the lathes of Kent or the ridings of Yorkshire and Lindsey. Within the wapentakes, there was a smaller unit called a hundred, which was in no way the equivalent of hundreds elsewhere, but was a subdivision of the wapentake for fiscal purposes. In addition to these were the boroughs, whose court met every 3 weeks. It was in the boroughs that coins were minted, markets held and craft industries were located. Most boroughs were under royal control, very few were in private hands, and many had been created by the King. The lowest unit of government was the township, what we now call the parish, in which the local people would organise their economic and social lives. An average township would have contained about 125–150 people. Cutting across these geo-political units were the complex estates of the landlords, organised around the manor. Many of these were granted the right to hold their own courts with delegated powers. Private landlords or even monasteries could be granted the right to hold the courts of particular hundreds or groups of hundreds. All freemen had the duty of attending the courts and were deemed to be able to take on legal responsibility at the age of 12.

An important feature of local government and military service was delegation of power. Kings granted rights over land to many thanes. In return they expected service. Such grants might include whole hundreds. In which case the thane, Bishop or abbey became responsible to the King for administering justice within the hundred and for the military service due from it. The most well known example was the jurisdiction granted to Bury St Edmund's Abbey over western Suffolk, but there were many others on a lesser scale than this. All thanes were liable for military service to the King (Abels 1988). Many would have to find a set number of soldiers for service. They could do this by leasing land to such soldiers or keep them in a paid retinue. The King himself would do likewise and had his household troops to give him a standing armed force. For specific emergencies, mercenary troops might also be hired. Furthermore, expressing personal loyalties through commending oneself to a powerful lord may have involved military obligation although the evidence on this is unclear and it could come into conflict with service based on land.

**Finance**  The income of the crown came from various sources. Royal estates contributed traditional renders of food or money. The courts imposed fines for many offences which went to the crown and Aldermen. The King could charge fees for services, such as drawing up land charters. However, the most sophisticated source of income was taxation. All land was assessed in units known in most of the country as the hide. Taxes could be charged at a certain rate from each hide. The hide could also be used as the basis for levying troops (Abels 1988) by requiring one man from so many hides (often every five hides) to serve in the army.

## The Church in England (Map 3)

The English Church consisted of two provinces; Canterbury and York. Each was separate from and equal in status to the other, and was made up of different sees. In Canterbury, there had been thirteen Bishops with a further four in York, but not all of these would survive the Viking invasions of the 9th century. New sees were created in the 10th century which gave Wessex a dominant position in the Church hierarchy. Some sees had junior Bishops to assist the diocesan Bishop, e.g. St Martins in Canterbury or St Germans in Crediton. Below the level of the see, ecclesiastical provision was made by the old minster churches. These served large parochial areas and were staffed by several priests. The minsters would administer baptism and other important functions. There were also newer private chapels belonging to some landlords, which could serve people on the lord's estate, for ordinary functions of regular worship. It was these proprietary churches which became the local parish churches found in every village or township. These probably became the churches of most of the population during the 10<sup>th</sup> and 11<sup>th</sup> centuries. Churches were a common feature of the landscape by the time of the Domesday Book (Morris 1989) and most people would have been within walking distance of religious services.

**Finance** The the Church (Barlow 1979) was financed by income from land, fees and taxes. The Bishops and major monasteries were major landowners and collected enormous wealth from their manors. Parish churches would be less fortunate and might rely more on the fees and taxes for their income. Tithes were collected as a tenth of all farm produce. A law of Æþelred laid down that tithes were to be divided into three parts; a third for church buildings, a third for supporting the clergy and a third as charity for the poor. Other dues were church scot, collected from all freemen in the form of grain or money, soul scot which was a fee for burial, light dues which were paid to churches for their lighting, and plough alms which was a tax of a penny on all ploughs. Church dues went to all the ancient minsters, while proprietary churches were supposed to be supported by the estate which established them. Inevitably, as proprietary churches became parish churches they began to intrude into the minster's rights. However, minsters remained important throughout the period and in the 12<sup>th</sup> century many became the centres of rural deaneries. There is no evidence that such deaneries existed before then. Under the Bishop, the only official mentioned in the sources is the archdeacon, first noted in the 11<sup>th</sup> century.

**Sees** The Viking invasion of 865–79 disrupted sees in the east and north. Several ceased to exist. The Church after the tenth century (Map 3) was marked by a scarcity of bishoprics in the Danelaw and Northumbria compared with Wessex and western Mercia. The two provinces of Canterbury and York were grossly unequal. Canterbury had all England south of the Humber (Nottingham was later transferred to York). York was left with only Durham and a vague and theoretical supervision of Scottish sees. It became common to link York with richer sees to the south by allowing its Archbishops to hold a southern diocese at the same time, usually Worcester. Papal objections ended this practice in the 11<sup>th</sup> century. Bishops commonly held more than one see, sometimes temporarily but often for long periods. Even those regarded as saints were guilty of what was technically uncanonical. For a short while, Archbishop Dunstan held both London and Worcester as well as Canterbury. In York and Elmham the large size of the diocese was mitigated by the use of some minsters to act as regional centres, almost like semi-cathedrals. By contrast, Wessex was well provided for, perhaps over provided as some sees were amalgamated by 1066. The large Dorchester see was sometimes provided with an assistant Bishop in Lindsey for the north of the diocese.

Some cathedrals were sited in old Roman towns; Canterbury, London, Rochester, Winchester, York. Others had towns grow up around them; Durham, Hereford, Worcester. However, some were sited in rural areas; Selsey, Sherborne, Ramsbury, Wells, Crediton, St German's, Lichfield, Dorchester, Elmham. Part of the 11th century Papal reforms was to insist on Bishops residing in towns. A start was made on this by moving the combined sees of Crediton and St German's to Exeter in 1050. Other moves were made after the Norman Conquest both by Bishops who had been appointed under Eadward III, or had been one of Eadward's chaplains, and by Norman newcomers. Hereman moved the combined sees of Sherborne and Ramsbury to a new site at Salisbury around which a town soon grew up. Gisa of Wells moved his see to the monastery of Bath. Lichfield was moved to Chester and thence to Coventry. Dorchester ended up at Lincoln, Selsey at Chichester, while Elmham moved to Thetford and thence to Norwich. The only new sees added after 1066 were Ely in 1109 and Carlisle in 1133.

Some sees, notably Hereford and Worcester, preserved the boundaries of old Mercian provinces which did not coincide with the newer shire boundaries. This can only have complicated the sittings of the shire courts which were to be presided over by the Alderman and Bishop jointly. The old names of provinces were sometimes still used, especially *Magonsæte* for Hereford (preserved in modern Maund) and *Hwicce* for Worcester (preserved in Wychwood).

**Bishops**    Bishops' clerical duties were: 1. to administer baptism and confirmation; 2. to ordain priests and consecrate churches; 3. to instruct the clergy and laity in a Christian way of life and duties, 4. to administer canon law and legislate for their diocese (Barlow,1963). After the monastic reform under Eadgar I, many Bishops were monks and had links with monasteries outside their sees. Some cathedral chapters were monastic, with the Bishop acting as Abbot (Canterbury, Sherborne, Winchester, Worcester). Others had colleges of secular canons, some with a communal rule (Durham, Exeter, Hereford?, London, Wells, York). Existing monastic chapters were kept and new ones added after 1066: Bath, Carlisle, Coventry, Durham, Ely, Norwich, Rochester. Appointment was by a pragmatic mixture of royal appointment and election by the chapter, which sometimes came into conflict.

Bishops (Appendix 3) and Abbots were important people in the world of politics. They not only exercised the moral authority of the Church but they were also major landowners with all the rights and obligations that entailed. They were prominent at court and several individual clergy played important political roles. Examples of this are many. For instance, Archbishops Dunstan and Oswold probably secured the succession of Eadward II. During the minority of Æþelred, a key role seems to have been played by Bishop Æþelwold of Winchester. A major influence on the legislation of Æþelred and Cnut was Archbishop Wulfstan of York. At a local level, Bishops were to preside at the county court alongside the Earl.

**Learning**   The Church was important in the cultural life of England since it provided the only schools. Also, since most of the surviving manuscripts of the period are ecclesiastical, our image of the art and literature of the period is shaped the taste and skills of successive priests, Bishops and monks. The important Winchester style of manuscript illumination was a product of the monastic reformation in the 10th century and can still produce feelings of awe and admiration among people of the 20th century. Old English poetry, much of it composed by clergy, would be largely unknown if it were not for the collections preserved in monastic and cathedral manuscripts.

**Reform**   The Norman Conquest brought about one definite effect on the English Church, the acceptance of the reforms pursued by the papacy since the Council of Rheims in 1049. Reform would probably have come about anyway but the Church of late Anglo-Saxon England was definitely a pre-reform Church. The two most obvious features that showed this were the existence of married clergy, even Bishops, and the intimate relationship between Church and state. The Church played its part in upholding royal authority and the King played his part by supporting and defending the Church. However, the reforming effect of the conquest can be exaggerated. Married Bishops were still being appointed after 1066, e.g. Herfast of Elmham, Samson of Worcester and Robert Bloet of Lincoln.

**Summaries of Sees**   All values listed below in Table 6 are for the lands of the Bishop and chapter in 1066, calculated from the Domesday Survey and should be regarded as approximate given the uncertainties of that survey.

### Table 6 —England's Bishoprics
### Canterbury Province

*Nine sees survived the Viking invasions by 871:*

| See | Value | Chapter | |
|---|---|---|---|
| Canterbury | £1,200 | monastic | |
| Winchester | £1,180 | monastic | |
| London | £490 | collegiate | |
| Worcester | £440 | monastic | |
| Hereford | £270 | collegiate | |
| Sherborne | £200 | monastic | held with Ramsbury after 1058 |
| Selsey | £160 | | |
| Rochester | £110 | | |
| Lichfield | £70 | | |

*Four sees disappeared during the Viking invasions:*

| See | Kingdom |
|---|---|
| Dunwich | East Anglia |
| Elmham | East Anglia |
| Leicester | Mercia |
| Lindsey | Mercia |

*Six new sees were created after 871:*

| Date | See | Value | Chapter | |
|------|-----|-------|---------|---|
| 879 | Dorchester | £360 | | moved from Leicester |

| Date | See | Value | Chapter | |
|------|-----|-------|---------|---|
| 909 | Crediton | £250 | collegiate | moved to Exeter in 1050 |
| 909 | Ramsbury | £310 | | held with Sherborne after 1058 |
| 909 | Wells | £200 | collegiate | |
| 928 | Saint German's* | | collegiate | held with Crediton after 1027 |
| 955 | Elmham | £220 | | |

\* St German's was established as the seat of a bishopric when Cornwall was finally incorporated into England, but was subordinate to the bishopric of Crediton until 994.

*One minster acted as a semi-cathedral:*
Hoxne in Elmham diocese

**York Province**

*Two sees survived the Viking invasions by 871:*

| See | Value | Chapter | |
|-----|-------|---------|---|
| York | £350 | collegiate | |
| Lindisfarne? | | collegiate | moved to Chester le Street in 883, Durham 995 |

*Two sees disappeared during the Viking invasions:*

Hexham
Whithorn

*Three minsters acted as semi-cathedrals:*
Beverley in York diocese
Ripon in York diocese
Southwell in York diocese

**Monasteries** A major feature of the 10th century was the monastic reformation which reached its peak under Eadgar I. Monasteries had been founded in the early decades of Christianity in England. They followed varying rules and by the 9th century the status of many would be regarded as uncertain by later 10th century standards. The reform was an English adaptation of the continental Cluniac revitalisation of monastic life, through the inspiration of Fleury and Ghent. It led to the founding of many new monasteries and the reorganisation of existing ones on stricter lines. Monasteries became important landowners, the greatest of which rivalled the Bishops in wealth. They were also important centres of learning, literature and art. We have only to think of Abbot Ælfric of Eynsham or the Winchester art style to realise the contribution of the monastic reformation in these fields. By the 11th century the monastic hierarchy consisted of the Abbot and his deputy the provost (the post-conquest prior), several deans and other officers.

Several cathedrals adopted collegiate rules and some became monastic chapters headed by the Bishop. The wealthiest abbeys were concentrated in four areas: East Anglia and the Fens, the Thames, south central Wessex and the see of Worcester. Communal religious life in areas without monasteries was often provided for by secular minsters, some of whom had powerful patrons (e.g. Waltham patronised by Harold II). However, the monasteries were generally wealthier and have left abundant documentary materials for the historian and so tend to dominate our picture of religious life at the time. The monasteries shown on Map 3 are those whose wealth was equal to that of the Bishops (over £120). No more than one major monastery occurs in any one shire although some shires also had a major nunnery, and Canterbury and Winchester had both a monastic cathedral as well as a major monastery. The exception is Worcestershire with a monastic cathedral (Worcester) and two major monasteries (Evesham and Pershore).

Those which existed by 1066 are listed in Table 7. Nunneries are indicated by (n). The monasteries had varying fortunes over the following centuries. However, eight of the top ten Anglo-Saxon abbeys were still in the top sixteen abbeys at the dissolution in 1536–40. All values given are those for the abbeys' lands at 1066, calculated from the Domesday Book.

## Table 7 — Monasteries

| Abbey | Value | Shire | Reform or Foundation | Earlier Foundation | Reformer or Founder |
|---|---|---|---|---|---|
| Ely | £730 | Cambridge | 970 | (n) 673 | Bp Æþelwold |
| Glastonbury | £670 | Somerset | 940 | early | Abp Dunstan |
| Abingdon | £430 | Berkshire | c954 | 675 | Bp Æþelwold |
| St Augustine's | £420 | Kent | c960 | c600 | Abp Dunstan |
| Ramsey | £390 | Huntingdon | c969 | - | Abp Oswold |
| Westminster | £390 | Middlesex | c959 | - | Abp Dunstan |
| St Edmund's | £320 | Suffolk | 1020 | c633 | Bp Ælfwine & King Cnut |
| Wilton (n) | £310 | Wiltshire | c965 | 830? | Wulfþryð, wife of Eadgar I |
| New Minster | £280 | Hampshire | 964 | 901 | Bp Æþelwold (King Eadward I) |
| Shaftesbury (n) | £280 | Dorset | -980 | c888 | (King Ælfred) |
| St Alban's | £260 | Hertford | c970 | c793 | Abp Oswold |
| Chertsey | £200 | Surrey | -964 | 666 | Bp Æþelwold |
| Cerne | £170 | Dorset | -987 | - | Ald Æþelmær |
| Barking (n) | £160 | Essex | c946/c965 | c666 | Abp Dunstan? |
| Malmesbury | £140 | Wiltshire | 965 | c637 | Abp Dunstan |
| Evesham | £140 | Worcester | c970/c995 | +701 | Bp Ealdwulf (Abp Oswold) |
| Peterborough | £130 | Northampton | c966 | 655 | Bp Æþelwold |

| Abbey | Value | Shire | Reform or Foundation | Earlier Foundation | Reformer or Founder |
|---|---|---|---|---|---|
| Romsey (n) | £120 | Hampshire | 967 | c907 | Bp Æþelwold (King Eadward I) |
| Pershore | £110 | Worcester | c970 | c689 | Abp Oswold |
| Coventry | £100 | Warwick | 1043 | - | Earl Leofric |
| Milton | £90 | Dorset | 964 | - | Bp Æþelwold |
| St Benet's | £80 | Norfolk | 1019 | c800 | King Cnut |
| Winchcombe | £80 | Gloucester | c970 | 798 | Abp Oswold |
| Abbotsbury | £70 | Dorset | 1044 | - | Orc, thane |
| Bath | £70 | Somerset | c963 | (n) c676 | Abp Dunstan |
| Tavistock | £70 | Devon | 975/80 | - | Ordwulf, thane |
| Thorney | £60 | Cambridge | 973 | -675 | Bp Æþelwold |
| Crowland | £50 | Holland | +971 | +716 | Ald Æþelwine |
| Gloucester | £50 | Gloucester | c1022 | (n) -679 | Abp Wulfstan |
| Amesbury (n) | £50 | Wiltshire | c979 | - | Queen Ælfþryð |
| Nunminster (n) | £50 | Hampshire | 963 | c900 | Bp Æþelwold (Queen Ealhswið) |
| Muchelney | £40 | Somerset | c950 | -693 | Abp Dunstan |
| Cranborne | £40 | Dorset | c980 | - | Æþelward, thane |
| Wherwell (n) | £40 | Hampshire | c986 | - | Queen Ælfþryð |
| Athelney | £20 | Somerset | c960 | c880 | Abp Dunstan (King Ælfred) |
| Burton | £20 | Stafford | 1002/04 | - | Wulfric, thane |
| Eynsham | £20 | Oxford | 1005 | - | Ald Æþelmær |
| Chatteris (n) | £20 | Cambridge | 1006/16 | - | Bp Eadnoð |
| Buckfast | £15 | Devon | 1018 | - | Ald Æþelward |
| Horton | £15 | Dorset | c1050 | (n) c970 | Ordgar, thane, or son Ordwulf |
| Polesworth (n) | ? | Warwick | c980 | -839 | Abp Oswold? |

Note: names of earlier founders or reformers are in brackets  (n) = nunnery

Most abbeys had earlier foundations which either did not at first succeed or, if successful, were disrupted during the Viking invasions. The only monasteries founded before the 9th century that are thought to have survived throughout were Glastonbury and St Augustine's. Not all the later monastic foundations or refoundations were successful. A number failed to thrive up to 1066 and we have only the sketchiest information about such places. Among those known about are Bedford, Cholsey, Leominster (n), Reading (n) and Westbury (transferred to Ramsey). Others had to be refounded after initial failure, e.g. Evesham.

**Priories and cells**  Some monasteries were dependencies of foreign abbeys, or near neighbours. The four foreign dependencies were Deerhurst (under Paris, £35), Mersea (under Rouen, £25), Lewisham (under Ghent, £15), and Lapley (under Rheims, £5). Other dependencies were Alkborough (cell of Spalding), Peakirk (under Crowland), Rumburgh (under St Benet), St Ives (under Ramsey), St Neots (under Ely), Spalding (under Crowland), and Tewkesbury (under Cranborne).

## English Society

**Thanes**  Society in late Anglo-Saxon England was very hierarchical. The people whom we see in the historical record are merely the tip of the pyramid. At the top of that pyramid was the King and royal family. This was a relatively small group. Underneath royalty, there was a threefold classification of the population into nobility, commoners and slaves. The nobility were referred to as thanes, a term which covered groups that would later be differentiated into various levels of lords, and 'lesser gentry'. The highest group of nobility was the Aldermen or Earls. These did not form a closed group but depended on royal appointment. Underneath these, the wealthier landowners were the King's thanes, granted land by the King in return for services. These included army service, repair of bridges and maintenance of fortifications. Granting land was a traditional means of rewarding the King's servants. King's thanes varied in wealth from people who could approach the Earls in influence and power to those whose influence was limited to the shire or just a few townships. Earls and larger thanes might themselves have their own thanes, owning or leasing land in return for services to their lord. There is some evidence (Fleming 1979) that a group of larger thanes, with over £40 of land, were thought of as a separate section of the nobility. These would be equivalent to the later medieval barons. Thanes could be granted rights of justice over their lands. In many cases, this would involve holding their own courts but might involve them merely collecting the fines imposed on their men in the public courts of the hundred or shire. A powerful means of binding thanes, and even commoners, into political connections was by means of commendation. This was the voluntary acceptance of someone's lordship. The patron would defend the client and further his interests while the client would provide his patron with a body of supporters to bolster his political position.

**The Elite of 1066**  The documentary sources allow us to identify who formed the elite of the country by 1066. Underneath the King were the 6 Earls and 14 Bishops whose power and influence stemmed from their office. The larger landowners with lands worth more than £40 consisted of 90 thanes (Clarke 1994) and 25 Abbots. Of more local importance, but powerful enough to be actors on the national stage were the 34 Sheriffs and perhaps the greater merchants. Identifying the latter is difficult in the absence of urban records. We may perhaps assume that the moneyers who were licensed to mint the nation's coinage in the boroughs comprise this class. Under Harold II, there were perhaps a little over 150 moneyers.

Of these, only 30 were of more than local significance. To this elite, we must add the royal court and its officials. The total core elite of England then amounted to just under 250 people. The wider elite who controlled the regions and localities would include the 4–5,000 named thanes of the Domesday survey, the lesser merchants, reeves of the hundreds, Abbots of the smaller monasteries, archdeacons, priors and others. It would be difficult to make all these add up to anywhere near 10,000, unless we accept the military service of one man from every 5 hides of land as a general rule (Abels 1988). In which case the military elite would amount to around 13,000 men. This would represent only about 4% of the households in the country.

**Local Society**  Society was truly unequal. It was also a local society. For most people, their judicial and social world was that of the shire, hundred and township. The 4–5,000 named thanes of the Domesday survey would be thinly spread at a local level. There would be perhaps 100–150 of them in an average shire and may be only 6 in a representative hundred. There were certainly too few for each of the approximately 13,500 townships to have its own resident thane. The more local the arena, the greater was the potential influence of the common people. The customs of the manor might enshrine the lord's entitlements from his men, but would also set limits to what he could exact. Commoners were still freemen with rights. A lord's power was not arbitrary and at the local level could only be exercised through his local officials, themselves part of the local commoner society. England at this time was still a society where most people could have dealings with one another face-to-face. The average township contained just 100–150 people, while even the hundred would only have 2000–2500.

**Commoners**  The commoners could be classified into various groups (Loyn 1991). All commoners were freemen, they were not yet legally defined as serfs. However, the term freeman is sometimes reserved specifically for an upper group of commoners who held land freely, although they might lie within the court jurisdiction of a particular thane. Commoners who had the right and duty to attend local courts were often termed sokemen (soke being a court jurisdiction), and were not tied to the manor. Most commoners would hold land from a particular lord in return for agricultural services or rents. These could be substantial farmers, or smallholders whose main income came from labouring on other people's farms or from pursuing craft activities like blacksmithing. An aspect of medieval society that is commonly forgotten is social mobility. Commoners could thrive to become thanes and thanely families could become extinct or be dispossessed. However, at any one time, there was a sharp distinction between the two.

**Slaves**  There would also be a large pool of people who owned no land but made their living solely by working for others. Some of these would be legally slaves, with no civil rights in the courts. However, slaves were protected in law and had some basic rights, even though they were technically the property of their owner. Reducing a person to slavery was one of the punishments available to the courts for criminal offences. People might also sell themselves into slavery in times of hardship, being willing to trade their civil status for secure accommodation, clothing and food. Slaves were allowed to work on their own behalf and could accumulate enough money to buy their freedom. Lords would also free slaves themselves as an act of charity and a number of documents survive recording this.

**Gender**   A major social divide was that between men and women. Politics, government, office-holding and warfare were definitely men's activities. The woman's world was one of looking after the household, bearing and caring for children. Wider opportunities for women were rare. However, late Anglo-Saxon England did allow women more of a role than they would have later in the medieval period (Fell 1984). Women could be landowners in their own right and could bequeath land freely. Records survive of women taking action, and defending themselves, in the courts successfully against male relatives. Women could escape their limited role by turning to the cloister. Becoming a nun or lay sister was an attractive alternative to many.

**The Church**   Parallel to the secular hierarchy was that of the Church with its well defined grades and offices. An Archbishop was rated as equal to a Prince of the realm while Bishops were the equivalent of Earls. It is uncertain where Abbots rated but they were certainly equal to the Bishops and greater thanes in wealth. Priests would come from various social backgrounds and in proprietary churches must have been very much subject to their lords. However, Church writers were keen to improve the stature and standards of the clergy and would have liked celibate priests to be given the rank of thane. Priests were important members of society with their position as intermediary between God and man, and their lengthy education and training.

**Urban Society**   Towns lay outside the usual pattern of lordship and landholding that belonged to rural estates. It was in the boroughs that merchants were concentrated, pursuing an economy very different to that of the landlords in the countryside. One tract of the period suggests that the wealthier merchants would rank alongside thanes in status. Other professions that are difficult to fit into the rural pattern would have been physicians and lawyers. It is uncertain whether there were true lawyers at this period but there are people described as lawmen in certain boroughs. These may be influential citizens of the borough fulfilling legal functions rather than specialists in the law. The boroughs were a source of great profit to the King, to the nobility and the merchants. This profit came from market tolls, court fines, property rents and taxes.

# Language and Literature
# (Godden and Lapidge 1991, Mitchell 1995)

One feature that marked England out from its continental neighbours was its rich tradition of writing in its own spoken language. Outside the Byzantine Empire, Latin was the language of writing. Only in England and Ireland before the 12th century was the language of the people used to any extent as a written language. Occasional examples of English survive from the 8th and early 9th centuries. The reign of Ælfred saw English used for an important series of translations and original works. The monastic reformation under Eadgar I saw the establishment of a written standard based on the Church schools of Winchester. This became the written language of the whole country alongside Latin.

The stage of English spoken and written during the period is called Old English. Surviving documents of the time are in four main dialects, Northumbrian (north of the Humber), Mercian (the midlands), Kentish (the far south-east) and West Saxon (south of the Thames). Most of the differences are in pronunciation (accent), but there are also differences in grammar and words used. West Saxon was the basis of King Ælfred's English and of the later standard Old English. The other dialects are represented by rare early works and a few later ones. Modern Standard English developed in the 15th century from the language spoken in London. Then its dialect was that of the south-east midlands. Hence, Modern English and Old English represent different dialects.

**Literature** Writings in English that survive from this period (Renwick and Orton 1966) can be divided into three main types: religious prose, secular prose (Swanton 1975), poetry (Bradley 1982). Since most manuscripts survive from monastic archives, we have far more religious material than secular. Monasteries and cathedrals were not only essential for preserving manuscripts of the period, but were also the main translators, composers and collectors of literary works.

Religious works include a large number of homilies, with lesser numbers of saints' lives, liturgical works, and translations of sections from the Bible. Secular prose shows a great variety. These include charters and writs, letters, administrative records, laws and legal treatises, wills and scientific works. Major works are the chronicles, and the translations (both secular and religious) of major Latin works by King Ælfred and his circle. There are also a few anonymous prose fictional narratives. The most important authors of English works after Ælfred were Abbot Ælfric, Archbishop Wulfstan and the monk Brihtferð. About 30,000 lines of poetry survive, over three quarters on religious themes. The longest and most well-known poem is Beowulf, but there are also over 100 other poems, collections of riddles and translations of the psalms. Most of the poetry survives in just six manuscripts of the late 10th and early 11th centuries.

**Old English**   There are many differences between Old and Modern English. These differences are of four types.

–   spelling: even where pronunciation has changed little, their spelling may be quite different; e.g. *scip* for *ship*, *ecg* for *edge*, *geolu* for *yellow*, *cirice* for *church*.
–   vocabulary: many words have dropped out of use, being replaced by Latin or French equivalents; e.g. *dema* by *judge*, *astigan* by *ascend*, *gelome* by *frequently*. Where words survive they have often changed their meaning; e.g. *modig* (moody = spirited), *woh* (woe = wrong), *dysig* (dizzy = foolish).
–   endings: Old English made greater use of endings to show the precise meaning of a word within a sentence; e.g. *seo sunne scinð* for *the sun is shining*, but *seo sunne scine* for *the sun may shine*. Word order was less important, *se dogga bitt þone mann* and *þone mann bitt se dogga* both mean *the dog is biting the man*. For *the man bites the dog* you need to write *se mann bitt þone doggan*.
–   pronunciation: this has changed a great deal in most words, but usually in predictable ways; e.g. *stan* to *stone*, *hus* to *house*, *hafoc* to *hawk*, *cyning* to *king*.

**Pronunciation**   Pronunciation of English changed during the period covered by this book. The outline given here is for the situation as it may have been in 1066 and is meant only as a general guide. A more accurate account can be found in Campbell (1959). The Old English alphabet differed slightly from Modern English, the letters *j* and *q* were missing, and *k* and *z* (ts) were used only rarely. There were three letters not found in the modern alphabet, *Þ þ, Ð ð* (both used to represent the *th* sound), and a letter resembling *P p* but with a pointed bow, used for *w*. The letters *f* , *þ* and *s* were used for the *f*, *th* (as in *bath*) and *s* sounds, but also the *v*, *dh* (spelled *th* as in *bathe*) and *z* sounds. They signified the latter sounds when they stood between vowels (e.g. *fot* = *foot*, *lufu* = *love*, *self* = *self*). The letter *h* was like the modern *h* only when at the beginning of a word. Elsewhere, it was pronounced like the *ch* in Scots *loch*. Some combinations of letters had one sound; *sc* was like modern *sh*, e.g. *scip* (*ship*), and *cg* was like modern *dg*, e.g. *ecg* (*edge*). In other combinations of consonants, all the letters were pronounced, even where it would be difficult today, e.g. *cnawan* (to know). There are only two letters that cause problems, *c* and *g*. The letter *c* was pronounced:

•   as *k* in most positions; e.g. *cuppe* (*cup*), *cneo* (*knee*)
•   as *ch* when next to the letters *e* and *i*, and mostly when after *æ* and *y*; e.g. *cinn* (*chin*), *cycene* (*kitchen*).

The letter *g* covered three different sounds:

•   as modern *y* when next to *e*, *i* and *y*, also when after *æ*; e.g. *gese* (*yes*), *dæg* (*day*)
•   otherwise as modern *g* only at the beginning of a word; e.g. *god* (*good*)
•   or in the middle of words, like a more heavily breathed version of the *ch* in *loch*, which in Modern English has been replaced by *w*; e.g. *dragan* (*to draw*)

There are exceptions to these rules for *c* and *g* but they will serve for pronouncing most of the personal names found in this book.

There were seven letters used as vowels; *a, æ, e, i, o, u, y*. Each had a short and long version. Table 8 shows how they might have been pronounced by 1066 using modern words with a similar sound.

### table 8 — Pronunciation of old english vowels

|   | short | long |   |   | short | long |
|---|-------|------|---|---|-------|------|
| *æ* | *at* | *air* |   | *a* | *car* | *card* |
| *e* | *met* | *may* |   | *o* | *rod* | *road* |
| *i* | *sin* | *seen* |   | *u* | *but* | *boot* |

The letter *y* was similar to the Scots 'tight' *u* in words like *foot* and *hus (house)*. There were two combinations of vowels used in spelling by the 11th century: *ea* which was like *æ, eo* which was almost like *her* (short) and *herd* (long).

An example of late Old English is a writ of Cnut from 1035:

> Cnut cyngc gret Eadsige b. & Ælfstan abb. & Ægelric. & ealle mine þegenas on Cent freondlice. & ic cyðe eow þæt ic hæbbe geunnan Æþelnoðe arcebisceope. ealre þare landare þe Ælfmær hæfde. & mid rihte into Cristes cyricean gebyrað. binnan birig & butan. on wuda & on felda. swa full & swa forð swa Ælfric arceb. hyre weold oþþe ænig his forgengena.

> (Cnut, King, greets Eadsige, Bishop, & Ælfstan, Abbot, & Ægelric. & all my thanes in Kent friendly. & I declare to you that I have granted to Æþelnoð, Archbishop. all of that landed property which Ælfmær had. & which rightly belongs to Christ Church. within borough and without. in wood and plain. as full and as completely as Ælfric, Archbishop, possessed it or any of his predecessors.)

## Personal Names (Reaney and Wilson 1991)

**Spelling Names**  The modern practice in printing of medieval personal names varies a great deal. Names after 1066 are usually printed in their modern form. So, we have William instead of Willelm, Geoffrey instead of Goisfrið etc. For names before 1066, this is not the case. Few Old English names survive into Modern English as forenames, although many do as surnames. Those which do survive as modern forenames are often spelled in the modern way, while the others are not. Using indexes thus becomes frustrating as Edward (Eadward) and Ethelred (Æþelred) may be widely separated from Eadwig and Æþelwold. This practice also tends to emphasise the difference between English history before and after 1066. That coming after being full of familiar names, while that before has names that seem outlandish and hard to pronounce. A further inconsistency is that modern editors of the Domesday survey have used 13th century Icelandic spellings for names of Norse origin used in England in the 11<sup>th</sup> century. Thus emphasising the ethnic origin of a name by using spellings not in use at the time gives a false impression of the ethnic affiliation of the person holding the name. To be consistent, all names below, whether English, Danish or Norman, are given in their late Old English form. These are the forms occurring in the sources of the time. Danes may have their Danish spelling given in brackets. Variations in the spelling of the time do occur, e.g. Ædward and Rotbeard for Eadward and Rodbert, but these are not listed as they are readily recognisable when encountered. Modern works often use 9<sup>th</sup> century forms of names, e.g. Eadward as Eadweard. One major variation is the element Æþel- appearing as Ægel- (becoming Ail- in the 12<sup>th</sup> century), hence Ægelred for Æþelred. Another is that Eald- (pronounced *aild*) was the West Saxon form of Anglian Ald-, so Bishop Aldhun of Durham would be known as Ealdhun in a Winchester document. Women's names are given in italics as those who are not familiar with Old English names may not be able to distinguish the women from the men. For instance, Ælfgar was a man, while *Ælfgyfu* was a woman.

Pronunciation of personal names is straightforward, using the guide to Old English outlined above: e.g. Ælfred = *Alvred*, Eadgyfu = *Airdyüver*, Æþelmær = *Adhelmair*, Ecgwynn= *Edgwün*. Note that Ceol- is pronounced with *ch*, Ceolmund = *Cherlmund*, but Cen- is not, Cenwulf = *Kenulf*.

**The Formation of Names**  Old English names were of three types. The commonest were formed of two elements, each a word in its own right but divorced from its meaning when used in names. Most elements were restricted to either first or second position. For instance, Eadward was formed of Ead (happy, blessed) and ward (ruler). Elements could be combined in a large number of combinations, e.g. Ead + ward, mund, gar, ric, red, wig, wulf, or -wine with Ead-, Ælf-, Æþel-, Wulf-, God-, Leof- etc. Second elements were often altered or shortened, e.g. frið – ferð, wulf – ulf, briht – berht. A second type of name was to use a word with the ending -ing, e.g. Bruning, Hearding or Lyfing. The third type consisted of just one element, without any obvious meaning, e.g. Beocca, Odda. This traditional stock of English names was increased by the Viking settlements and Danish conquest. Viking names were made in similar ways to English, sometimes with the same elements but often with certain preferred words that were not found in English, e.g. Þor-. Some of the elements could be anglicised, e.g. As- to Os-, -geir to -gar, while others were kept as alternatives, e.g. Norse Ulf- and English Wulf-.

Norman names were of Norse or Frankish origin, and a few were the same as those used in England, e.g. Baldric, Þurstan. The English Odda/Oda, was found among the Normans as Odo. The Norse Osbeorn occurred in Normandy as Osbern, and Osmund could be either English or Norman. The Norse name Stigand was shared by the English Archbishop of Canterbury and a Norman Bishop of Rochester. Bishop Ulf of Dorchester was a Norman, but with a Norse name. Archbishop Stigand's brother had the English name of Æþelmær.

It is important to realise that the use of a name does not imply ethnic affiliation. There are many examples. The English Earl Ælfgar had two sons, one with an English name (Eadwine) and the other with a Danish name (Morcere). The Breton Rodbert FizWymarc gave his son the Danish name of Swegn. The Danish follower of Cnut Tofig gave his son the English name of Æþelstan.

**Survival of Names**  English and Norse names found in this guide which survive to the present, or were revived for modern use, are:

### English

| | | |
|---|---|---|
| **Ælfmær (Elmer)** | Eadgar (Edgar) | Norþman (Norman) |
| Ælfred (Alfred) | *Eadgyð* (Edith) | Oswold (Oswold) |
| *Ælfþryð* (Audrey) | Eadmund (Edmund) | Wilferð (Wilfred) |
| Ælfwine (Alvin) | Eadward (Edward) | Wynstan (Winston) |
| Cuðberht (Cuthbert) | Eadwine (Edwin) | |
| Dunstan (Dunstan) | Ecgberht (Egbert) | |

### Norse

| | | |
|---|---|---|
| Anlaf (Olaf) | Harold (Harold) | Magnus (Magnus) |
| Guþfrið (Godfrey) | Hawerd (Howard) | Rægnald (Ronald) |
| Hacun (Hakon) | Inwær (Ivor) | Yric (Erik) |

There are many that survive as surnames, often with variant forms (by the 12th century, some name elements had become confused with one another in pronunciation, e.g. Ælf-, Æþel-, Eald-, Ealh- could have become Al-, and might lead to the same modern surname). Those found in this guide are:

### English

| | | |
|---|---|---|
| Ælfgar (Algar/Elgar) | Æþelric (Etheridge) | Cola (Cole) |
| Ælfgeat (?Allott/Eliot) | Æþelward (Aylward) | Cuðwulf (Culf) |
| Ælfheah (Elphick) | Æþelwig (?Alaway) | Cynemund (?Kinman) |
| Ælfhere (Alvar) | Æþelwine (Aylwin) | Cynesige (Kinsey) |
| *Ælflæd* (Alflatt) | Æþelwulf (Ayloffe) | Cyneward (Kenward) |
| Ælfnoð (Allnatt) | Beocca (Beck) | Cynric (Kerrich) |
| Ælfric (Aldrich) | Brihtmær (Brihtmore) | Eadred (Errett) |
| Ælfsige (Elsey) | Brihtwig (Brighty) | Eadric (Edrich) |
| Ælfstan (Allston) | Brihtwine (Brightween) | Eadwig (Eddy) |
| *Ælfþryð* (Audrey) | Bruning (Browning) | Eadwulf (Eddols) |
| Ælfward (Allward) | Burgheard (Burrard) | Ealdhun (?Alden) |
| Ælfwig (Elvey/Alvey) | Burhred (Burrett) | Ealdred (Aldred) |
| Ælfwold (Elwood) | Burgric (?Burridge) | Ealhstan (Elston) |
| *Æþelgyfu* (Ayliffe) | Burhwold (Burall) | Garwulf (Gorrell) |
| Æþelmær (Aylmer) | Ceolmund (?Chillman) | *Godgyfu* (Goodeve) |

Godric (Goodrich/Godrich)
Godwine (Goodwin/Godwin)
Guðheard (?Goddard)
Hearding (Harding)
Hereward (Hereward)
Leofgar (Loveguard)
Leofric (Leveridge)
Leofsige (Lewsey)
Leofwine (Lewin)
Lyfing (Levinge/Livings)
Odda (Odd)

Ordgar (Orgar)
Osmund (Osmond/Osman)
Sideman (Seedman)
Sigegar (Siggers)
Sigered (Sirett)
Sigeric (Search)
Spearhafoc (Sparrowhawk)
Swetman (Sweetman)
Uhtred (Oughtred)
Wada (Wade)
Walþeof (Walthew/Waddilove)

Wigmund (Wyman)
Wulfgar (Woolgar)
Wulfhun (?Woolven)
Wulfmær (Woolmer)
Wulfnoð (Woolner/Woolnoth)
Wulfric (Woolrich/Wooldridge)
Wulfsige (Wolsey)
Wulfstan (Woolston)
Wulfwig (Woolaway)

## Norse

Beorn (Barne)
Bondig (Bond)
Brand (Brand)
Cnut (Knott)
Coll (Coll)
Copsig (Copsey)
Ðurig (Thorey)
Gamal (Gamble)
Grim (Grimm/Grimes)
*Gunnhildr* (Gunnell)
Gunner (Gunn/Gunner)

Guþrum (Goodrum)
Healfdene (Haldane)
Hemming (Hemming)
Osbeorn (Osborn)
Oscytel (Ashkettle)
Osgod (Osgood)
Oslac (Haslock)
Rægnold (Reynold)
Siward (Seward)
Stigand (Styan)
Swegn (Swain)

Tofig (Tovey)
Tolig (Tooley)
Þurcyll (Thurkell)
Þurcytel (Thurkettle)
Þurferð (Tollfree)
Ulf (Ulph)
Ulfcytel (Uncle)
Urm (Orme)
Wigod (Wiggett)

French and German names, which historians usually give their modern forms, are found in 11th century English sources as:

Alan
Baldwine (Baldwin)
Breon (Brian)
Carl (Charles)
Conrad (Konrad)
Drogo (Dreux)
Duduc
Earnald (Ernald – Arnold)
Earnulf (Ernulf/Arnulf)
Eustatius (Eustace)
Gerbod

Gisa
Henrig (Henry)
Hereman (Herman)
Hloðhere (Lothaire)
Hloþwig (Louis)
Hugo (Hugh)
*Leodgeard* (Liutgard)
Leodulf (Liudolf)
*Mahtild* (Matilda)
Odda (Otto)

Philippus (Philip)
Raulf (Ralph)
Regenbald
Ricard (Richard)
Rodbert (Robert)
Walter (Walter)
Willelm (William)
*Ymme* (Emma)

Welsh and Scottish names mostly survive to the present. Those found in late Old English documents include:

## Welsh

| | | |
|---|---|---|
| Asser | Cradoc (Caradog) | Hris (Rhys) |
| Bleðgente (Bleddyn) | Cunan | Ieoþwel (Idwal) |
| Cadwgaun (Cadwgan) | Etwin (Edwin) | Rigwatlan (Rhiwallon) |
| Censtec | Griffin (Gruffydd) | |
| Comoere | Howel (Hywel) | |

## Scottish

| | | |
|---|---|---|
| Cynað (Cinaed – Kenneth) | Dunecan (Duncan) | Macbeth) |
| Dufenal (Domhnall – Donald) | Iehmarc (Echmarcach) | Mælcolm (Mælcolum – Malcolm) |
| | Iuchill (Iocaill) | |
| | Macbeoþen (Macbethad – | |

Biblical, saints' and papal names were beginning to be used during the period:

| | | |
|---|---|---|
| *Agatha* | *Cristina* (Christine) | Iago (Iago – Jacob) |
| Alexander | Daniel | *Margareta* (Margaret) |
| *Beatrice* | Dauid (David) | *Maria* (Mary) |

# Effects of the Norman Conquest

**The Aristocracy**  The Norman Conquest did not create England. Nevertheless, it did have some profound effects. The most obvious of these was the displacement of the native higher aristocracy. The 4–5,000 English thanes of 1066 had been replaced by a group of under 200 Norman tenants-in-chief of the crown and a number of lesser thanes. The group that would later become the barons of the realm were overwhelmingly Norman. Out of 78 landowners with land worth more than £100 in 1086, there were just four Englishmen (Eadward of Salisbury, Swein of Essex, Ælfred of Marlborough and Þorcyll of Warwick), two of whom were of Norman parents settled in England before 1066 (Swegn and Ælfred). A further seven had land worth over £40 (Colswegn of Lincoln, Ælfred of Lincoln, Princess *Cristina*, Godric the Steward and Brihtric of Wiltshire, with two of French origin Harold son of Raulf and Osbeorn FitzRicard). In all, Englishmen counted for only 5% of the new tenants-in-chief. Some former tenants-in-chief were left in place with less land under new Norman lords. For instance, Siward of Shropshire was a kinsman of Eadward III who held 95 hides of land before 1066. After the conquest he held 12 hides as a tenant of Earl Roger, Osbern FitzRicard and Roger de Lacy. The lesser thanes that would become the later knightly class were probably a mixture of Norman and English. Modern research suggests that a great many English survived at the lower levels of the elite and the proportion of native English would be greatest among the lowest group of thanes that would later be called the gentry. There was a large number of English King's thanes identified in the Domesday Survey with only small amounts of land. Among the officeholders, Normans monopolised the offices of Earl, Sheriff and central administration. The native English were confined largely to the lesser, but essential, local offices of reeve, bailiff and geld collector. The Normans also brought with them their servants and many merchants came over to settle in the towns. However, the native English remained the main element within the merchant class and monopolised the group from whom the moneyers were drawn. The placing of castles in towns involved the destruction of much urban property and had a short term negative effect on urban prosperity. However, many new towns were created around new castles by lords eager to create profitable markets. They were also eager to exploit their landed estates to the full and financially exploited their lands more intensively than their native predecessors.

**Land and Service** The displacement of the native aristocracy led to new patterns of landholding. The proportion of land held by the King was greatly increased, although this had already come about with the accession of Harold to the throne, merging his own vast holdings with those of Eadward III. The new aristocracy was less dominated by a few over-wealthy Earls and landholding was spread more widely among the major tenants in chief. The great regional earldoms were not continued after the 1070s and instead smaller compact lordships were created in sensitive border areas like the Welsh marches and Channel coast. The conquest was a military event and was symbolised by the Norman innovation of the castle, a few of which had been built before 1066 by Norman followers of Eadward III. These acted as the centres of lordships with administrative as well as military functions. It is the latter which were a Norman innovation and altered the nature of military campaigning henceforth. The use of mounted knights as cavalry in battle was also new, although the Normans would also fight on foot when necessary. The levy of men for the army continued but by the 12th century this took the form of knight service quotas owed by landlords which could be turned into a money payment (scutage) for the hire of mercenaries. The arrangement is different in terminology and detail but perhaps not in actual operation from the native English method of levying men according the rating of the lands held by the landlord, which could also be used to levy money to hire mercenary troops.

**Law and Coinage** In law and administration, there were few changes. Trial by combat became a part of English judicial procedure and special fines were created to protect the new French settlers from English attacks. However, the laws of England remained those in force before 1066 and the hierarchy and functions of the public courts remained unaltered. One major innovation was the introduction of forest laws to carve out areas of royal monopoly of hunting, no matter on whose land. The use of writs to link central and local government continued, although after the 1070s, they were usually in Latin instead of English and had their date of issue and a list of witnesses added. Coinage remained as it had been, a royal monopoly with periodic recoinage minted locally from centrally produced dies. The only changes were a standardisation in weight of the penny and a different way of levying tax on the moneyers (by borough instead of individually).

**The Church** The Church was taken over by Norman Bishops and Abbots. English Abbots were few by the end of Willelm's reign. The Church itself was brought within the reform movement sooner than it otherwise might have been by the appointment of continental leaders. Archbishop Lanfranc held a series of reforming synods from 1072 to 1076. Part of this reform was the rebuilding of churches in Romanesque building styles and the move of sees to the towns and wealthy abbeys. These might have happened anyway as the first moves in both were made under Eadward III. Reform was limited, as strong royal control over the Church was accepted by all the new Bishops and such control was one of the 'abuses' being attacked by the Papal reformers. The purchase of ecclesiastical office and married clergy were also aspects of the Anglo-Saxon Church which continued unreformed. A new feature however was the creation of territorial archdeaconries as subdivisions of the diocese. Canon law cases were removed from the jurisdiction of the hundred courts, although not from the shire court where the Bishop continued to preside alongside the Sheriff. A dispute between Canterbury and York over the primacy of England was also a product of the conquest. The unique feature of monastic cathedral chapters was retained and expanded with Durham and Rochester added to the list, as were some of the new cathedrals (Bath, Carlisle, Coventry, Ely and Norwich). A new monastic liturgy was created by Lanfranc at Canterbury which was adopted elsewhere while others, like Winchester, kept to the traditional liturgy of the *Regularis Concordia*. There was an increase in lands held in England by foreign (mostly Norman) abbeys, and priories set up as dependencies of foreign abbeys. However, the new landlords also patronised existing English abbeys and soon founded new ones. Amongst these were the first Cluniac priories in England. The re-establishment of monasteries in Northumbria came after the conquest but Anglo-Saxon monks had a key hand in this along with the Normans. Relations between monks and their new Norman Abbots or Bishops were at times troubled but most of the Normans fostered the traditions of their institution, including the veneration of English saints. However, there was much disruption and higher ecclesiastical offices were largely closed to the English leaving them to form the bulk of the monks and parish priests.

**Art and Architecture** The Romanesque building style used for the new cathedrals was based on a concept of size, space and ornament that was fundamentally different to the native English aesthetic taste. It has often been said that native tastes emerged again in the 12th century Cistercian building style (an important founder of Cistercian ideals was an English monk, Harding). The rebuilding of Canterbury cathedral and St Augustine's abbey during the 1070s in the Romanesque style began the process of replacing native architectural traditions. However, Eadward III's new Westminster abbey was also Romanesque and English features continued to be used as part an English Romanesque distinct from that of Normandy. The traditional fine art styles were the native Winchester and the Danish Ringerike styles. By 1066, the Winchester style was adopting traits that foreshadow the continental Romanesque. By the 1080s, there are manuscripts showing a mix of Romanesque and Winchester features and native characteristics that continued until the first fully Romanesque style art appears by the 1120s. The Ringerike style also continued and even its successor, the Urnes style was adopted alongside the native and continental styles.

**Language**  The court, upper nobility, most of the Sheriffs and leadership of the Church spoke French and the tradition of using standard English as an official written language ceased. Only occasional writs in English survive after the 1070s. Standard Old English continued to be used for the versions of the Anglo-Saxon Chronicle written at various monasteries and for the collection of laws made at Rochester in the 1120s. The standard Old English ceased to be written after the 1130s by which time it no longer reflected how the language was really spoken. Written English (used for a wide variety of literary works and homilies) was henceforth that of the dialects and a new standard had to be forged 300 years later from the spoken language of London.

**Names and People**  The dominance of a Norman ruling class led those English who survived at this level to assimilate in order to be accepted. One sign of this was that English parents began giving their children Norman names. The large variety of English names was replaced over the next 150 years by a more restricted and repetitive list of continental names. In 1066, we know the names of 48 men who were royalty, Earls, Bishops or Sheriffs. They had 47 names between them. By 1154, we know of 68 men in the same positions who shared just 27 names. Seven of these names accounted for 46 of the men (William, Robert, Richard, Henry, Hugh, Walter, Geoffrey). One consequence of the conquest might be that the lines between nobility and commonalty were more tightly drawn and perhaps made stricter by differences of culture, an Anglo-French gentry looking down on Anglo-Saxon rustics. Writers of the time remarked on the arrogance and superiority of the Normans and the uncouthness of the Anglo-Saxon peasant and his language. By the mid 12th century native English names were restricted to the lower classes who gradually abandoned them in favour of the continental upper class names during the 13th century. One important social effect of the conquest was to downgrade the status and rights of women. They had little place in the male, military world of the Norman baron. However, this should not be overemphasised. The role of women before 1066 was limited and there were women who played important political roles after 1066.

**The Link with France**  The tying of England to possessions in France led to frequent absences of the King from England. This can only have helped the development of an independent central government machine that becomes so obvious under Henry I after 1100. The new Kings of England had extensive possessions on the continent and the involvement, both politically and militarily, in France was aided by the revenues of the rich country of England. Whether the long series of wars in France that England was involved in for the rest of the medieval period was of benefit to England or not, it was an endless source of activity for the new nobility.

**Conclusion**    The Norman Conquest had an important impact on England. However, apart from changes in personnel few institutional changes of substance resulted in the short term, and much of the basic framework of England stayed the same. Some changes would have come anyway as Anglo-Saxon England was constantly changing in response to its links with the continent and its internal pressures. England's relations with its neighbours, both on the continent and in the British Isles were fundamentally changed and England received a new aristocracy but the power and rights of the crown, the legal system and laws, the public administration through shire, hundred and township, the central administrative machine, the coinage system, the sees and parishes of the Church, and the language of the people are only a few of the things that survived from late Anglo-Saxon England. It was not until the reign of Henry II after 1154 that the mould created by the Anglo-Saxon Kings, 150 years before the Norman Duke set foot on English soil, was substantially altered.

# Sources of Evidence

## Historical Sources (Gransden 1974)

There are a number of documentary sources that survive from this period. The most important narrative is the Anglo-Saxon Chronicle (*C*), begun in 892. This was a monastic chronicle that survives in six versions, sharing many sections but also largely independent for some of their entries. A Latin version was produced by Alderman Æþelward (*Æ*) in the late 10th century. Two works referring to specific events are an account of the monastic reformation by Bishop Æþelwold (*Æw*) and an account of the family of the Earls of Northumbria (*OD*). After the Norman Conquest, Latin translations of the chronicle were produced which in some cases were based on English versions no longer surviving, at Worcester (*Wo*), Durham (*SD*), Melrose (*Me*) and by Henry of Huntingdon (*Hu*). Continental historians are useful for the Danish and Norman Conquests and the reign of Cnut. For the Danes (Ashdown 1930), Snorri Sturluson (*Sn*), Saxo Grammaticus (*Sx*), Knytlingasaga (*Ks*) and Thietmar of Merseburg (*Th*) are useful. For the Norman Conquest (Allen Brown 1984), Guy of Amiens (*GA*), William of Jumieges (*WJ*) and William of Poitiers (*WP*) are important. A unique type of narrative work is the Bayeux Tapestry (*BT*), still the subject of debate among historians as to its purpose and meaning. Proper narrative histories also appear in England from the 12th century and some contain traditions about or references to late Anglo-Saxon people and events. The chief of these are by Geoffrey Gaimar (*GM*), Roger of Howden (*RH*), William of Malmesbury (*M*), Orderic Vitalis (*O*), Ralph Diceto (*RD*) and Roger of Wendover (*RW*). In addition to chronicles and histories, there are various lives of saints and others which shed a great deal of light on the period. These are overtly biased works and need to be treated with due caution. The three most important are probably the lives of King Ælfred (*As*), of Queen *Ymme* (*EE*) and of King Eadward III (*VÆ*). A life of King Æþelstan was used by William of Malmesbury (*Æs*). There are lives of the three leaders of the monastic reform, Archbishops Dunstan (*Du*) and Oswold (*VO*), and Bishop Æþelwold. Other saints and ecclesiastics were also subject to biographies. Monasteries were keen assemblers of data about their own past and information about the late Anglo-Saxon period can be found in a number of later monastic histories, chiefly Abingdon (*Ab*), Durham (*Dh*), Ely (*Ey*), Evesham (*Ev*), Pershore (*Pe*), Peterborough (*Pb*), Ramsey (*Ra*), St Edmund's (*SE*), Waltham (*Wþ*) and Wells (*We*).

None of the above works can be taken at face value however. Some are overtly biased politically, many accept rumour and romantic tales as historical fact and even the date and purpose of composition, and therefore accuracy, of some is questioned by many modern historians. For instance, the biography of King Ælfred by the Welsh Bishop Asser only survives in a transcript of a late copy, whose authenticity was challenged until Dorothy Whitelock's effective refutation of these challenges in 1959. However, the debate was reopened in 1995 when Alfred Smyth put forward a new case for it being a later Anglo-Saxon forgery. I personally think that Whitelock's defence of Asser still stands and have used the work as a source below, but the reader should read the modern references cited for current academic debates and make up their own minds.

The English government machine was highly literate and it has left behind several types of administrative document of the greatest value for reconstructing the events and institutions of the periods. These include charters (*S*), writs (*WH*), laws (*L*) and wills (*w*). These have been intensively studied by historians but can still yield new insights when skilfully analysed. Unfortunately, the purpose of charters was to show entitlement to lands and they were often preserved as later copies in which entries had been enhanced or as outright forgeries. Anyone who seeks to determine which charters are genuine beyond reasonable doubt will soon run into a quagmire of conflicting claims. Some charters are obviously original and some obviously forged but many are the subject of debate. I have tried to show this in referencing the charters but I make no claims to infallibility, relying on the documentation of debate about charters as listed by Sawyer (1968).

## Archaeology (Richards 1991)

Although the life of ordinary people is seldom revealed by historical documents, they are the stuff of archaeology which can reveal a great deal about matters invisible in the documents. The period began with the Viking attacks and settlement of the late $9^{th}$ century. Their activity is revealed by finds of hoards of money and silver. Examples of probable Viking raiders' hoards are those of Cuerdale and Croydon, while hoards made by the English to defend their wealth are probably represented by Bolton Percy and Beeston Tor Cave. Viking fortification certainly exists at Repton and others may have been found at Shillington, Wimblington and Shoebury. The Repton site has produced the famous mass Viking grave of 250 people, 80% of them adult men. Permanent reminders of the Vikings remain in the place names of the Danelaw and Northumbria, such as Derby, Grimston, Scunthorpe, Lowestoft and Micklethwaite (Cameron 1977). Our language also is sprinkled with Viking words. Many are common, everyday words like window, husband, they, egg, skin, take and law.

Some settlements of the period have been excavated. These include royal sites (Cheddar), ecclesiastical (North Elmham) and aristocratic (Portchester, Sulgrave and Goltho). Village sites investigated include Raunds, Wharram Percy and Mawgan Porth. Single farmsteads have also been investigated, e.g. St Neots, Little Paxton, Ribblehead, Gwithian and Hound Tor. These all help to provide a picture of life at the time, and of the changes in settlement pattern and society occurring during the period.

An important aspect of late Anglo-Saxon life is the towns and associated industries. London, York, Winchester, Gloucester, Chester, Wareham, Wallingford, Lincoln and Stamford are just some of the important towns to produce information about life at this time. Sometimes, excavations can add to our understanding of particular events or Kings. The deliberate planning in the layout of Winchester which can be attributed to Ælfred is an example. Another might be the deliberate slighting of the defences of Wareham in the 11th century which could be attributed to Cnut. Technological developments revealed by excavation include the use of foundations to improve building standards, either wooden sill beams set in the ground, or stone and rubble foundations for wooden houses. An increasing use of stone for building can be seen from the evidence of the parish churches and greater minsters/cathedrals. Many of the parish churches begin their structural life in the 10th century.

A major industrial innovation of the period is the use of the potter's wheel and sometimes glazing to produce new types of ceramic table and kitchen ware. Stamford led the way in this but other towns soon followed, like Winchester, Northampton, Thetford and Stafford. Other town-based crafts were wood and leather working. Stone, iron and glass working were also occurring. Textiles may well have been one of the major industries of the country. The price of wool was even regulated at one point in the laws of Eadgar I. The level of trade and taxation is revealed by the coinage of the period. England developed a sophisticated system of minting coins, reformed by Eadgar I to ensure only coins of a standard design circulated throughout the country. This involved periodic recoinage, calling in the old currency and issuing coins with new designs from the mints placed in the boroughs. From the time of Æþelstan, only the King's coins were accepted as legal tender, neither private coinage nor foreign coins were allowed to circulate. The administration of the coinage system is one concrete example of the sophistication of the late Anglo-Saxon administration.

## Dating Methods and Dates

In all documentary sources, there is confusion between different methods of dating that can trap the unwary. Today we use calendars and diaries that begin the year on 1st January. In the 10th and 11th centuries, this would be considered odd. Unfortunately, there was no general agreement as to when the year should begin. There were three options (Garmonsway 1954, Harrison 1976); 1st September (the old Roman Imperial tax year), 25th December (the birth of Christ), 25th March (the Annunciation). Thus, the death of Ælfred occurred in 899 by modern reckoning, but in 900 by reckoning that began the year on 1st September. Harold II would have succeeded in 1065 and died in 1066 if the year began on 25th March. It seems that 25th December was the most usual beginning of the year but every document needs to be carefully read before this can be assumed. The regnal years of Kings could also be used for dating. These were sometimes reckoned from his accession and sometimes from his coronation.

Specific dates were often referred to by using religious festivals. Common festivals used were Easter (varying from 15th March to 18th April), Whitsun (varying from 13th May to 6th June), Michaelmas (29th September), Martinmas (11th November), Christmas (25th December). If dates were specified it was according to the Roman calendar where days were reckoned leading up to three times of each month (Cheney 1981): the kalends (1st), nones (5th or 7th), ides (13th or 15th). So, the 9th May would be the 7th before the Ides of May, VII Id. Mai. In so far as the seasons were closely defined, they were deemed to begin on the following dates: spring on 7th February, summer on 9th May, autumn on 7th August, winter on 7th November.

Of greater interest to the common people of the time may have been the yearly holidays. The laws of Ælfred and his successors laid down statutory public holidays: Christmas (25th December–5th January), the harrowing of hell (15th February), St Gregory (12th March), Easter fortnight (15th–29th March to 18th April–2nd May), St Edward (18th March) St Dunstan (19th May), Sts Peter and Paul (29th June), Marymas (8th–15th August) and All Hallows (1st November).

# Kings and Events

## Introduction

The following sections of the book are based on the reigns of the Kings of England from Ælfred to Eadgar II. They give details about the date of birth, succession, coronation, death and burial of each King, with information about the King's title in charters and coins of the period. In some cases, there is information about portraits, or supposed portraits, surviving in manuscripts of the period; and description of appearance or character. The wives of each King are listed with their children and relevant personal details, and then notices of any people described as the King's kinsmen. The King's children are listed in order of seniority at the time, i.e. men first in order of birth and then women in order of birth. For all these entries, references to primary, or medieval, sources are given in brackets as abbreviations. The sources are listed in the bibliography.

The main features of the reign are described under various categories: politics and government, the Church, art and literature. These are then followed by a chronicle of events listed under each year of the King's reign. Care has been taken to be as accurate as possible. However, the nature of the evidence means that certain events cannot be assigned a precise date, or the date is subject to dispute. This is usually noted in the entry. The interpretation of many events in the period is open to dispute and I have chosen to let the events speak for themselves in the chronicle section. Hence, the reader will find it an unordered succession of disparate happenings. Modern accounts of people, reigns and events can be found in the bibliography by those who wish to study the period in more detail.

A summary of the Kings is given in Table 9.

**Table 9 —A Summary of Kings from Ælfred to Eadgar II**

| King | date of accession | age | date of death | age | regnal years |
|---|---|---|---|---|---|
| Ælfred | 23 Apr 871 | 22 | 26 Oct 899 | 50 | 29 |
| Eadward I | 26 Oct 899 | 28 | 17 Jul 924 | 53 | 25 |
| Æþelstan | 18 Aug 924 | 30 | 27 Oct 939 | 45 | 16 |
| Eadmund I | 27 Oct 939 | 18 | 26 May 946 | 24 | 7 |
| Eadred | 26 May 946 | 23 | 24 Nov 955 | 32 | 10 |
| Eadwig | 24 Nov 955 | 13 | 1 Oct 959 | 17 | 4 |
| Eadgar I[1] | 1 Oct 959 | 16 | 8 Jul 975 | 32 | 16 |
| Eadward II | 8 Jul 975 | 15 | 18 Mar 978 | 18 | 3 |
| Æþelred[2] | 18 Mar 978 | 10 | 23 Apr 1016 | 48 | 39 |

| King | date of accession | age | date of death | age | regnal years |
|------|------------------|-----|---------------|-----|--------------|
| Eadward II | 8 Jul 975 | 15 | 18 Mar 978 | 18 | 3 |
| Æþelred[2] | 18 Mar 978 | 10 | 23 Apr 1016 | 48 | 39 |
| Eadmund II | 23 Apr 1016 | 26 | 30 Nov 1016 | 26 | 1 |
| Cnut[3] | Dec 1016 | 28 | 12 Nov 1035 | 47 | 19 |
| Harold I | 26 Nov 1035 | 18 | 17 Mar 1040 | 23 | 5 |
| Harðacnut[4] | 18 Jun 1040 | 22 | 8 Jun 1042 | 24 | 3 |
| Eadward III | 8 Jun 1042 | 37 | 5 Jan 1066 | 61 | 24 |
| Harold II | 5 Jan 1066 | 43 | 14 Oct 1066 | 44 | 1 |
| Eadgar II | ?16 Oct 1066 | 14 | *ab. Dec 1066* | *14* | 1 |

Notes:

1 Eadgar was first made King in Mercia and Northumbria in 957 as a result of a revolt against Eadwig.

2 Swegn of Denmark was accepted as *de-facto* King late in 1013 (aged 48?) after invading England but died on 2nd Feb 1014.

3 Cnut became King in Mercia and Northumbria after a treaty with Eadmund II following the Battle of *Assandun* on 18th October 1016.

4 Harðacnut, although absent in Denmark, was King in Wessex while Harold I was King elsewhere from 1035 to 1037.

The average length of reign from 871 to 1066 was just 12½ years. This is rather shorter than the average of 16 years for neighbouring Germany and France at the same time. In part, this is because the average age of natural death for those not murdered or killed in battle was 39. Some had their natural lives cut short. Eadmund I (24) was killed during a brawl, Eadward II (18) was murdered, Eadmund II (26) probably died of wounds acquired in action, Harold II (44) was killed in battle. By succeeding at the age of 43, Harold II must have been seen as an elder statesman by comparison with his predecessors. The average age at accession was only 23 and five Kings succeeded under the age of 16. Ironically, the longest lived of the Kings had the shortest reign, Eadgar II who was still living at over 70 in the 1120s.

To distinguish the Kings before 1066 from those after, it became common to add a descriptive by-name rather than a number. Some were already in use by the 12th century but others have been coined in more recent times. The commonest of these are given in Table 10.

## Table 10 —Kings' Bynames

| | |
|---|---|
| Ælfred | the Great |
| Eadward I | the Elder |
| Eadgar I | the Peaceable |
| Eadward II | the Martyr |
| Æþelred | the 'Unready' (a mistranslation of *unræd* meaning ill advised) |
| Eadmund II | Ironside |

**Table 10 —Kings' Bynames** (continued)

| | |
|---|---|
| Swegn | Forkbeard |
| Cnut | the Great |
| Harold I | Harefoot |
| Eadward III | the Confessor |
| Harold II | Godwineson |
| Eadgar II | Æþeling (the Old English for Prince) |

# Summary of the Period 871–1074

The period covered by this book is about 200 years. Conditions in England did not stay the same throughout and a greater sense of the changes and major themes of the period can be gained by breaking it into smaller units.

## Unification 879–927

This period is dominated by the efforts of the Kings of Wessex to bring under their control all the former Anglo-Saxon Kingdoms. Up to 879, the Viking armies were destroying and settling each of the Anglo-Saxon Kingdoms. The threat to Wessex was overcome in 878 and by 879 Mercia was no longer under an independent King but in the hands of Alderman Æþelred who was subordinate to Ælfred and later married his daughter *Æþelflæd* (who herself ruled Mercia on the death of Æþelred). Their daughter *Ælfwynn* briefly exercised authority before Mercia was formally incorporated into England by *Æþelflæd's* brother Eadward I in 918. East Anglia and Danish Mercia were conquered jointly by Eadward and *Æþelflæd* in 917–18 and Northumbria was annexed by Æþelstan in 927 to complete the process. Unification was by no means a foregone conclusion. Although it could be portrayed as a reconquest of England from the Vikings, it could also be seen as a conquest by Wessex of areas never before under its direct control. The growth in status and power of the Kings from being Kings of Wessex to being Kings of England was remarkable. The trio of Ælfred, Eadward I and Æþelstan, along with *Æþelflæd*, deserve to be commemorated more widely as the founders of England.

## Definition 927–955

Two features mark this period. The struggle between England and Dublin for control of York, and the definition of the administrative and legal framework of the English state. York need not have become part of the England. It looked as much northwards and westwards as to the south. During the previous 200 years, it had stood largely apart from the Mercian and West Saxon struggle for dominance south of the Humber, had a coinage system that developed separately from the south and was an ecclesiastical province separate from and equal to Canterbury. On the other hand, it was part of the English nation, had provided the whole of the English with their 'national' historian Bæda and rule from Dublin was just as foreign as rule from Winchester. Also, England was strategically weak with a northern frontier on the line of the Mersey or Ribble and the Humber, up which fleets of ships could easily sail. In the end, the north accepted being part of England and the Kings left it to continue with its own distinctive features of administration, law and social customs. To the south of the Humber, England developed a sophisticated machinery of government balancing central and local power, based on the court, Bishops and Aldermen acting within a system of declared law and operated through public courts. This was also a time when towns were beginning to grow, with their associated trade networks and industries like pottery manufacture.

## Achievement and Crisis 955-1009

This was in many fields the 'Golden Age' of late Anglo-Saxon England. It was time of great achievements but also a time of political conflict with the potential for disaster. The achievements included bringing internal peace with accompanying economic growth and prosperity, and the officially sponsored growth of monasticism with all that entailed for learning, literature and the arts. Perhaps the greatest symbols of England's achievement were the Winchester style of decorative art, whose beauty can still take the breath away after 1000 years, and the development of a relatively standardised form of written English; apart from Greek, the earliest official language to be based on people's spoken tongue in Europe. The period is dominated by two Kings, Eadgar and Æþelred. Both succeeded to the throne in an atmosphere of intrigue and division. Increasing royal control over the new Kingdom had been achieved by creating a class of powerful noble families whose members were the regional Aldermen. Various marital and social links bound these families to the throne but tensions between them would be inevitable. Attempts to upset the existing order and bring in new families led to loyalties being strained to breaking point. Eadgar seems to have been able to stand above the factional rivalries while Æþelred was not. The latter sided with factions instead, and levels of mistrust and intrigue reached dangerous proportions near the end of his reign.

## Danish Conquest 1009-1018

England's incorporation into the Nordic Empire of Swegn and Cnut was a painful process but was a natural consequence of the preceding period. The state was wealthy which made it a tempting prize, and was well administered which made it easy for any conqueror to maintain his grip on the Kingdom. Attempt at conquest was helped by the divisions within the nobility that had marked the 'Golden Age'. Danish armies had attacked England for much of Æþelred's reign but had been fairly successfully dealt with, although the gloomy and damning description of events in the chronicles does not always reveal this as they were often written with hindsight or with political motives in mind. The Danish campaign of 1009-12 however was different and its devastation of the wealthy south-east left Swegn free to profit from the factional dissatisfaction with Æþelred in other parts of the country. Swegn's early death gave England a reprieve but resistance to his son Cnut was bedevilled by division and mistrust, the legacy of Æþelred's earlier policies. This ensured that Cnut would find English supporters and that the conquest would not lead to the wholesale displacement of the English ruling elite.

## New Orientations 1018–66

This was a period of relative stability in which England developed greater links with the continent in many spheres. Paradoxically, this went hand in hand with a developing sense of English nationhood and independence. Although Cnut ruled as King of Denmark and later also Norway, he was careful to portray himself as first and foremost King of England. Danes were given important places at court, made Earls and given landed estates but there was always a place for English families alongside them, some traditional and some newly made families. Cnut was a King who looked outwards and links with Germany were part of his foreign policy. These were reflected in the continental links of the Church where one Lotharingian priest became Cnut's chaplain and later a Bishop. The links shifted away from Scandinavia and Germany to Germany and France with the succession of Eadward III, and the foreign born element contributed greatly to England's ruling elite. Alongside this increasing integration of England into the wider European family, there was an increasing sense of English nationhood, perhaps the inevitable result of foreign conquest. This revealed itself on Cnut's death with a strong party declaring for his English born son Harold, the ready acceptance of Eadward's return representing the old royal line and the return from exile in Hungary of Prince Eadward and his family. The chief expression of this desire for independence was the support for Godwine after his exile when a pro-Norman faction was seen as having gone too far in exploiting his downfall. It could also be seen in the resistance to Church reform and the only sporadic appearance of Romanesque architecture in church building.

## Norman Conquest 1066–74

Just when Europe was beginning a new phase of its history with the Papal reforms and growing intellectual renaissance, England was dragged by force into a far closer connection with the continent. The conquest by Willelm differed in important respects from that of Cnut. Harold at his accession did not face the divided nobility that existed in 1016. This was partly due to his own overwhelming dominance (through his experience, royal support and wealth) but also to his willingness to sacrifice family for the sake of wider unity (the exile of his brother Tostig). As a result, there was no extensive native faction willing to support Willelm and widespread dispossession of the English nobility was the result. Willelm also had a strong Church in his native land, unlike Cnut, that he could use to find clerics to take over the higher positions in the English Church. Also, Cnut had faced an adult opponent capable of rallying the nobility, Eadmund II. Eadmund's grandson Eadgar II was still too young to take on that role and opposition to Willelm lacked vital focus.

# Ælfred

Born – 849 at Wantage, Berkshire; son of Æþelwulf of Wessex and *Osburh* (*A*)
Succeeded – 23<sup>rd</sup> April 871 (*H*) on the death of his elder brother Æþelred (*A, C*)
Died – 26<sup>th</sup> October 899 (*C*)
Buried – at Winchester Cathedral, translated to New Minster, Winchester (*H*)

Title – King of the West Saxons in charters up to 878, also in the laws and his will. King of the Anglo-Saxons in charters from 891 (or 887/93) and in Asser's biography of him (893). One charter of 889 has King of the English and Saxons. Coins usually have King of the Saxons, and there is one coin with a short form of King of the English (*Rex Anglo* for Rex Anglorum) between 880 and 885.

## Wife

*Ealhswið* (*C, w*)
   married 868 (*A*), daughter of Alderman Æþelred and *Eadburh* (*A*), died 5<sup>th</sup> Dec. 902 (*C*)

## Children:

**King Eadward I** (*A*)
   born 871? (2<sup>nd</sup> child), died 924

**Æþelward** (*A*)
   born after 877? (5<sup>th</sup> child), died 16<sup>th</sup> Oct. 922 (*W*)
   married ?
   children:
   – **Ælfwine** – born ?, died 937 (*M*)
   – **Æþelwine** – born ?, died 937 (*M*)

**Æþelflæd** (*A*)
   born 869 (1<sup>st</sup> child), died 12<sup>th</sup> June 918 (*C*)
   married Alderman Æþelred of Mercia (*A*) by 887 (*S217*), ruler of Mercia after his death 911, buried at Gloucester (*W*)
   children:
   – **Ælfwynn** – ruler of Mercia until c.4<sup>th</sup> Dec. 918/19 (*C*)

**Æþelgyfu** (*A*)
   born 873? (3<sup>rd</sup> child), died 9<sup>th</sup> December
   abbess of Shaftesbury (*A, S357*)

**Children:** (continued)

*Ælfþryð* (*A*)

born 875? (4th child)
married Baldwine Marquis of Flanders (*Æ*), [*descendants – Counts of Flanders and Counts of Boulogne*]

## Kinsmen

brother's (Æþelred) sons: **Æþelhelm** and **Æþelwold** (*w*)
sister: *Æþelswið* (*C*), married 853 to King Burhred of Mercia (died 874), died **888**
**Oswold**, Prince, signed charters 868–875 (*S343, 1201, 1203*), son of Æþelred?
**Osferð** (*w*), related to his mother?

## The Main Features of the Reign

### *Politics and Government*

Ælfred began his reign as one of four Anglo-Saxon Kings in England. He ended as the only King, claiming lordship over all the English not under Viking rule. A large Viking army had arrived in England in 865, probably under the command of King Inwær of Dublin and his brother Healfdene. This army took over the Kingdom of Northumbria after 876. Another army under Guþrum arrived in 871 which partitioned Mercia in 877 and took over East Anglia in 879. Ælfred precariously, but successfully, defended Wessex against both armies and his later enhancement of its power enabled his son and grandson to take over all of England in the 30 years after his death. The collapse of three Kingdoms in the face of Viking attack underlines Ælfred's achievement in defending Wessex and the seriousness of his plight up to 878. An Alderman, Æþelred, succeeded the last King of Mercia (Ceolwulf II) as ruler of western, English Mercia in 879 and he was acknowledging Ælfred as his overlord by 883 (and by 887 had married his daughter). One of Æþelred's subordinate Aldermen was Ælfred's brother in law, while another originally came from Somerset and so also had links to Ælfred. The Welsh Kings also made alliance with him seeking his support. If the coronation rite used for his son (Ordo 2, Nelson 1986) has been correctly identified, he is explicitly mentioned as uniting two peoples in one Kingdom, the Angles (Mercia) and Saxons (Wessex). Hence, he may have portrayed himself as he was described in the Chronicle, lord of all the English not under Danish rule.

In the 890s, Ælfred faced renewed Viking attack from new groups crossing over from France. The help they received from the settlers in East Anglia and York meant that relations with the Viking states to the north of Wessex were sure to dominate the politics of his son and successor. The Viking threat to Wessex was not finally overcome until the war of 910 under Eadward I.

Ælfred issued one code of laws, incorporating a reissue of Ine's laws (688–726) and his own chapters covering oaths, treason, sanctuary, breach of the peace, assault and compensation for injury. Ælfred reorganised the military forces of Wessex, both on land and at sea. He also began a policy of building fortified boroughs in Wessex as places of refuge and trade. These fostered urban economic life as well as being strongholds for defence against the Vikings. A treaty with the Vikings in East Anglia settled the border between them and Wessex, and guaranteed legal rights for the English under Danish rule.

He reformed the household into a system of shifts and organised his income into earmarked portions. One half was devoted to secular purposes, to pay his household, his craftsmen and foreign guests, and the other half was devoted to religious purposes, to the poor, to his monasteries, to foreign monasteries, and to the court school. He fostered cathedral schools in Wessex and Mercia, to educate future public officials so that they could read and write, and to improve the educational standards of the clergy.

## The Church

Ælfred founded a monastery at Athelney and a nunnery at Shaftesbury. The nunnery of Wilton was also rebuilt at this time. He established strong relations with the Papacy renewing the payment of a Papal tax to Rome. However, he had been criticised by an earlier Pope for his negative attitude to the Church at Canterbury. His relations with foreign clerics extended to the nearby Archbishop of Rheims and the more distant Patriarch of Jerusalem (a 10th century reference has him being sent medical recipes by the Patriarch).

## Art and Literature

Ælfred's reign saw the first extensive use of English for literary translation and composition (it was already increasing in use for records such as charters and wills). He was responsible for a series of translations of works from Latin into English as part of a scheme of education. Some he did himself, others he commissioned. His own translations were:

a. *Liber Regula Pastoralis* of Pope Gregory (written in c590, also called *Cura Pastoralis*)
b. *De Consolatione Philosophiae* of Boethius (c520)
c. *Soliloquia* of Augustine (c380)
d. Psalms 1–50

Others translations which were produced at this time were:

e. *Historia Ecclesiastica Gentis Anglorum* of Bede (731)
f. *Dialogi* of Pope Gregory (593)
g. *Historia Adversus Paganos* of Orosius (c410)

Ælfred was probably also responsible for the compilation of the Anglo-Saxon Chronicle in 892, the major source for the history of England up to 1154 and the source for the 'authorised version' of West Saxon history and the reign of Ælfred. A collection of medical recipes, *Bald's Leechbook*, may also date from Ælfred's reign, as may the *Martyrology*, a collection of saints' lives.

He had a keen sense of history, insisting that we learn from the examples of the past. This is reflected in his probable sponsorship of three historical works (Orosius, Bede and the Chronicle). History was also a way of living in people's minds after death; as he wrote 'it has ever been my desire to live honourably while I was alive, and after my death to leave to them that should come after me my memory in good works.' His translations reveal something of his own thought by the changes he made to the texts. Ælfred altered Boethius to put forward a view that people had freedom of choice within the overall plan ordained by God, and that choice would lead to right decisions only through having wisdom. Hence his emphasis on learning and literacy, and his innovations during his reign which showed that people did not have to accept fate but could fight and strive for better things. Ælfred also saw government as a duty, rather than a right, and that the three orders of clergy, warrior nobility and labouring commoners (a common way of dividing society at the time) had to be fostered equally for a healthy Kingdom.

The main art style of Ælfred's time was the Trewhiddle Style, chiefly surviving in metalwork. A good example is the Fuller Brooch. A rare wooden example is the Coppergate saddle bow from York. The most famous artefact of the period is the Alfred jewel, possibly ordered by Ælfred himself.

## Chronicle of Events

871   Ælfred succeeded during a Viking invasion of Berkshire and Wiltshire, and after several battles made peace with them by paying them tribute.

874   The Vikings drove out King Burhred of Mercia, Ælfred's brother-in-law.

875   The Viking army split, with Guþrum staying in the south and Healfdene heading north.

876   The Vikings under Guþrum returned to Wessex, taking Wareham. Ælfred was unable to expel them. Healfdene took over part of Northumbria, creating a Kingdom at York.

877   The Vikings moved to Exeter, where they were besieged by Ælfred. They agreed to leave after a storm destroyed their fleet off the coast at Swanwick. Going to Mercia, they divided it, taking the east for themselves and leaving the west under King Ceolwulf.

878    Wessex was overrun by Guþrum (January) after an attack on Ælfred at Chippenham. Ælfred took refuge in Athelney, recovered and decisively beat them at Edington (May). Guþrum made peace and left for Mercia.

879    A second Viking army camped at Fulham, leaving in 880. King Ceolwulf of Mercia died and was succeeded by Æþelred who accepted Ælfred's lordship. The Vikings moved to East Anglia to settle down.

883    Pope Marinus sent a relic of the cross to Ælfred. Sigehelm and Æþelstan took alms to Rome and India.

885    Vikings came from France to Rochester, which was relieved by Ælfred and the Danes departed overseas. Ælfred sent the Kentish fleet against East Anglia in the Stour estuary.

886    Ælfred occupied London and all the English submitted to him, except those who were under the Danes. He entrusted London to Æþelred of Mercia.

887    Ælfred began learning Latin, to begin his series of translations.

892    Vikings arrived in Kent from France, encamped at Appledore and Milton. They were blockaded by Ælfred.

893    The Vikings, helped by Northumbria and East Anglia, were beaten at Farnham and their base at Milton was attacked. They moved into Essex and were beaten again, at Benfleet. The Vikings moved to Buttington by the Severn where they were besieged and defeated, and then onto Chester for the winter. Ælfred moved against a second Viking force that had attacked Exeter.

894    Exeter was secured and the Danish fleet expelled. The first Viking force in Chester left for a base above London.

895    Ælfred blockaded the Viking force above London, which later fled through the Danelaw to Mercia at Bridgnorth.

896    The Danes finally dispersed. Vikings from Northumbria and East Anglia harried the Wessex coast.

# Eadward I

Born – 871? (*A – 2<sup>nd</sup> child of Ælfred*)
Succeeded – 26<sup>th</sup> October 899 on the death of his father, Ælfred.
Crowned – 8<sup>th</sup> June 900 (*Æ*)
Died – 17<sup>th</sup> July 924 (*H*) at Farndon on Dee (*C*)
Buried – at New Minster, Winchester (*H*)

Titles – Usually King of the Anglo-Saxons. Occurs as King of the English on two charters of 900 and 904, King of the Saxons of a charter of 901, and King of the West Saxons in a charter of 904. On coins only King of the Saxons. There are no charters surviving after 909.

## 1<sup>st</sup> Wife

*Ecgwynn* (*H, M, W*)

## Children:

**King Æþelstan**
born 893/4, died 939

*Eadgyð* (RW)
married Sihtric King of York 30<sup>th</sup> Jan. 926 (*C*), died 15<sup>th</sup> July at Polesworth (RW)

## 2<sup>nd</sup> Wife

*Ælflæd* (*H, M*)
married by 901* (*S363*), daughter of Alderman Æþelhelm (*M*), divorced, still living 939/46 (*S1719*), buried at Wilton (*M*)
* by 900 if coronation rite, Ordo 2, applies to her (see Nelson)

## Children:

*Ælfward* (*Æ, C, H, R, W*)
born 901? (*S364*), died 2<sup>nd</sup> Aug. 924 at Oxford (*C*)
Listed as King with a reign of 4 weeks (*R – this may be due to a misreading of the entry in the Anglo-Saxon Chronicle*), crowned with royal insignia (*H*)

**Eadwine** (*H, M, W*)
born after 902, died at sea 933 (*C*), buried at St Bertins, Flanders (*Fw – styled King*)

*Eadflæd* (*H, M*)
nun, buried at Wilton

## Children: (continued)

*Eadgyfu* (*Æ, F, H, M*)
married Carl of France 916/19 (deposed 923, died 929), Queen Mother of Hloðwig
VI 936–54 [*descendants – Kings of France to 987, Dukes of Lorraine to 1012*]
married Herebert 951 (Count of Meaux and Troyes 967, died 995/6)

*Æþelhild* (*H, M*)
lay sister at Winchester, buried at Wilton

*Eadhild* (*Æ, F, H, M*)
died c.935
married Hugo, Count of Paris 926

*Eadgyð* (*Æ, F, H, Hr, M*)
died 26th Jan. 946 (*Wd*)
married Odda of Germany (*C*) 929 [*descendants – Dukes of Swabia to 982, Kings of Germany to 1254 and of Sicily to 1410*]

*Ælfgyfu* (*Æ, H, M, Hr*)
(variously named: *Hr – Eadgifu, M – Ealdgyð, Ælfgyfu*)
married ? (*Æ – a King near the St Bernard pass*, see Poole 1911 under *Hr*)

## 3rd Wife

*Eadgyfu* (*H, M, W*)
married 919, daughter of Alderman Sigehelm, died 966/67

## Children:

**King Eadmund I** (*H*)
born 920/1, died 946

**King Eadred** (*H*)
born 922/4, died 955

*Eadburh* (*H, M*)
nun at Winchester, buried there, died 15th June, saint

*Eadgyfu* (*H, M*)
married Hloðwig of Aquitaine

## Kinsmen

cousin: **Æþelwold** (*C*), exiled 899 in a dispute over the inheritance of manors from Ælfred, killed leading an invasion of Danes 902

Osferð (*S1286, S378*), signed charters 899–934, Alderman 909, Prince (*S1286-904*), relative of his grandmother?

## The Main Features of the Reign

### *Politics and Government*

The major political event at Eadward's accession was the revolt of Æþelwold (son of his father's elder brother). This may have been over the inheritance of family property, although some modern historians would see Æþelwold as making a bid for the throne. This is possible but the evidence is slight and circumstantial for such an interpretation. However, Æþelwold did soon become a serious threat to Eadward by taking over York, and later allying with Eadward's opponents in the Danelaw. These included a member of the former Mercian royal house and Æþelwold's attack on Eadward must be regarded as a serious attempt to undo the work of Ælfred and his son.

Following Æþelwold's defeat and death, the main achievement of Eadward was the conquest of the Danelaw, carried out with his sister *Æþelflæd.* (see Appendix 5) This had to wait until the defeat of the powerful Viking Kingdom of York in 910, and was carried out in stages between 911 and 918. Once this was complete, Eadward was ruling directly over the whole of England south of the Humber. Eadward's regional governors were the Aldermen, of whom there were 11 in Wessex when he succeeded, usually one to each shire. This situation remained up to 909. There is then a gap in the charter evidence until 925, when the number of Aldermen was 9 covering the whole of the area south of the Humber. It is reasonable to suppose that the reorganisation of Aldermen was made by Eadward after his conquest of the area north of the Thames. This would have been part of the wholesale rearrangement of administration and landholding which ensured the incorporation of the newly annexed areas into England. For instance, the conquest of England south of the Humber was achieved partly by building fortified boroughs in Mercia and the Danelaw. These often became the focus for the later shires of the midlands which had no basis in the earlier history of Mercia. Evidence of Eadward's establishment and recognition of the midland shires survives in the document known as the County Hidage (Hart 1992). Eadward's achievement in creating the administrative framework of England has seldom been recognised and he is usually regarded as purely a warrior king. However, as well as refashioning local government, he also issued two law codes:

I   trade and the ownership of goods, disputes over land, and perjury.
II  Exeter – the administration of justice.

Early in his reign he seems to have confirmed, or made a treaty, with the Danes to regulate relations with them. This was included in collections of laws made in the 11th century.

## The Church

Eadward found Nunminster and New Minster abbeys in Winchester. The nunnery of Romsey was also founded in his reign. New sees were created at Crediton, Wells and Ramsbury.

## Art and Literature

The Anglo-Saxon Chronicle was continued with a new section being added in 924.

# Chronicle of Events

899 Dispute with Æþelwold who occupied two manors illegally and was refused permission to marry a woman in holy orders. He fled to Northumbria where he was accepted as King.

902 Æþelwold arrived in Essex, securing its allegiance. The Vikings were expelled from Dublin by the Irish and began settling in north-west Mercia and Northumbria.

903 Æþelwold, Eohric of East Anglia and Prince Brihtsige of the former Mercian royal house invaded Mercia and Wessex. They were pursued back as far as the Fens. The Kentish contingent was attacked at Holme (Huntingdonshire?) where Æþelwold, Eohric and Brihtsige were killed, ending the threat to Eadward.

904 Peace was made at Tiddingford with both East Anglia and Northumbria.

907 *Æþelflæd* fortified Chester.

909 West Saxon and Mercian levies raided the Danes in the north.

910 Northumbria harried Mercia, being intercepted by levies from Wessex and Mercia on their way back, at Tettenhall on 5th August, where Kings Eowils and Healfdene were killed. *Æþelflæd* fortified *Bremesburh*.

911 Alderman Æþelred died, Eadward took over direct rule of London and Oxford, and fortified Hertford.

912 Eadward advanced into Essex and built a fort at Witham. The Danish area around Maldon submitted. *Æþelflæd* built forts at Bridgnorth and *Scergeat*.

913 Tamworth and Stafford were fortified by *Æþelflæd*. Danes from Northampton and Leicester raided the area to the south.

914 Vikings from Brittany harried south Wales, a Welsh Bishop was ransomed by Eadward and the Vikings were beaten by forces from Hereford and Gloucester. They attacked near Watchet and Porlock before departing. *Æþelflæd* built a fortress at Eddisbury and fortified Warwick. Eadward built fortresses at Buckingham. Earl Þurcytel of Bedford submitted, also some of the Danes of Northampton.

915 Fortresses were built at Chirbury, *Weardburh* and Runcorn.

916 Mercian forces attacked the Welsh in Brecon. Eadward fortified Maldon.

917 Eadward fortified Towcester before Easter, and *Wigingamere*. The Danes from Northampton and Leicester besieged the fortress of Towcester but were beaten off. Danes from Huntingdon and East Anglia built a fortress at Tempsford and attacked Bedford, and *Wigingamere*. Tempsford was captured by Eadward during the summer, and the Danish King was killed. English forces took Colchester in the autumn, while Danes from East Anglia failed in an attack on Maldon. In early August, *Æþelflæd* took Derby. After the autumn, the Danish Earl of Northampton submitted and English forces took over Huntingdon. Before Martinmas, Eadward rebuilt Colchester and the Danes in East Anglia and Cambridge submitted to him.

918 Eadward marched to Stamford in June, the Danes submitted. Leicester submitted to *Æþelflæd*. *Æþelflæd* died at Tamworth 12<sup>th</sup> June after arranging an alliance with York against Rægnald from Ireland. The Mercians submitted to Eadward, who also occupied Nottingham. The Welsh of Gwynedd and Deheubarth also gave their allegiance. *Æþelflæd's* daughter *Ælfwynn* was deprived of authority in Mercia and taken to Wessex in December.

919 Rægnold of Waterford stormed York. In late autumn, Eadward built a fortress at Thelwall and occupied Manchester.

920 Sihtric, Rægnold's brother, attacked Cheshire. Eadward built a fortress at Nottingham before midsummer and then another at Bakewell. The Scots, Bamburgh and Strathclyde recognised his lordship.

921 Eadward built a fortress at the mouth of the Clwyd.

924 A revolt in Chester, supported by the Welsh, was put down. Edward died at Farndon on Dee.

# Æþelstan

Born – 893/4 (*M – 30 in 924*), brought up by his aunt *Æþelflæd* in Mercia (*M*)

Succeeded – 18th August 924 (*C – reign length adjusted to the correct year*), after the death of his father. His half-brother Ælfward was a potential rival but died shortly after Eadward I.

Crowned – 4th September 925 (*S394*) at Kingston (*C*)

Died – 27th October 939 at Gloucester (*C*)

Buried – at Malmesbury (*W*)

Portrait – in Bede's Life of Cuthbert (Wilson 1984)

Description – medium height, thin, fair haired (*M*)

Title – Usually King of the English after 928, once in 925. King of the Anglo-Saxons in charters of 926, King of All Britain on charters after 931, King of All Albion in a charter of 937, Emperor of the English in a charter of 939. On coins, King of All Britain and King of the Saxons.

## Unmarried

## No known children

## The Main Features of the Reign

### *Politics and Government*

It was Æþelstan who became the first King to rule over the whole of the later area of England by his annexation of Northumbria in 927. His power was recognised by other Kings in Britain, which was reflected in his choice of title (see above). It was also recognised abroad, as several foreign rulers were keen to ally with him by accepting his sisters in marriage, and he often intervened in other countries on behalf of favoured rulers. He had contacts with monasteries abroad and foreign scholars were welcome at court, as they had been under Ælfred. Æþelstan ensured the loyalty of the Church by collecting relics and distributing gifts.

The politics of the reign seems to have been dominated by the presence of an adult heir, Eadwine, whose position may have been threatened by his stepmother, *Eadgyfu*, and her two young children, Eadmund and Eadred. *Eadgyfu* was linked with the family of Aldermen Ælfstan, and Æþelstan his brother, who were appointed to office by the King in the early 930s. Shortly after this, Eadwine went into exile and died. Up to then, the dominant Earl was the kinsman of King Ælfred, Osferð, who may have been killed in the campaign against Scotland in 934.

Æþelstan legislated to control the coinage by making it a royal monopoly with a set number of moneyers in the boroughs. Charters begin to survive in large numbers from his reign and show that he had an organised secretariat at court. In administering justice, he leaned towards leniency by banning execution of criminals under 15.

Æþelstan issued four law codes:
I   on tithes and Church dues.
II  Grateley – various chapters on theft, lordless men, lordship, trade, fortress repair, coinage, and administration of justice.
IV  Thundersfield – measures against criminals.
V   Exeter – administration of justice.

(The so-called code III was a letter to the King from Kent on the implementation of code II, and code VI was a set of guild rules for London.)

## Literature and Art

Æþelstan presented various gifts to St Cuthbert's shrine, including fine embroidered textiles, a copy of the gospels and a copy of Bede's Life of St Cuthbert. These are artistically important survivals of the period showing the early stages of development of the typical late Anglo-Saxon Winchester style (the textiles were made c910 under Eadward I). Æþelstan was reputedly a great donor of books, ornaments and lands to various churches. He founded the monasteries of Milton and Muchelney. Æþelstan's reputation was as a learned King, interested in literature and entertaining foreign scholars.

### Chronicle of Events

924  He succeeded his father in spite of opposition from a party of the nobility, and after the death of his brother.

926  Æþelstan met Sihtric of York at Tamworth, 30th January, and gave him his sister *Eadgyð* in marriage. Another sister, *Eadhild*, was married to Count Hugo of Paris.

927  Sihtric died and Æþelstan took over Northumbria, driving out Sihtric's brother Guþfrið, and Ealdred of Bamburgh. The Scots, Strathclyde, and Ealdred submitted to him at Eamont, 12th July.

928? Cornwall was subdued and its boundary fixed at the Tamar.

928? Gwynedd, Dyfed and Gwent submitted to Æþelstan at Hereford. The Welsh Kings often attended Æþelstan's court after this.

929  Æþelstan's sister *Eadgyð* was married to Odda of Germany.

933  Prince Eadwine was drowned at sea going to Flanders either fleeing or having been exiled.

934  Æþelstan invaded Scotland as far as Dunottar, Kincardine, and sent his fleet as far as Caithness.

?  Hacun of Norway who had been fostered at Æþelstan's court returned to Norway to overthrow his brother Yric.

936  Æþelstan's nephew Hloþwig returned to France as King. Alan of Brittany was helped to return and expel the Vikings from Nantes.

937  Æþelstan defeated an alliance of Scots, Strathclyde and Dublin Vikings, who had invaded England through the Humber, at the Battle of *Brunanburh* (site unknown).

939  A fleet was sent across the channel to help Hloþwig of France in Lotharingia.

# Eadmund I

Born – 920/1 (*C – 18 at accession*)
Succeeded – 27th October 939 on the death of his half-brother Æþelstan (*C*)
Crowned – 24th November 939 (*C – length of reign*)
Died – 26th May 946, accidentally killed during an affray at Pucklechurch (*C*)
Buried – at Glastonbury (*W*)

Title – Usually King of the English. King of the Anglo-Saxons (940–42), King of All Albion (945–46) and Emperor of the English were also used (940).

## 1st Wife

*Ælfgyfu* (*Æ, W*)
   married 940, died 18th May 943/4, buried at Shaftesbury, saint

## Children:

**King Eadwig** (*C, W*)
   born 939/42, died 959
**King Eadgar I** (*W*)
   born 943, died 975
*Eadgyfu*
   Abbess of Nunminster in 964/75 (*S1449*), described as King's daughter and may be daughter of Eadmund. Witnessed *S1454* of 990/92.

## 2nd Wife

*Æþelflæd* (*C, W, w*)
   married 944, daughter of Alderman Ælfgar, remarried Alderman Æþelstan Rota, will dated 975/91.
   no children

## Kinsmen

   wife of Alderman Ælfheah: *Ælfswið* (*S462*)

# The Main Features of the Reign

## *Politics and Government*

The reign was dominated by the King's family; his mother *Eadgyfu* and brother Eadred. Their main supporters seem to have been Alderman Æþelstan, whose younger brothers were made Aldermen in 940 and 942. Æþelstan was a close friend of Abbot Dunstan (later Archbishop) and Prince Eadgar was fostered by his wife after the death of *Ælfgyfu*. The foundation was being laid of the political connections that were instrumental in the monastic reformation in the 960s. The Viking rulers of Dublin made determined efforts to secure the rule of York during his reign, which he eventually overcame after initial setbacks.

Eadmund issued three law codes:
I London – Church dues, behaviour and protection of the Church.
II Feud and breach of the peace.
III Colyton – action against thieves.

## *The Church*

Glastonbury Abbey was reformed by Dunstan, appointed by Eadmund. This was the beginning of Church reform, brought to fruition under Eadgar I. Eadmund also acted as a protector of foreign monks. Members of the monastery of St Bertins in Flanders found refuge under Eadmund during a dispute with their Count.

## Chronicle of Events

939 Anlaf of Dublin (son of Sihtric) took over York.

940 Anlaf marched south to Northampton, Tamworth and Leicester. A treaty with Eadmund, mediated by Archbishops Oda and Wulfstan, gave the Five Boroughs to Anlaf.

941 Anlaf attacked Tiningham and Lindisfarne.

942 Eadmund won back the Five Boroughs. Anlaf I died. Idwal and Elisedd of Gwynedd were killed fighting the English in Wales.

943 Anlaf II of York (son of Guþfrið) successfully stormed Tamworth. Later he was besieged with Archbishop Wulfstan in Leicester. Eadmund received Anlaf in baptism and later also Rægnold (Anlaf I's brother).

944 Eadmund drove out Anlaf and Rægnold, and took over Northumbria.

945 Eadmund overran Cumbria but left it to Mælcolm of Scotland. He visited the shrine of St Cuþberht, making gifts there.

946 Diplomatic attempts were made to aid the restoration of King Hloþwig in France.

# Eadred

Born – 922/4 (youngest son of Eadward I)
Succeeded – 26th May 946 on the death of his brother Eadmund (*C*)
Crowned – 16th August 946 at Kingston (*W*)
Died – 23rd November 955 at Frome (*C*)
Buried – at Winchester Old Minster (*C*)

Title – King of the English with lesser use of King and Chieftain of All Albion (951-55), King and Emperor of All Britain (955), King of the English, Ruler of the Northumbrians, Emperor of the Heathen, Protector of the Britons (946–55). King of the English and King the Saxons on coins.

## Unmarried

## No known children

## Kinsman

Ælfheah (*S564*), Alderman 959

## The Main Features of the Reign

### Politics and Government

Eadred had succeeded as King because Eadmund's sons, Eadwig and Eadgar, were under age. His succession secured the position of the Queen Mother and her supporters, Æþelstan and his family. Eadred was said to have suffered from chronic illness for much of his life. English control of Northumbria was again threatened by the Kings of Dublin, and also by Yric Bloodaxe of Norway, but Northumbria was finally secured after the people of York turned against Yric in 954.

### The Church

Monasteries were founded at Abingdon and Muchelney. The see of Elmham was established as independent of London.

### Literature and Art

The *Leechbook of Bald* was compiled c950, consisting of medical recipes. About this time also, manuscript Paris 8824 was written, containing a translation of the Psalms. In 955, additions were made to the Anglo-Saxon Chronicle (version A at Winchester).

## Chronicle of Events

946   Eadred succeeded, took all Northumbria under his power and the Scots gave him oaths.

947   Eadred came to Tanshelf (Pontefract), Wulfstan and Northumbria pledged allegiance but broke it soon afterwards by accepting Yric of Norway as King.

948   Eadred harried Northumbria, destroying Ripon. His rearguard was attacked at Castleford. Northumbria deserted Yric and made reparation to Eadred.

949   Anlaf Cuaran took over Northumbria. Cadwgaun of Glywysing in south Wales was killed by the English.

952   Eadred imprisoned Archbishop Wulfstan of York. Northumbria expelled Anlaf and received Yric again as King. Citizens of Thetford were executed for the murder of Abbot Eadhelm of St Augustine's.

954   Northumbria expelled Yric, who was betrayed and killed by Oswulf of Bamburgh, and Eadred succeeded to Northumbria. Oswulf was made Earl of Northumbria to govern it under Eadred. Archbishop Wulfstan was freed.

# Eadwig

Born – 939/42 (elder brother of Eadgar), occurred in a dubious charter of 941 (*S477*)

Succeeded – 24th November 955 on the death of his uncle Eadred (*C*)

Crowned – 25th January 956? (*C* – reign length amended to the nearest Sunday, +2 days instead of -2 days) at Kingston (*W*)

Died – 1st October 959 (*C*)

Buried – at New Minster, Winchester (*W*)

Title – usually King of the English. Other titles include King of the English and Britons/All Britain (956–59), King of All Britain (957), King of the English and All Albion (956–57), King of the Saxons (958). A variety of titles were used on charters of 956: King of all races of the island; King and Chieftain of All Albion; King of the Anglo-Saxons and All Albion; Ruler of all the island of Albion; Monarch of Albion; King and Monarch of the Island of Britain; King of the Anglo-Saxons; Ruler of the Gewisse, East, West and North Saxons; King of the Anglo-Saxons, Ruler of the Northumbrians, Emperor of the Heathen, Protector of the Britons. King of the Saxons occurs on coins.

## Wife

*Ælfgyfu* (*C, D, w*)

daughter of *Æþelgyfu*, married 956, dissolved 958 on grounds of kinship (related to Alderman Æþelward?, a descendant of Ælfred's brother Æþelred), kinsman of Eadgar I (*S737, S738*), will dated 965/75.

## No children

## Kinsmen

**Ælfhere** (*W*) signed charters 955–83 (Alderman 956), brother **Ælfheah** (*S585, S586*), Alderman 959

wife of Ælfheah: **Ælfswið** (*S662*)

**Ælfgar** (*S651, C*) signed charters 951–62, died 962, brother **Brihtferð** (*S651*) signed charters 949–70

# The Main Features of the Reign

## *Politics and Government*

Becoming king at the same time as reaching adulthood (at c15), Eadwig seems to have decided to break with his mother's supporters and pursue his own independent policies. He patronised an opposing faction, that of Alderman Ealhelm's sons, Ælfhere and Ælfheah, and also the nobility of western Wessex under Alderman Eadmund. A large number of land grants were made to thanes in Wessex by Eadwig, attempting to build up a party of supporters. His marriage may have been an attempt to ally with powerful West Saxon nobility against the interests of Æþelstan's family. However, his policies led to the adoption of Eadgar as King in Mercia and Northumbria in opposition to him. In spite of this, the same noble families held lands and offices in both Mercia and Wessex, and civil war was avoided.

## *The Church*

Eadwig quarrelled with Dunstan, the chief promoter of the new monasticism but was not antagonistic towards the Church itself. The monastery of Westminster was reformed at this time under Eadgar as King of Mercia.

### Chronicle of Events

956   Dunstan was exiled, going to Ghent.

957   Mercia and Northumbria deserted Eadwig, choosing Eadgar as King. Dunstan was recalled by Eadgar, soon succeeding as Bishop of Worcester.

958   Eadwig and his wife *Ælfgyfu* were separated by Archbishop Oda. Dunstan was given the see of London by Eadgar.

# Eadgar I

Born – July/Oct. 943 (*C – 16 at accession*), fostered by *Ælfwynn*, wife of Alderman Æþelstan (*Ra*)

Succeeded – 1ˢᵗ October 959 on the death of his brother Eadwig (*C, W*), having been King of Mercia and Northumbria since 957 (*C, D, W*)

Crowned – 24ᵗʰ June 960? (*Æ – reign length amended to correct year*). His coronation on 11ᵗʰ May 973 at Bath was an imperial coronation to emphasise his overlordship in Britain as a whole (*C*)

Died – 8ᵗʰ July 975 (*C, W*)

Buried – at Glastonbury (*W*)

Portrait – in the Regularis Concordia and New Minster Charter (Backhouse et al. 1984)

Description – extremely small (*M*)

Title – the commonest title on charters is King (or Ruler) of All Britain, with other common titles being King of the English and King (and Chieftain) of All Albion. He is also called Emperor of All Britain (967–69), of All Albion (970) and Emperor of the Kings and peoples of Britain (967). King of All England occurs on a charter of 961, King of the whole island realm in 966 and King of the English, Ruler of the Northumbrians, heathens and British peoples in 968. Before 959 he was styled King of the Mercians or Mercians, Northumbrians and Britons. Coins have King of the English or King of All Britain.

## 1ˢᵗ Wife

*Æþelflæd* (*W, M*)
married 959/60?, daughter of Ordmær (*M*)

## Children:

**King Eadward II** (*W*)
born c960, died 978

## 2ⁿᵈ Wife

*Wulfþryð* (*G, W, M, Ed, Wu*)
married 962 (may have been a mistress only), divorced, Abbess of Wilton, died 21ˢᵗ Sept. 1000, saint

## Children:

*Eadgyð* (*Ed*)
born 962/4, died 16ᵗʰ September 985/7 aged 23 (*M*), nun of Wilton (*W*), saint (*M*)

## 3<sup>rd</sup> Wife

*Ælfþryð* (*C, S724, M*)
  married 964 (*W*) or 965 (*C*), daughter of Ordgar, widow of Alderman Æþelwold (*VO*) and had two sons by him – Leofric and Æþelnoð, died 17 Nov (*H*) 1001 (*S904 – referred to her as dead in 1002*)

## Children:

**Eadmund** (*W, S745*)
  born 966, died 971
**King Æþelred** (*W*)
  born 968, died 1016

## Kinsmen (see also under Eadwig)

  *Ælfheah* (*S702*), Alderman 959
  *Ælfgyfu* (*S737, S738*), sister of Alderman Æþelward?, ex-wife of Eadwig
  **Brihthelm** (*S695*), Bishop of Winchester, Selsey and Sherborne

## The Main Features of the Reign

### *Politics and Government*

Eadgar seems to have steered a middle course between the various factions. Ælfhere and Ælfheah had a prominent place at court alongside Æþelstan's sons, Æþelwold and Æþelwine. Other powerful nobles were also included and the politics of the reign were stable. He had a reputation for welcoming foreigners into the country. There was no threat of foreign invasion during his reign and later tradition said that he kept a powerful navy that deterred any aggression. When he became King, there was no obvious heir. There were possible claimants abroad, descended from the sisters of Eadgar's father Eadmund. These included the son of Emperor Odda of Germany, who concluded a treaty with Eadgar soon after his accession.

Eadgar issued four law codes.
I    holding of hundred courts.
II   Andover – tithes and Church dues.
III  Andover – administration of justice.
IV   *Wihtbordestan* – Church dues, trade, Danelaw rights.

One important feature of his laws was the judicial autonomy granted to the Danish settled shires in eastern England (the Danelaw).

## The Church

A major reformation of monasticism was begun with Eadgar's support, under the leadership of Archbishop Dunstan of Canterbury, Bishop Æþelwold of Winchester and Archbishop Oswold of York. The abbeys founded or reformed were New Minster, St Augustine's, Chertsey, Horton, Milton, Exeter, Malmesbury, Bath, Pershore, Evesham, Winchcombe, Deerhurst, Westbury, Crowland, Peterborough, Thorney, Ramsey, Ely, St Neots, St Albans, Huntingdon and Bedford, and the nunnery of Barking. Winchester and Worcester cathedrals were also given monastic chapters.

## Art and Literature

The first fruit of the monastic reformation may have been the writing of homilies. The collection known as the Blickling Homilies was put together in 971. The Vercelli collection of homilies may also have been made at this time. Bishop Æþelwold translated the Benedictine Rule as part of the monastic revival, of which he also wrote a description some time before he died in 984. Additions were made to the Anglo-Saxon Chronicle (version A) in 968. The Vercelli manuscript (containing the poems *The Dream of the Rood, Andreas, Fates of the Apostles, Soul and Body* and *Elene*) may have been written during Eadgar's reign (or during Æþelred's).

The Winchester Style of art was fully developed during Eadgar's reign. This is mainly preserved in manuscript illumination and illustration. Important examples from Eadgar's reign are the New Minster charter, the Benedictional of St Æþelwold and possibly the Ramsey Psalter.

Dating architecture to particular reigns is very difficult but a number of churches or fragments of churches survive from the late 10th century. Perhaps it was Eadgar's support for the Church and monasticism that was resposible for new churches being built and others being rebuilt in stone. Examples might include Breamore, Barnack, Dover and Earl's Barton.

### Chronicle of Events

959 Brihthelm was deposed from Canterbury by Eadgar, and was replaced by Dunstan.

Emperor Odda I sent gifts and made a treaty with Eadgar.

960 Oswold was made Bishop of Worcester at Dunstan's request.

962 There was a great plague this year. Odda of Germany was crowned Emperor.

963 Æþelwold was consecrated Bishop of Winchester 29th November.

964 Eadgar expelled the canons from Winchester, New Minster, Chertsey and Milton, replacing them with monks.

966 Þored of Northumbria harried Westmorland (part of Strathclyde).

967 Nuns were placed in Romsey by Eadgar.

Gwynedd was harried by the English under Alderman Ælfhere.

969 Eadgar had Thanet ravaged for attacking merchants from York.

Eadgar ordered monks to be placed in the greater Mercian monasteries.

? A national synod at Winchester drew up a common rule for the reformed monasteries, the *Regularis Concordia.*

972 Oswold became Archbishop of York.

973 Eadgar was crowned at Bath 11th May; and then led his fleet to Chester where he was joined by eight rulers from the rest of Britain, Cynað of Scotland, Mælcolm of Cumbria, Magnus of the Isles, Dufenal of Strathclyde, Iago and Howel of Gwynedd, Sigeferð, Iuchill. Lothian was ceded to Scotland.

974 There was an earthquake over all England.

975 Edward, Edgar's son , succeeded to the kingdom.

# Eadward II

Born – 960? (elder brother of *Eadgyð*)
Succeeded – 8th July 975 on the death of his father Eadgar, opposed by his stepmother (*C, W*)
Crowned – 18th July 975? (*H* – reign length)
Died – 18th March 978 at Corfe, murdered by supporters of his stepmother (*C, PE*)
Buried – at Wareham, translated to Shaftesbury 980 (*C*)

Title – King of the English and King and Chieftain of All Albion occur on charters. King of the English occurs on coins.

## Unmarried

## No known children

## The Main Features of the Reign

### Politics and Government

Eadgar's death split the nobility with different factions supporting Eadward or his younger brother. Eadward's supporters included Aldermen Æþelwine and Brihtnoð while Ælfhere supported Eadward's stepmother, *Ælfþryð*, and her son Æþelred. Eadward was assassinated by supporters of *Ælfþryð* but it is not clear that this was done with her knowledge. There was no proscription of Eadward's supporters after his death. He had a reputation for an unpredictable and violent temper. He came to be regarded as a martyr and his cult was fostered later by his brother Æþelred and by Cnut.

### Art and Literature

The Exeter Book, containing a large number of poems, may have been written at about this time.

### Chronicle of Events

975 There was a division over the succession, Archbishops Dunstan and Oswold led the Bishops, Abbots and Aldermen in choosing Eadward, who was then crowned.
976 There was a great famine.
   Alderman Ælfhere attacked monasteries founded by Æþelwold, opposed by Aldermen Æþelwine and Brihtnoð.
   Earl Oslac of Northumbria was exiled.
977 Synods were held at Calne and Amesbury.

# Æþelred

Born – 968 (*M – 10 at accession and scarcely 7 in 975*)
Succeeded – 18th March 978 on the murder of his half-brother Eadward (*C*). In exile from Christmas 1013 to Lent 1014 in the face of a Danish invasion (*C*).
Crowned – 4th May 979 (*C*) or 14th April 978 (*W*) at Kingston
Died – 23rd April 1016 (*C*)
Buried – at London (*W*)

Title – King of the English is the commonest title. Also occurring are King of All Albion and King of All Britain. Rarer titles are Emperor of the English (987–1002), of All Albion (995–1012), King of the whole island of Britain (978/84–987). On coins and in the laws there is simply King of the English.

## 1st Wife

*Ælfgyfu* (*W*)
married 984, daughter of Alderman Þored (*AR*)

## Children:

**Æþelstan**
born 988? (1st charter), died 25th June 1014 (*w, Cant.*)

**Ecgberht**
born 989?, died 1005 (charters)

**King Eadmund II**
born 990? (1st charter), died 1016

**Eadred**
born 992?, died 1012 (charters)

**Eadwig**
born 997? (1st charter), died 1017 (*W*), buried at Tavistock (*M*)

**Eadgar**
born 1001, died 1008 (charters)

***Eadgyð***
married Eadric by 1009 (*W*) [*descendants – Seward family*]

***Ælfgyfu***
married Uhtred (*OD*) [*descendants – Earls of Dunbar and Neville family*]

***(unnamed)***
Abbess of Wherwell in 1048 (*C*)

***? Wulfhild*** (*J*)
married Ulfcytel

## 2$^{nd}$ Wife

*Ymme* (*C*)
  married 1002, daughter of Ricard of Normandy, adopted the English name *Ælfgyfu*

## Children:

### King Eadward III
  born 1005? (1$^{st}$ charter), died 1066

### Ælfred
  born 1013? (1$^{st}$ charter), died 5$^{th}$ February (*Ely*) 1037 (*C, W*)

*Godgyfu* (*M, OV*)
  married Drogo of the Vexin (died 1035) [*descendants – Lords Sudeley to 1473*]
  married Eustatius of Boulogne (*M, W*) ?1036 (*EE – Ælfred received help from Boulogne in 1036*)
  died 1048? (*An – Eustatius was excommunicated for marriage to his second wife in 1049*)

## Kinsmen

**Æþelmær** (*S937*), son of Alderman Æþelward
**Æþelstan** (*C*), brother of Queen *Ælfgyfu*, killed at Ringmere 1010
**Brihtwold** (*H*), related to Æþelred's uncle Ordwulf?

## The Main Features of the Reign

### *Politics and Government* (see Appendix 6)

Æþelred succeeded when under age, and when he was old enough to assume the government himself he began to favour one particular aristocratic faction as a means of asserting his independence. He was thus unable to rise above faction and be neutral between the different noble families and his reign was characterised by consecutive periods of dominance by particular political groupings. However, he came to distrust the traditional nobility and he may have attempted to break their stranglehold on power by promoting newer families who would be more loyal, and relying on local Sheriffs to counterbalance the regional power of the Aldermen. All this undermined his position and helped Swegn to take over the country in 1013. Swegn's attack of that year was the culmination of a series of escalating attacks by Viking fleets. Æþelred employed mercenary forces to help in the defence of the country and paying for these involved heavy taxation. A way of avoiding this was to pay geld to the Danes but this was also a heavy financial burden which would have added to his unpopularity. However, he did also inspire loyalty for he was recalled on Swegn's death and the army refused to fight the Danes in 1015 without his presence. Æþelred had no heir until 988. Possible claimants included the family of Emperor Odda in Germany. One of Æþelred's Aldermen, Æþelward, wrote a history of England for a member of this family, Abbess *Matilda* of Essen.

Æþelred issued four major law codes:

I     Woodstock, 996 – administration of justice.

III   Wantage, 997 – breach of the peace, land disputes, administration of justice, and coinage.

V    Enham, 1008 – a large code with various chapters on church behaviour, festivals, social behaviour, coinage, weights and measures, defence, treason, and unjust practices. (VI was an expanded version of this for Northumbria).

VIII  Woodstock, 1014 – extensive code on church matters

(The so-called code II was a treaty with Anlaf of Norway, code IV a set of regulations on trade and coinage for London, code VII a proclamation of national penance in response to invasion, code IX a fragment of code VIII, and code X a fragment of code V.)

One of the great successes of government in England during the late Anglo-Saxon period was the development of close central supervision of local administration. This was achieved partly through the writ, a letter written in English transmitting commands and information to the shire court. The earliest surviving examples of writs may date from Æþelred's reign.

## The Church

Monasteries continued to be founded: Cranborne, Cerne, Tavistock, Cholsey, Burton, Evesham, Eynsham, and nunneries at Wherwell, Polesworth, Chatteris, and Reading. Canterbury and Sherborne cathedrals were also turned into monasteries. The see of St Cuthbert left Chester le Street and moved to Durham for greater security against Danish attack.

## Art and Literature

Æþelred's reign was the golden age of literature. The two main writers were Abbot Ælfric of Eynsham and Archbishop Wulfstan of York. Ælfric wrote a large number of homilies as well as treatises, educational works and translations of sections of the Bible between 989 and 1006. Wulfstan wrote some homilies also but was mostly concerned with legal and political treatises. He also had a great influence on the drafting of law codes. A scientific manual was produced by Brihtferð, a monk of Ramsey, c1011. Another important scientific collection, the Tiberius Bv manuscript, was put together probably in the 990s. A copy of the Anglo-Saxon Chronicle (version B) was made c1000 at Abingdon, and the last addition was made at Winchester to version A in 1001. As regards manuscripts containing poetry, the first section of Bodleian Junius 11 (*Genesis, Exodus, Daniel*) was written c1000, as was Cotton Vitellius Axv (*Beowulf, Judith*). The Vercelli manuscript may have been written in the early part of Æþelred's reign, before 1000, or Eadgar I's. Most of the poems in these collections were originally written much earlier than this. A poem that may have been written at this time is *The Battle of Maldon*, relating the story of Alderman Brihtnoð's death fighting the Danes in 991.

Important examples of Winchester style art were the Bosworth Psalter, the Benedictional of Archbishop Robert and two ivory carvings of the Virgin Mary and St John. A rare survival is the Winchester cantatorum preserving musical notation of the period.

## Chronicle of Events

978 Æþelred was under age, Queen Mother *Ælfþryð* and Bishop Æþelwold dominated the government. Lleyn and Clynnog Fawr in Gwynedd were ravaged by Howel and the English.

980 Eadward II was reburied with honour at Shaftesbury by Alderman Ælfhere.

Southampton was raided by Viking pirates, also Thanet and Chester.

981 Devon and Cornwall were attacked by Vikings, as was Southampton.

982 Three ships of Vikings harried Portland.

The Emperor's nephew Odda, who was Æþelred's cousin, died.

983 Brycheiniog in Wales was ravaged by Alderman Ælfhere.

984 Bishop Æþelwold died 1st August. Queen Mother *Ælfþryð* stopped signing charters. Æþelred probably began his personal rule, supported by Alderman Ælfric of Wessex, Ælfsige, Ælfgar and Æþelsige.

985 Alderman Ælfric of Mercia was exiled.

Howel, son of Ieuaf of Gwynedd, was killed by the English.

986 The King ravaged the see of Rochester in a dispute with Bishop Ælfstan.

There was a great epidemic of disease among cattle and people.

988 Watchet was harried by the Vikings who were defeated.

Archbishop Dunstan died, 19th May.

991 Vikings attacked Ipswich, killing Alderman Brihtnoð at Maldon 10th August. The Danes were paid off for the first time (£10,000). The Papacy mediated a treaty between England and Normandy, who had been supporting the Vikings.

992 The Danes were caught at sea and beaten, although they had been joined by Alderman Ælfric. Etwin son of Einion and English under Æþelsige ravaged Deheubarth in Wales.

993 Æþelred ordered Ælfgar, son of Alderman Ælfric, to be blinded. Ælfric's faction fell from power. *Ælfþryð* returned to court. The dominant factions were now Alderman Æþelward, Ordulf (*Ælfþryð's* brother), and Alderman Ælfhelm. Bamburgh was destroyed and Danes came to the Humber harrying Lindsey and Northumbria. An army gathered to fight them fled.

994 Vikings Anlaf and Swegn attacked London 8th September but were beaten off with heavy losses. They then harried Essex, Kent, Sussex and Hampshire. Peace was made for £16,000. Æþelred sponsored Anlaf's confirmation, and he agreed to make peace and leave England, becoming King of Norway.

995 Swegn ravaged the Isle of Man.

996 Æþelred issued his first major law code.

997 Danes raided the Severn estuary and destroyed the monastery at Tavistock.

998 Danes attacked Somerset and Dorset, occupying the Isle of Wight.

999 The Danes came into the Thames and up the Medway to Rochester. The Kentish forces opposed them, fighting a sharp battle, but eventually fled. The King gathered the fleet and army but with no result.

1000 The Danes sailed away to Normandy. Æþelred ravaged almost all of Cumbria and the fleet harried the Isle of Man.

1001 The Vikings returned to Wessex, beating the English at *Æþelingadene* and Pinhoe but were repulsed at Exmouth. They then went to the Isle of Wight and peace was made with them. Æþelred may have sent a force to attack Normandy. Eadward II was reburied in a new tomb at Shaftesbury Abbey.

1002 The Vikings were paid £24,000. Alderman Leofsige was later banished for killing a King's high reeve (Sheriff). Æþelred married Ricard of Normandy's daughter *Ymme*. The King ordered a massacre of Danes living in England 13th November.

1003 Exeter, Wilton and Salisbury were taken by the Vikings under Swegn. Alderman Ælfric failed to stop them.

1004 Swegn sacked Norwich. Ulfcytel decided to buy peace but the Danes stole away to Thetford, where he brought them to battle.

1005 There was a great famine throughout England, and the Danes left. Ordulf and Æþelmær retired from court.

1006 Alderman Ælfhelm was killed and his family were disgraced. They were replaced as the main faction by Eadric and his family. Danes raided Kent and Sussex, Æþelred raised an army but the Danes would not meet him. They went to the Isle of Wight and then attacked Hampshire, Berkshire and Wiltshire, defeating the Wiltshire forces by the Kennet.

Mælcolm of Scotland besieged Durham but was decisively beaten by Uhtred who was then made Alderman. He later married a daughter of the King.

1007 £36,000 was paid to the Danes. Eadric was made Alderman over all Mercia and at some point married the King's daughter.

1008 Æþelred ordered ships to be built from every 300 hides of land.

1009 The ships were gathered at Sandwich but were dispersed by a quarrel between Eadric's brother Brihtric and Wulfnoð (father of the later Earl Godwine), and by a storm. The fleet then withdrew to the Thames.

The Danes under Þurcyll came to Sandwich shortly after 1st August. Canterbury and east Kent bought peace for £3,000. The Danes moved to the Isle of Wight and harried Hampshire, Sussex and Berkshire. Æþelred called out the army against them, even surrounding them on one occasion but no result ensued.

(1009) In November, the Danes moved to the Thames, and attacked London unsuccessfully. A national penance was decreed. Eadric became dominant at court.

1010 The Danes destroyed Oxford before moving to Ipswich where they were fought by Ulfcytel on 18th May at Ringmere. The dead included the King's brother in law, Æþelstan. The Danes harried East Anglia for three months, destroying Thetford and Cambridge, and then moved through Oxfordshire, Buckinghamshire, Bedfordshire, Hertfordshire, Northamptonshire and Wiltshire. The army failed to make contact and shires were uncoordinated in their response.

1011 Æþelred sued for peace from the Danes. Counties overrun were East Anglia, Essex, Middlesex, Oxford, Cambridge, Hertford, Buckingham, Bedford, Huntingdon, Kent, Sussex, Hastings, Surrey, Berkshire, Hampshire, Wiltshire. They took Canterbury, capturing the Archbishop, Ælfheah.

1012 £48,000 was paid to the Danes in April, but Archbishop Ælfheah was killed by the Danes on the 19th. They dispersed after being paid and 45 ships under Þurcyll were taken into Æþelred's service.

St David's was ravaged by the English under Eadric and Ufic.

1013 Before August, Swegn came to Sandwich and then up the Humber and Trent to Gainsborough. Alderman Uhtred of Northumbria submitted straightaway, and the Five Boroughs, and soon all the Danelaw, and gave hostages. He crossed Watling Street and began harrying. Oxford and Winchester in turn surrendered. He was repulsed at London, defended by Æþelred and Þurcyll. Swegn went through Wallingford to Bath and received the submission of Æþelmær and the south-west. He returned to his ships having been accepted as King by many. London then submitted. Æþelred was with the fleet in the Thames, and sent *Ymme* to Normandy. Princes Eadward and Ælfred were sent abroad with Bishop Ælfhun. Æþelred went to the Isle of Wight at Christmas. Þurcyll's fleet lay at Greenwich awaiting supplies.

1014 After Christmas, Æþelred went to Normandy. Swegn died 3rd February, his fleet choosing Cnut to succeed him. The English negotiated with Æþelred for his return and he came back during Lent. Cnut was supplied by Lindsey which was harried by Æþelred. Cnut then left. Þurcyll's fleet at Greenwich was paid £21,000. Prince Æþelstan died 25th June.

1015 Eadric betrayed two thanes, Sigeferð and Morcere, who were killed. Sigeferð's widow was brought to Malmesbury, and married by Prince Eadmund. Eadmund then seized the property of Sigeferð and Morcere in opposition to Eadric.

Cnut came to Sandwich, and then harried Dorset, Wiltshire and Somerset while Æþelred was lying ill. Eadric and Eadmund joined forces but parted in distrust before taking action. Eadric took 40 ships with him and went over to Cnut who secured control of Wessex.

1016 Cnut with 160 ships and Eadric crossed the Thames at Cricklade and harried Warwickshire. Eadmund gathered the army but without the support of the King and London, they dispersed. The army gathered again and was joined by the King but he later withdrew, distrusting its loyalty. Eadmund joined forces with Uhtred and began harrying Staffordshire, Shropshire and Cheshire. Cnut harried Buckingham, Bedford, Huntingdon, Lincoln, Nottingham and York. Uhtred of Northumbria was then forced to submit to Cnut but was killed. Cnut travelled westwards to his ships in March. Eadmund went to London to his father, who died 23rd April.

# Swegn (SVEINN)

Born – c. 965 (*Th – old enough to attack Slesvig in 983*)
Succeeded – 987 (*AB*) to Denmark, invaded England 1013, recognised as King (*C*)
Died – 3$^{rd}$ February 1014 at Gainsborough (*C*)
Buried – at York (*SD*), translated to Roskilde (*EE*)

## 1$^{st}$ Wife

*Gunnhild*
  daughter of Mieczyslaw of Poland, divorced and still living in 1014 (*Th*)

## Children:

**Harold (Haraldr)**
  born ?, died 1019 (*EE, Th* – King of Denmark 1014–19?)

**King Cnut (Knutr)**
  born 988?, died 1035

*Gyða*
  married Earl Yric of Hlaðir (*Sn*) (exiled – *M*, 1023 – *last charter*)

*Estrið (Astriðr)*
  married Earl Ulf Þorgilsson by 1015 (*AB, Ks*) (died 1026? – *Sx, Rk*)
  married Duke Rodbert of Normandy, divorced 1035 (*RG*)

*Santslaue* (*H*)
  *? (W)*
  married Wyrtgeorn of the Wends

## 2$^{nd}$ Wife

*Sigrið* (*Sn*)
  c995, widow of King Yric of Sweden

## Chronicle of Events

see under Æþelred 1013–14.

# Eadmund II

Born – 990? (1st charter witnessed)
Succeeded – 23rd April 1016 on the death of his father Æþelred, chosen by the
  citizens and councillors in London during the invasion of Cnut (*C*)
Died – 30th November 1016 (*C*) at London (*W*)
Buried – at Glastonbury (*C*)

## Wife

*Ealdgyð* (*C, W*)
  married August 1015, widow of Sigeferð

## Children:

### Eadmund

  born 1016 (elder son), married a princess of Hungary (*AR*), died 10th January
  (*Crow.*) 1046/54 in Hungary (*W*)

### Eadward

  born 1017?, died 19th April (*Crow.*) 1057 (*C*)
  married *Agatha* (*C, W, AR*), 1043?, half-niece of Emperor Henrig III (*LE*)
  children: (*C*)

  – **King Eadgar II**, born 1052?, died after 1125
  – *Margareta* (*VM*), married Mælcolm of Scotland 1070 (d. 1093), died
      16th November 1093, saint 1249
  – *Cristina*, nun at Romsey (*C*)

## The Main Features of the Reign

### Politics and Government

Eadmund had taken the leadership of the opposition to his father's favourite,
Alderman Eadric in 1015. When Cnut invaded in that year, Eadmund was the heir to
his ailing father and Eadric defected to Cnut to preserve his position. Eadmund had
the support of the traditional nobility, Aldermen Ælfhelm, Ælfric, Æþelmær and
Ulfcytel, but his reign was occupied with fighting Cnut's invasion. In this, he was
largely successful until the final battle at Assandun, which was a major defeat. He
was forced to divide England with Cnut and accept that each of them would be the
other's heir. No doubt the war would have continued had he lived but his death
handed the whole of England to Cnut.

## Chronicle of Events

1016 The councillors and citizens of London chose Eadmund as King. In May, Cnut came to Greenwich and onto London besieging the city. Alderman Eadric of Mercia supported Cnut. Eadmund went to Wessex, taking its submission, and defeating the Danes at Penselwood, and after midsummer at Sherston.

Eadmund then relieved London, and defeated the Danes at Brentford, pursuing them through Otford to Sheppey. Eadric submitted to Eadmund at Aylesford.

The Danes went into Essex and on to Mercia. Eadmund overtook them at *Assandun* on 16th October. Eadric deserted Eadmund at the battle leaving Cnut victorious. The English dead included Bishop Eadnoð, Abbot Wulfsige, Alderman Ælfric, Alderman Godwine, Ulfcytel, Æþelward (son of Alderman Æþelwine) and others.

Cnut followed Eadmund to Gloucestershire and a treaty was made at Alney. Eadmund was to hold Wessex and Cnut Mercia, with each to be the other's heir. The Danes went to London which bought peace from them.

# Cnut (Knutr)

Born – 988? (*Kd – at attack on Norwich 1004, Ks – 37 at death, mistake for 47?*)

Succeeded – December 1016 on the death of Eadmund according to treaty (*W*). He was chosen King by the Danish fleet on the death of Swegn in 1014 but left England (*C.*) He invaded in 1015 and was accepted by a party of the English on the death of Æþelred (*W*). A treaty with Eadmund in October 1016 gave him Mercia and Northumbria (*C*).

Crowned – in London (*RD*)

Died – 12$^{th}$ November 1035 at Shaftesbury (*C*)

Buried – at Winchester Old Minster (*C*)

Portrait – in the Liber Vitae of New Minster (Backhouse et al. 1984)

Title – Usually King of the English, sometimes King of All Britain. Rarer titles were Emperor of the English (1019), King of the Anglo-Saxons (1021/3), King of the whole island of Britain (1021/3), King of All Albion (1032). King of All England occurs on a charter of 1022, and of All England and the Danes in 1035, as well as in the law code Cnut I of 1023. Coins have King of the English.

## 1$^{st}$ Wife (Concubine?)

*Ælfgyfu* (*C, W*)

married 1015?, daughter of Alderman Ælfhelm

## Children:

**Swegn** (*W, Sn*)

born 1016?, King of Norway 1030, died 1035

**King Harold I** (*C, W*)

born 1017/18?, died 1040

## 2$^{nd}$ Wife

*Ymme*

married July 1017 (*SD, EE*), widow of Æþelred, died 7$^{th}$ March 1052 (*Ely, H, Cant.*), or 6$^{th}$ March (*C*), portrait in the Liber Vitae of New Minster and the Encomium Emmae (Fell 1984)

## Children:

**King Harðacnut** (*C*)
  born 1018?, died 1042

*Gunnhild* (*SD*)
  born ?, died 1038
  married Henrig son of Emperor Conrad II, 1036 (*M*)

## Kinsman

Ælfward (*Ev*), Abbot of Evesham 1014, Bishop of London 1035, died 1044

## The Main Features of the Reign

### Politics and Government

Cnut came to power as a foreign conqueror and he established his supporters as a powerful party in government, especially Þurcyll. By 1018, he had exiled or executed potential English opponents identified with the old regime. However, he did trust and use English families. After 1023, the dominant Earl was Godwine. He and Earl Leofric were heads of the two most important English families to survive. The court was balanced between English and Danish nobles, with the latter taking precedence but not overwhelming the English element.

There were three law codes issued by Cnut.
0  Oxford, 1018 – a revised version of Æþelred V.
I  Winchester, 1023 – church matters.
II  Winchester, 1023 – a large code dealing with a wide variety of secular matters. It reiterated and updated earlier codes.

### The Church

Abbeys founded were Buckfast, Gloucester, St Benet's and St Edmund's. The sees of Crediton and St German's were united. Cnut was careful to placate English opinion and patronised English saints, both royal saints like Eadward II and *Eadgyð*, and martyrs killed by Danes like Eadmund of East Anglia and Archbishop Ælfheah.

### Art and Literature

Archbishop Wulfstan continued his writings until his death in 1023, and was still the dominant influence on legislation. A collection of his works made c1050 included an anonymous translation of the Greek romance *Apollonius of Tyre*, which could have been done about this time. The second section of manuscript Bodleian Junius 11, containing the poem *Christ and Satan*, may have been written during Cnut's reign.

The Winchester Style of art continued under Danish rule, producing such examples as the Missal of Robert of Jumieges, the Harley Psalter and the Liber Vitae of New Minster. The Danish art style of the period was the Ringerike Style. An example of this is the gravestone of one of Cnut's followers from St Paul's, which preserves original painting on its carved surface.

## Chronicle of Events

1016 Cnut gathered the nobility in London who agreed that Cnut succeeded to the whole of England by the terms of the treaty at Alney.

1017 England was divided into four – Wessex under Cnut himself, East Anglia under Earl Þurcyll, Mercia under Alderman Eadric, Northumbria under Earl Yric. Prince Eadwig was outlawed and afterwards killed. Eadmund's sons Eadmund and Eadward were sent to Sweden. Before 1st August, *Ymme* was brought to be Cnut's Queen. The following were executed on 25th December; Alderman Eadric, Norðman, Æþelward and Brihtric.

1018 Cnut imposed a tribute of £72,000 and £11,500 from London. 60 Ships stayed with Cnut, the rest returned to Denmark. English and Danes came to agreement at Oxford to keep Eadgar's laws. The dominant figures at court were the Danish Earls Þurcyll and Yric, and the thanes Þored and Oslac.

Eadwulf of Bamburgh and Mælcolm of Scotland fought at Carham, Lothian was finally lost to the Scots.

1019 Cnut went to Denmark and stayed there the winter.

1020 Cnut returned to England. Alderman Æþelward was outlawed 17th April at Cirencester. Cnut went to *Assandun* with Archbishop Wulfstan and Þurcyll for the consecration of the minster he had ordered for those who were killed there. The church was given to Stigand the priest.

1021 Þurcyll was outlawed 11th November.

1022 Cnut went with his fleet to the Isle of Wight.

1023 Cnut returned to England from Denmark having been reconciled to Þurcyll, entrusting him with Denmark and his son, taking Þurcyll's son with him to England. Ælfheah's relics (who had been killed by the Danes in 1012) were translated from London to Canterbury on 15th June. Archbishop Wulfstan died 28th May.

1025 Cnut took his fleet to Denmark against Ulf and Eglaf at the Holy River, and was beaten by the Swedes, losing many Danes and English.

1026 The dominant figures at court were now Earl Godwine, Osgod and Tofig.

1027 Cnut bribed the Norwegians to accept himself as King instead of Anlaf. He visited Rome from Denmark for Emperor Conrad's coronation.

1028  Cnut went to Norway with 50 ships and expelled King Anlaf, annexing the whole country. His son Harðacnut was left as King in Denmark under Cnut.

1029  Cnut returned to England.

Earl Hacun was banished, being sent to Norway.

1030  Anlaf returned to Norway and the people gathered against him, killing him in battle. Earl Hacun died at sea. Prince Swegn was made King of Norway under Cnut. Cnut may have made a second visit to Rome.

1031  On his return, Cnut went to Scotland where King Mælcolm submitted to him with two other rulers, Macbeoþen of Moray and Iehmarc of the Isle of Man.

1033  The court became less Danish with Earls Godwine and Leofric, and Ælfwine dominating the chief remaining Danes, Earl Siward, Osgod and Tofig. There was the threat of an attack by Rodbert of Normandy.

1034  Anlaf son of Sihtric of Dublin was killed by the English.

1035  Cradoc son of Rhydderch of Gwent was killed by the English.

# Harold I

Born – 1017/18 (2nd son)

Succeeded – 26th November (*C – reign length*) 1035 on the death of his father Cnut to Mercia and Northumbria, with Harðacnut to Wessex (*C, W*); to the whole of England 1037 (*W*)

Crowned – Archbishop Æþelnoð refused to crown him (*EE*)

Died – 17th March 1040 at Oxford (*C*)

Buried – at Westminster (*C*), disinterred, remains buried at London (*W*)

## Wife

*Ælfgyfu* (*SF*)

## Children:

**Ælfwine** (*SF*)
  prior of St Foi 1060

## The Main Features of the Reign

### *Politics and Government*

Cnut's death resulted in a struggle for power between his widow, *Ymme*, supporting her absent son, Harðacnut, and the nobility who wanted an English King without Danish ties. Their candidate was Harold, who was in England and supported by Mercia and Northumbria. *Ymme* relied on Godwine's support in holding Wessex, but Harðacnut's failure to return from Denmark gave the advantage to Harold and she had to flee in 1037.

The split of the Kingdom in 1035 is revealed by the coins. The first issue of Harold was issued with Harðacnut's portrait and name from mints in Wessex.

### Chronicle of Events

1035 An assembly was held at Oxford, Leofric and most northern thanes chose Harold to hold all England for himself and Harðacnut his brother, in Denmark. Godwine and the West Saxons supported the absent Harðacnut. It was agreed that *Ymme* should be in Winchester to hold Wessex for her son. She later had Cnut's treasure taken from her, though she stayed in Winchester as long as she could.

1036 Æþelred's sons Eadward and Ælfred came from Normandy and Boulogne to see *Ymme*. Ælfred was arrested by Godwine on his way to see Harold, blinded and sent to Ely where he died. *Ymme* sent Eadward back to Normandy.

1037 Harold was chosen King everywhere and Harðacnut was repudiated, as he was still in Denmark. *Ymme* was expelled during the winter to Bruges.

1039 The Welsh attacked the border, killing Eadwine, Leofric's brother, Þurcyll and Ælfgeat and others.

Harðacnut arrived in Bruges to join *Ymme*.

# Harðacnut (Harðaknutr)

Born – 1018+ (parents married 1017)

Succeeded – King of Denmark 1028; 26th November 1035 (see Harold) succeeded to Wessex on the death of his father Cnut with Harold succeeding to the rest; absent in Denmark and was deposed 1037; 18th June (*C – reign length*) 1040 succeeded on the death of Harold (*C, W*)

Died – 8th June 1042 (*C*)

Buried – at Winchester Old Minster (*C*)

Portrait – in the Encomium Emmae (EE)

Title – King of the English and All Albion on the only authentic charter (1042).

## Unmarried

## No known children

## The Main Features of the Reign

### Politics and Government

Harðacnut was waiting in Flanders with a fleet ready to invade when Harold I died. With no obvious alternative in England, he was welcomed across the channel to take up the throne. It was probably *Ymme's* decision to send for Eadward, her son by Æþelred, to be Harðacnut's heir, as an attempt to bolster her position. This may have been done as a concession to the English faction that had supported Harold I who were clearly opposed to having a Danish King.

### Chronicle of Events

1040  Harðacnut was invited from Bruges. He came with 60 ships and imposed a tax at 8 marks to the oar to pay the fleet. He had Harold I exhumed and cast into a marsh. Bishop Lyfing of Worcester was charged with complicity in Prince Ælfred's death, his see was given to Archbishop Ælfric but he was restored next year. Godwine was also charged but cleared himself on oath and with a costly ship as gift for the King.

There was famine and a sester of wheat reached 54 pence and higher.

Dunecan of Scotland unsuccessfully attacked Durham.

1041 The tax for the fleet was collected, £21,099, and £11,048 was paid to 32 ships. Harðacnut ravaged Worcestershire, 12th November, for the death of his two thanes who were killed in May while tax collecting. Prince Eadward returned to England. Harðacnut betrayed Earl Eadulf of Bamburgh who was under his protection.

# Eadward III

Born – 1005? (1st charter witnessed) at Islip, Oxfordshire
Succeeded – 8th June 1042 as Harðacnut's recognised heir (*C, W*)
Crowned – 3rd April 1043 at Winchester (*C*)
Died – 5th January 1066 at Westminster (*C*)
Buried – at Westminster (*C*)
Canonised – 7th February 1161

Portrait – in the Encomium Emmae (EE) and Bayeux Tapestry (BT)
Description – tall, white hair, rosy face, long and thin hands (*VÆ*)

Title – Usually King of the English. Other titles were King of All Britain (46–60), King of All Albion (1045–50), King of the Anglo-Saxons (1061), King of England (1061), Emperor of All Albion (1048). Coins have King of the English.

## Wife

*Eadgyð* (*C, VÆ*)

married 23rd January 1045, daughter of Earl Godwine, died 18th December 1075, portrait in the Bayeux Tapestry

## No children

## Kinsmen

**Gospatric** (*VÆ*), great nephew, grandson of Ælfgyfu and Uhtred, Earl 1067
**Odda** (*M*), signed charters 1014–50, Earl 1051, brother **Ælfric**, possibly grandson of Alderman Ælfhere (*Pe*)
**Raulf** (*Ra*), nephew, died 1057, son of *Godgyfu* and Earl Drogo of the Vexin 1049
**Rodbert** (*VÆ*), staller, in writ 1052/3, signed charters 1060–65, and son **Swegn** (*WH92*) in writs 1057/66 – 1066/75, Sheriff of Essex after 1066
**Rodulf** (*Ab*), Abbot of Abingdon 1051–52, a Norwegian Bishop
**Siward** (*OV*), signed charters 1062–65, and brother **Ealdred**, possibly grandsons of Alderman Eadric and *Eadgyð*, daughter of Æþelred
**Wigod** (*WH104*), signs charter 1062/65, in writ 1065/6
**Wulfric** (*LibE*), Abbot of Ely 1045 (55?)-65

## The Main Features of the Reign

### Politics and Government

A notable feature of the early years of the reign was the demotion and disappearance of the Danish element at court. After 1046, the government was thoroughly English and dominated by Godwine's family. Earl Godwine's power however had limits. Eadward did not favour his support for his nephew Swegn in Denmark, and his daughter's failure to produce an heir after marrying Eadward must have harmed his position. Eadward brought over various French and German followers on his return to England in 1041. These were given lands and positions but were only prominent in the Church. The Norman Rodbert was made Bishop of London and later Archbishop of Canterbury, and became the main focus of political opposition to Godwine. The exile of Godwine and his family in 1051 was the culmination of this opposition, to be reversed the next year. The main alternative noble family was that of Leofric, whose son Ælfgar was the focus of opposition to Godwine's heir Harold. It was only after 1057 that Earl Harold was able to exceed his father's power and only after Ælfgar's death, probably in 1062, that his position became totally dominant.

The question of the succession was the crucial matter of the whole reign. Eadward's nearest male kin were in exile in Russia and later in Hungary, only to return in 1057. An attempt had been made to grant the succession to the Duke of Normandy in 1051, but this would have been nullified by the return of Godwine to power in 1052. The main military threat to Eadward in the early part of the reign was from Magnus of Norway, claiming to be Harðacnut's heir by treaty. Cnut's nephew, Swegn eventually succeeded to Denmark after the death of Magnus, and later claimed that Eadward had made him his heir in 1042.

### The Church

Monasteries reformed or founded were Abbotsbury, Coventry, Deerhurst and Horton. Ramsbury and Sherborne sees were united, and the see of Crediton was moved to Exeter. Stigand's appointment to Canterbury after the exile of Rodbert was not recognised by the new reform minded Papacy. The English Church was slow to accept the reforms that would have weakened royal control over the Church. Eadward kept strict control, appointing many of his chaplains as Bishops. Adoption of Papal reforms would have to wait until after the Norman Conquest.

### Art and Literature

Eadward's reign saw the copying of the Anglo-Saxon chronicle version C, and its contemporary updating, along with contemporary additions to versions D and E. Version D may well have been sponsored by Archbishop Ealdred of York while he was Bishop of Worcester.

Good examples of the Winchester style still occurred, the Tiberius Psalter and Crowland Psalter. However, the style was moving towards a more Romanesque appearance, exemplified by the Hereford Gospels and Troper.

A number of churches, or major parts of churches, have survived from Eadward's reign, built in a native architectural style. These include Odda's chapel at Deerhurst, Worth, Sompting, Greensted, Bosham and Kirkdale. A move towards a more Romanesque style of building may be seen in Stow on the Wold. Eadward's rebuilding of Westminster Abbey is known to have been in a fully Romanesque style.

## Chronicle of Events

1043 Eadward and the Earls deprived *Ymme* of the treasures in her possession, claiming that she had not done enough for him before or after his accession. Stigand had been made Bishop of East Anglia but was deprived for being *Ymme's* closest adviser.

1044 There was great famine, the sester of wheat reaching 60 pence and more. The fleet was gathered at Sandwich. Stigand returned to his bishopric. *Gunnhild*, Cnut's niece, was exiled. She went to Bruges and afterwards to Denmark.

1045 Eadward married *Eadgyð*, daughter of Earl Godwine. The fleet was gathered again at Sandwich due to the threat from Magnus of Norway, who was occupied fighting Swegn in Denmark.

1046 Osgod the staller was outlawed. Earl Swegn (Godwine's son) invaded Wales abducting the Abbess of Leominster on his return. It was a severe winter into 1047, many people and livestock died of cold and hunger. Princes Eadmund and Eadward (sons of Eadmund II) probably left Russia for Hungary under King Andras I, in opposition to the Emperor Henrig.

1047 Swegn asked for help against Magnus of Norway, supported by Godwine, but was turned down. Magnus drove out Swegn and took over Denmark, dying the same year. Earl Swegn fled to Bruges, staying over winter.

1048 Vikings attacked Sandwich and Essex, taking their spoil thence to Flanders for sale. Magnus died and Harold succeeded to Norway, which made peace with England. Swegn again appealed for help, supported by Godwine but was refused.

1049 Emperor Henrig III asked for Eadward's help in his war against Flanders. Eadward gathered his fleet at Sandwich until the end of the campaign. Godwine's son Swegn arrived asking for his lands back but this was objected to by Harold, and Beorn, who was murdered. Swegn was outlawed and fled to Flanders. Osgod attacked Essex but was later destroyed by a gale. Irish Vikings helped by Griffin of Deheubarth defeated Bishop Ealdred of Worcester 29th July. Godwine was sent with ships against them.

1050 Eadward paid off nine ships, keeping five, at Lent. Bishops Hereman and Ealdred went to Rome for the King before Easter. Swegn's outlawry was revoked.

1051 Eadward appointed Rodbert Archbishop and Spearhafoc Bishop of London. Eadward paid off his fleet and abolished the Danegeld. Spearhafoc was forbidden to succeed to London by the Pope and Rodbert refused to consecrate him. Eadward allowed him to occupy the see nevertheless. An offer of the succession may have been conveyed to Willelm of Normandy by Archbishop Rodbert. Eustatius, the King's brother in law, came to Dover and was involved in killings in the town. Eustatius was protected by the King at Gloucester. Godwine, Swegn and Harold gathered their forces on 1st September to demand Eustatius be surrendered, refusing to harry Dover, and that French thanes be expelled from Hereford. Leofric, Siward and Raulf came to support the King. They agreed to assemble in London to debate the issue on 24th September. Godwine's men fell away, Swegn was outlawed, and he fled. Godwine and his sons were all outlawed, he with Swegn, Tostig and Gyrð went to Bruges, Harold and Leofwine to Ireland. Bishop Ealdred was sent to intercept Harold but failed to do so. *Eadgyð* was sent to Wherwell abbey. Willelm was made Bishop of London in place of Spearhafoc.

1052 *Ymme* died 6th March. Harold attacked Somerset and Devon. Eadward gathered 40 ships at Sandwich under Raulf and Odda against Godwine at Bruges. Godwine nevertheless came and won over Kent, Sussex and Surrey. The fleet failed to catch him in bad weather. He joined up with Harold at Wight, gathering support and came to Sandwich with a large following, and on to Southwark where he came to an agreement with London. A settlement was mediated by Stigand. Godwine and his family were restored 15th September, and some of the Frenchmen were outlawed. Bishops Rodbert, Willelm and Ulf fled. Osbeorn and Hugo surrendered their castles in Hereford and went to Scotland. Bishop Willelm was later recalled. Stigand was appointed to replace Rodbert. Griffin of Deheubarth harried Herefordshire defeating a force of English and French near Leominster.

1053 Earl Godwine died. The Welsh killed a number of English on the border at Westbury after Hris, brother of the Welsh King, was executed.

1054 Earl Siward invaded Scotland and routed the Scots under Macbeoþen, on behalf of Mælcolm. Bishop Ealdred went to Germany for the King to negotiate with Hungary for the return of Prince Eadward.

1055 Earl Ælfgar was outlawed on 19th March for treason. He joined Griffin of Gwynedd and attacked Hereford 24th October. Earl Raulf's forces were defeated, fleeing after a fierce battle. Earl Harold restored the defences and came to a settlement. Ælfgar was restored.

1056 Bishop Æþelstan of Hereford died, succeeded by Leofgar who was killed with the army fighting Griffin of Gwynedd along with the Sheriff, 16th June. Peace was made by Earls Leofric, Harold and Bishop Ealdred.

1057 Prince Eadward returned to be heir to the throne but died soon after, 19th April. Earl Leofric and Earl Raulf died.

1058 Earl Ælfgar was expelled again but returned with the help of Griffin and Magnus of Norway. Bishop Ealdred went to Jerusalem, through Hungary.

1059 Mælcolm of Scotland visited Eadward.

1061 Mælcolm attacked Northumbria while Earl Tostig was in Rome.

1062 A Papal embassy came to see Eadward.

1063 After Christmas, Harold attacked Rhuddlan. Harold then took the fleet against Gwynedd on 26th May while Tostig attacked Wales overland. Griffin was killed by his own men 5th August. Wales was entrusted to Bleðgente and Rigwatlaun.

1064 Harold visited the continent, staying with Willelm II of Normandy and taking part in the latter's campaign in Brittany. He promised to support Willelm's candidacy for the succession to Eadward and brought home his nephew Hacun (a hostage with Willelm since 1051).

1065 Cradoc of Gwent attacked Harold's hunting lodge at Portskewet 24th August. Northumbrian thanes rebelled against Earl Tostig, choosing Morcere (brother of Earl Eadwine) instead. They were joined by Earl Eadwine and many Welsh, met by Harold and a settlement was reached after talks at Northampton and Oxford 28th October. Tostig left for Flanders.

# Harold II

Born – c. 1022 (2<sup>nd</sup> or 3<sup>rd</sup> child)

Born – c. 1022 (2$^{nd}$ or 3$^{rd}$ child)
Succeeded – 5$^{th}$ January 1066 by the grant of Eadward on his deathbed (*C, VÆ, WP, E*), Eadward's brother-in-law, Earl of East Anglia 1045, Earl of Wessex 1053
Crowned – 6$^{th}$ January 1066 (*C*) by Archbishop Ealdred of York (*W*)
Died – 14$^{th}$ October 1066, killed in the Battle of Hastings (*C*)
Buried – at Waltham (*M*)

Portrait – in the Bayeux Tapestry

Title – King of the English occurs on coins.

## 1$^{st}$ Wife

*Eadgyð (Wþ)*

## Children:

**Godwine** (*W*)
  raided Somerset in 1068

**Eadmund** (*W*)
  raided Somerset in 1068

**Magnus** (*W*)
  raided Somerset in 1068

**Ulf** (*W*)
  held captive by Willelm until 1087

*Gunnhild (M, VW)*
  nun at Wilton

*Gyða (Sn)*
  married Vladimir of Russia

## 2$^{nd}$ Wife

*Ealdgyð (O)*
  daughter of Earl Ælfgar

## Children:

**Harold** (*W, M*)

## Kinsmen

brothers (*C*): **Tostig,** Earl 1055–65, **Leofwine,** Earl 1057–66, **Gyrð,** Earl 1057–66,
   **Wulfnoð** (*E*), hostage in Normandy 1051–64
sister (*C*): *Eadgyð*, wife of Eadward III
nephew: **Hacun** (*E*), son of brother Swegn, hostage in Normandy since 1051

## The Main Features of the Reign

### *Politics and Government*

Harold was by far the most experienced and powerful layman in England at
Eadward's death. His military reputation was high after his successful invasion of
Wales and he had neutralised the opposition of Ælfgar's sons by marrying their
sister. There was no one who could have challenged his succession, which was
based on Eadward's bequest on his deathbed (Prince Eadgar was still under age).
However, he knew that a challenge would probably come from abroad; Denmark,
Norway or Normandy. Denmark waited until after the Norman Conquest before
making a move. The Norwegian attempt at invasion was decisively beaten at
Stamford Bridge, but Harold was killed fighting the Normans at Hastings.

### Chronicle of Events

1066  Harold succeeded according to Eadward's deathbed bequest. Harold went to
York to ensure its loyalty, returning to Westminster 16th April. A comet was
seen 24th April for one week.

Tostig came to Wight and raided the coast up to Sandwich, and thence to
Lindsey with 60 ships, to the Humber, where he was driven off by Eadwine
and Morcere. He was given shelter in Scotland for the summer.

Harold gathered the fleet at Wight and stationed troops along the coast
waiting for an invasion by Willelm of Normandy. The fleet dispersed
8th September when its supplies ran out.

Harold of Norway with 300 ships came to the Tyne, was joined by Tostig and
then went up the Ouse to York. Eadwine and Morcere were defeated with
heavy loss 20th September and York fell. Harold came straightaway from the
south and defeated them at Stamford Bridge 25th September. The Norwegians
sailed home with only 24 ships.

Willelm came to Pevensey 28th September and built a castle at Hastings.
Harold marched against him but Willelm attacked him before his army was
fully ready. Harold was killed and Leofwine and Gyrð, and many others on
14th October.

# Eadgar II

Born – 1052? (*O – same age as Rodbert of Normandy*)

Succeeded – 16th? October 1066, chosen by the army, councillors and citizens of London after the Battle of Hastings (*C, W, GA, WP, O*), claimed the throne 1068–74 (*C, W, SD, M, WP, WJ*). He was the acknowledged heir of Eadward before his death (*LE*)

Abdicated – December 1066 (*C, O, GA, WP*)

Died – after 1125 (*M*)

Buried – ?

## Unmarried

## No known children

## Kinsmen

sons of sister *Margareta*: **Eadward** died 1093, **Eadmund** King of Scots 1094–97, **Æþelred** Earl of Fife & Abbot of Dunkeld, **Eadgar** King of Scots 1097–1107, **Alexander** King of Scots 1107–24, **Dauid** King of Scots 1124–53

daughters of *Margareta*: *Eadgyð* died 1118, married Henrig I 1101, *Maria* died 1115/16, married Eustatius of Boulogne 1102

## The Main Features of the Reign

### Politics and Government

Eadgar was only 13 when Eadward III died. It was only after Harold's death that his succession stood any chance of success. Unfortunately, the English forces had been heavily mauled at Fulford and Hastings, and there must have been losses also at Stamford Bridge. Against this, the Normans could bring over reinforcements, having secured a bridgehead on the coast. Furthermore, Harold's brothers had been killed with him at Hastings and there was no one with enough experience who could unite the different factions in support of a now 14 year old King.

Eadgar's attempt to win back the crown began with his flight to Scotland supported by a party of English nobles under his cousin Earl Gospatric. The military strength of the Normans and the losses of the English by death and confiscation after the Norman takeover made foreign military support necessary for success. Also, the opposition to Willelm was on the edges of England, in the south-west, the Welsh marches and in the north. It was therefore difficult to co-ordinate military action and Willelm could suppress each area individually (anyway, it is not clear that all the attacks and revolts were linked and in support of Eadgar). A factor in Willelm's favour was that he was the consecrated King and so would have the support of the Church who would not want to see the sanctity of coronation undermined. After 1070, Willelm's destruction of the north made it impossible for Eadgar to secure a base of operations inside England and Scottish help alone was not enough. Danish help had proved less useful than hoped. By 1074, the higher nobility of England was predominantly Norman, as were the Bishops, and there was little likelihood of serious foreign support. Eadgar had no options left and returned to England to make peace rather than live in permanent exile.

## Eadgar's Life after 1074

Eadgar remained at Willelm's court until 1086 when he went to Apulia, joining the Normans in Italy. By 1091, he was in Normandy as a key adviser and ally of Duke Rodbert, Willelm's son. Later that year, he mediated a peace agreement between Mælcolm of Scotland and Willelm II, and acted as an ambassador to Scotland in 1093. After Mælcolm's death and the seizure of the throne by his brother Dufenal, Eadgar invaded Scotland and put his nephew, also called Eadgar, on the throne in 1097. He then joined the first crusade. Eadgar became King Henrig I's uncle-in-law after Henrig married his niece *Eadgyð*, but joined his old friend Duke Rodbert in opposition to Henrig at the Battle of Tinchebrai in 1106, where he was taken prisoner. He was released and was last mentioned as living in retirement in 1125.

### Chronicle of Events

1066 Archbishop Ealdred and London supported Eadgar as King. Eadwine and Morcere came to London, sending their sister Queen *Ealdgyð* to Chester. Eadwine and Morcere promised to fight for him but there were continual delays. While the army was preparing to fight Eadwine and Morcere returned home.

Abbot Leofric of Peterborough fell ill during the campaign at Hastings and died 31st October. Brand was chosen as successor, and was sent to Eadgar, who confirmed him in office.

Willelm waited for a surrender at Hastings but none was given. He marched through Sussex, Kent, Surrey (engaging the English in London at Southwark) and Hampshire, where Winchester surrendered. He crossed the Thames at Wallingford and cut off London from the north, receiving the submission of Archbishop Stigand. Eadgar, Bishops Ealdred, Wulfstan, Walter and Earls Eadwine and Morcere submitted at Berkhamstead in Hertfordshire.

1068 After the crowning of Willelm's wife *Mahtild* 11th May, the Earls Eadwine, Morcere and Walþeof threatened opposition to Willelm who marched against them and built castles at Warwick, Nottingham, Lincoln, York, Huntingdon and Cambridge. Eadgar fled England in the summer with his family, Earl Gospatric, Mærleswegn and others, to Scotland. He reluctantly gave consent for his sister *Margareta* to marry King Mælcolm. Harold's sons harried Bristol and Somerset.

1069 Durham rose up, killing the Norman Earl Rodbert and his men. Eadgar was accepted as King at York with the rebels, led by Earl Gospatric, Mærleswegn and Arncyll. Willelm came up from the south unawares and defeated them heavily, plundering York and advancing to Durham. Eadgar then returned to Scotland. Bishop Æþelwine of Durham was outlawed after the arrest of his brother, the former Bishop Æþelric. Harold's sons raided Devon, and were beaten off by Earl Breon, 24th June. The northern Welsh marches were raised in revolt by Eadric and Siward (Eadward III's kinsman). Other possible centres of opposition were the abbeys of St Benet's in Norfolk and St Augustine's in Canterbury.

Between 15th August and 8th September, Swegn of Denmark's sons came to the Humber after attacking Kent and East Anglia with 240 ships. They were met by Eadgar, Walþeof, Gospatric, Mærleswegn, Siward Barn and others. They marched on York 21st September, taking the castle, but the town had been burned by the French beforehand (Archbishop Ealdred having died there 11th September). Willelm came north and wasted the area of the rebellion, then reduced Stafford and Shrewsbury. The Danes were paid off by Willelm. There was a great famine, caused by the military devastation. Risings in western Wessex at Exeter and Montacute (Dorset) were also put down.

1070 Earls Gospatric and Walþeof made peace with Willelm after they had been pursued as far as the Tees, and were restored to office. Willelm reduced Chester before returning south. A council on 4th April with Papal legates deposed Bishops Stigand, Æþelmær and some Abbots, and on 23rd May also Bishop Æþelric (Bishop Leofwine had already resigned). Swegn of Denmark came to join his fleet and sent Earl Osbeorn to attack the Fens. They teamed up with Hereward at Ely to attack Peterborough which had been given a new Norman Abbot before he could arrive on 2nd June. The Danes were paid to leave by Willelm and returned to Denmark before 24th June. Eadric in the Welsh marches was reconciled to the King.

1071 Earls Eadwine and Morcere fled. Eadwine was killed by his own men on his way to Scotland. Morcere went to Ely, also Bishop Æþelwine of Durham and Siward Barn, joining Hereward, Siward of Maldon, Þurcyll and others. Willelm besieged them forcing them to surrender, except for Hereward. Æþelwine died that same winter. Abbot Ealdred of Abingdon was dismissed and imprisoned possibly for complicity in the revolts.

1072 Willelm invaded Scotland after 15th August. Mælcolm made peace and gave him hostages. Eadgar was forced to leave Scotland. Earl Gospatric was dismissed by Willelm.

1073 Willelm took English forces abroad, invaded and took over Maine.

1074 Eadgar came to Scotland from Flanders 8th July. King Philip of France offered him Montreuil castle as a base to attack Willelm but he was shipwrecked on his way there. Advised by Mælcolm to make peace with Willelm, he did so, being escorted to Willelm through England and across the channel.

# Appendices

# Appendix 1

# The Officials of the King's Household

Information about the King's household officials is scarce. Occasional notices in charters are the main source, whose reliability is often unsafe. However, even forged charters may copy genuine witness lists and so cannot be wholly dismissed. References below include the source for the reader to check to his/her own satisfaction. Dates given after the names are those of documents in which they are denoted by their office, not when they were appointed. See page 30 above for the organisation of the household. There was a tradition at Ely (LE) that Æþelred began a rota system for staffing the King's writing office (later the Chancery), using monks from Ely, Glastonbury and St Augustine's in turn.

Various names were used to denote the different offices of the household:

| *Modern* | *Old English* | *Latin* |
|---|---|---|
| Steward | Discþegn | Discifer, Dapifer |
| Chamberlain | Burþegn, Hræglþegn | Camerarius, Cubicularius |
| Butler | Byrele | Pincerna |
| Constable | Steallere | Constabularius |
| Chancellor | Canceller | Cancellarius, Sigillarius |

## Steward

**Deormod** 892 (S348): signed charters 878–909

**Wulfhelm** 926 (S396): signed charters 926–934

**Wulfgar** 927 (LVD)

**Brihtric** 927 (LVD)

**Ælfheah** 956 (S597), 956/57 (S1292): brother of Alderman Ælfhere, Steward of Eadwig, appointed Alderman of Wessex 959

**Ælfsige** 956 (S597)

**Ælfsige** 956 (S597), 973 (S792): signed charters up to 995

**Wulfgar** 957 (S658): signed S658 of 959 as *custos*, Steward of Eadwig

**Ealdred** 958 (S651): Steward of Eadwig

**Ælfwine** 968 (S768): brother of Aldermen Ælfhere and Ælfheah, granted land in 952, signed charters 956–70, followed Eadgar in 957

**Eanwulf** 968 (S768), 971 (S782): signed charters 958–75, follower of Eadgar

**Wulfstan**  968 (S768): signed charters 958–974, originally Steward of Queen *Eadgyfu*, follower of Eadgar
**Æþelward** 971 (S782), 973 (S792)
**Ælfward**  971 (S782), 973 (S792): brother of Æþelward, signed charters up to 986
**Æþelmær**  1002 (S914): signed charters 983–1005, son of Alderman Æþelward of the Western Wessex, appointed Alderman in succession to his father
**Ordwulf**  1002 (S914): son of Alderman Ordgar of the South-West, brother of Queen *Ælfþryð*, signed charters 975–1005, appointed Steward 994?, founded Tavistock Abbey
**Harold**  (H): signed at the head of the thanes in 1045 (S1007, S1012), later Earl of Wessex and King
**Ætsere**  1062 (S1036): signed also in 1059
**Lyfing?**  1062 (S1036): mistake for Constable
**Eadnoð?**  1066 (DB): mistake for Constable
**Alan**  1066 (DB)

## Chamberlain

**Ælfric**  892 (S348), 899/924 (S1445)
**Titstan**  962 (S706)
**Wynstan**  963 (S719), 972 (S789)
**Æþelsige**  963 (S713), 968 (S768): brother of Alderman Æþelwine, signed charters 958–87, died 13th October 987
**Leofric**  1002 (S914): signed charters 980–1005
**Hugo**  1044 (S1002), 1060 (S1030), 1061 (S1033), 1066 (DB): S1002, S1030 were forged by Osbert of Clare in the early 12th century
**Ælfric**  1066 (DB)
**Wynsige**  1066 (DB)

## Butler

**Sigewulf**  892 (S348)
**Ælfwig**  958 (S651): signed charters 956–61, follower of Eadwig
**Æþelsige**  959 (S658): under Eadwig
**Wulfgar**  1000 (S897): signed charters 997–1015
**Hearding**  1065 (S1042): the Queen's Butler in 1062 (S1036)
**Wigod**  1062 (S1036), 1065 (S1042)

## Constable

**Þored**  1016/35 (S981): signed charters 1018–45
**Tofig**  ? (IW): signed charters 1018–44
**Ælfstan**  1045 (S1471): signed charters 1042–50
**Osgod**  1046 (C): signed charters 1026–46, outlawed in 1046

**Rodbert**   1052/53 (H84), 1058/66 (H93), 1066 (VÆ, DB): signed charters 1059-65

## Constable (continued)

**Lyfing**   1053/55 (S1476, S1478): signed charters 1043–53/55
**Raulf**   1053/55 (S1476, S1478), 1060 (S1029, S1031), 1061/65 (S1426): signed charters 1050–65, later Earl of East Anglia
**Eadnoð**   1053/66 (H85), 1066 (DB), 1067 (C)
**Esgar**   1060 (S1030), 1053/66 (H98), 1057/66 (H93): signed S1029 of 1060 as dapifer, S1031 of 1060 as procurator, signed charters 1053/55–65
**Bondig**   1060 (S1031), 1061/65 (S1426), 1066 (DB): signed charters 1060–65

## Chancellor

**Ealdwulf**   (Pb) Abbot of Peterborough *980*–992, Archbishop of York 992–1002, said to have been Chancellor of Eadgar I
**Ælfric**   (SAb) Abbot of St Alban's *969*, Bishop of Ramsbury 990–1002, Archbishop of Canterbury 995–1005, Saint, said to have been Chancellor of Æþelred
**Leofric**   (FW) became Bishop of Crediton 1046
**Wulfwig**   1045 (S1011), became Bishop of Dorchester 1053: forged by Osbert of Clare in the early 12th century
**Regenbald** 1060 (S1030), 1061 (S1033), 1062 (S1036), 1065 (S1041), 1066 (S1043), 1066 (DB): S1030, S1041, S1043 were forged by Osbert of Clare in the early 12th century

# Appendix 2

# The Aldermen and Earls

Aldermen were the King's chief representatives in the regions of the Kingdom. From the time of the Danish conquest, under Cnut, the term Alderman was replaced by that of Earl. The duties of the Aldermen were as follows:

a. to lead the military forces of their district, both in defence of the district and when serving in the King's army.
b. to preside over the twice yearly shire and thrice yearly borough courts, alongside the Bishop.
c. to make sure the King's taxes were collected from their district.
d. to advise the King on matters of national importance.

We may assume that they had other functions which followed from the above. These might include supervising the repair of fortifications and the enforcement of the law. In practice, much of the day-to-day work would be done by the Sheriff, a royal official in each shire. To reward them in their work, they received a third of the profits of justice from the courts and had manors attached to their office. They would naturally attract their own personal following and have a network of clients in their district bound to them by personal ties of lordship. Their role at court as royal advisers and military assistants meant that they connected their local areas with national affairs and acted as a bridge between the crown and the locality. This could lead to a conflict of interests between their role as King's officials and as regional magnates. Holders of the office were appointed by the King. Although there was no automatic inheritance of the position, there was a strong tendency for Kings to appoint sons to succeed their fathers.

The laws of Cnut laid down the heriot (death duties) of an Earl as 8 horses (4 saddled), 4 helmets, 4 mailcoats, 4 swords, 8 spears, 8 shields and £25 (II Cnut c.71). This was double the fighting equipment of a King's thane and four times the amount of money.

Until the reign of Eadward I, the Alderman had charge of a single shire. After the conquest of the Danelaw, they had charge of groups of shires. At first there were nine provinces south of the Humber but the boundaries between them do not seem to have been fixed. Some were later combined with others and by the eleventh century, earldoms could be created for any combination of shires. Throughout the period, but especially in the reign of Æþelred, some provinces were left without an Alderman or Earl for periods of time. The usual number of Earls by the reign of Eadward III was six.

Dates given in *italics* show the earliest or latest mention of that person in the office. Dates in brackets are used where only one notice exists of the person holding the position. Split dates (e.g. 893/96) show that the true dates lies somewhere between the two. The names given to the Aldermen's provinces from Æþelstan onwards are purely for modern convenience. Names used at the time varied and often depended on the perspective of the writer. The name of one particular shire might be used, e.g. Alderman of Kent in eastern Wessex, or a wider regional name might occur, e.g. Earl of the Mediterraneorum in south-eastern Mercia. Sometimes an old folk name might be revived as in the Magonsæte for Herefordshire.

## Aldermen 871–909

Identifying the Aldermen and the shires they were responsible for depends on notices in the Anglo-Saxon Chronicle and the witness lists of charters. Secure identifications are underlined. Anglo-Saxon parents sometimes included elements of their own names in those of their children. Identifying successors on this basis is highly risky but has been used below (assumed successors are given in *italics*). Others can be assigned by default, other shires being allotted, or by assuming that they signed charters as the First of the Aldermen for their own shires (an unproven assumption).

### *Wessex*

Berkshire: **Ordwulf** *876–882*, *Oswulf 901–909*
Devon: Æþelstan (875), **Odda** (878), **Æþelred** *892–899*, **Ælfred** (900), Ælfwold (904)
Dorset: Æþelwulf (876)
Essex: **Brihtwulf** *–893/6* (in Danish hands after 879/86 and so no successor)
Hampshire: **Cuðred** *875–878/79*, **Wulfred** *878/79–893/6*, **Ordlaf** *898–909*
Kent (a): **Æþelwold** *–888*, **Ceolmund** *–893/6*, **Sigewulf** *898–902*, **Osferð** *909–934*
Kent (b): Ælfstan *–878*, **Garwulf** (882), **Sigehelm** *898–902*
Somerset: **Eadwulf** *–878*, **Æþelnoð** *878–893*, **Heahferð** *900–909*
Surrey: **Ælfred** *–871*,
Sussex: **Mucel** *–878*,
Wiltshire: **Wulfhere** *–878*, **Æþelhelm** *878–897*, **Ordgar** *900–909*

**Unknown shires in Wessex**

The following must cover Dorset, Surrey and Sussex.

**Beocca** *882–904*, **Osred** (909)
**Brihtnoð** (882), *Brihtwulf 903–909*
**Wullaf** *882–898*, *Wulfsige 901–909*

## Mercia (under Æþelred and Æþelflæd)

In the 880s, five Aldermen can be identified holding office at the same time under Æþelred. Their provinces probably covered the dioceses of Worcester, Hereford, Lichfield (perhaps 2 Aldermen) and that part of Dorchester not under Danish rule.

**Brihtnoð** *872–884*, **Eadwold** (888)
**Æþelwold** *875–888*
**Æþelferð** *883–916* (area may have included Buckingham, of West Saxon origin)
**Æþelwulf** *884*–902 (area included Worcester; brother of Ælfred's wife, Queen *Ealhswið*)
**Ealhelm** *884–900* (northern Mercia?)

By the 890s, only three Aldermen signed charters, **Æþelferð**, **Æþelwulf** and **Ealhelm**. Charters of 903 and 904 have only two, **Æþelferð** and a new name, **Ælfwold**. **Æþelferð** still signed under *Æþelflæd* in 916, and was joined by **Ælfred**.

## Aldermen and Earls From 925

Charter evidence only began again in 925 after a break since 909. Between these two dates, the Aldermen were reorganised to cover several shires each. The provincial boundaries are not easy to reconstruct and may not have been fixed. Some provinces seem to have been short-lived or intermittent. The title Alderman was replaced by that of Earl from the reign of Cnut. Earls found earlier than this were Danish Earls from the Viking settled east of England and may have been akin to later Sheriffs in function.

## Central Wessex

**Ælfwold** *925*–938/39: headed the list of Aldermen 934–38
**Ælfhere** 938/39–942: headed the list of Aldermen 939–40
**Eadric** 942–949: brother of Alderman Æþelstan of East Anglia, in charters since 940, signed as thane from 932
**Æþelsige** 949/51–958/59: signed as thane 945–949
**Ælfheah** 959–971: formerly Steward, brother of Alderman Ælfhere, in charters since 937, area included Southampton, Sussex, Wilton
*under Ælfhere of Mercia 971–75?*
*or Ælfweard?*
**Æþelmær** *977*–982: signed as thane 972–75
**Ælfric** 982–1016: killed at Assandun, son Ælfgar blinded on the King's order 993, headed the list of Aldermen 999–1009, area included Southampton and Wilton, in charters since 973
**Godwine** *1018*–1053: expelled 1051–52, daughter *Eadgyð* married Eadward III 1045, father of Earls Swegn, Harold, Tostig, Gyrð and Leofwine, supported Harðacnut in 1035, area included Berkshire, Kent, Southampton, legatee of Prince Æþelstan's will in 1014

**Harold** 1053–1066: formerly Earl of East Anglia, son of Godwine, brother–in–law of Eadward III, area included Berkshire, Devon, Dorset, Somerset, Southampton, also Hereford after 1057, succeeded as King Harold II in 1066

**Willelm** (FitzOsbern) 1067–1071: close associate of Willelm I, co–regent of England in 1067, brother of Osbeorn (chaplain of Eadward III)

## Western Wessex

**?Ordgar** *925–926*: Alderman under Eadward I since *900*, headed the list by 926

**?Æscberht** *930–934*

**Wulfgar** *939*–948/49: signed from 931, possibly since 928, granted land 921, headed the list of Aldermen 940–943

**Eadmund** 948/49–963/64: headed list of Aldermen 949–51 & 957–59 for Eadwig, granted land in 947, signed as thane after 931

**Ordgar** 963/64–971: daughter *Ælfþryð* married Eadgar I, signed as thane 958 (Eadwig)–64, area included Devon

**Æþelward** 971/75–998/1002: father of Æþelmær, headed the list of Aldermen 993-998, wrote a Latin version of the Anglo-Saxon Chronicle, patron of the writer Abbot Ælfric, signed as thane after 959

**Æþelmær** *1013*–1014/18: formerly Steward, retired from court 1005, signed as thane 983–1005, son of Æþelward, area included Dorset

**Æþelward** 1014/18–1020: signed as thane 1002, son-in-law of Æþelmær, exiled in 1020

**Sihtric** *1026–1031*

**Odda** 1051–52: appointed during the exile of Earl Godwine of Wessex, transferred to Worcester, died 1056 (as a monk), signed as thane 1014–50, area was Cornwall, Devon, Dorset, Somerset

## Eastern Wessex

**Osferð** 904/09–*934*: signed as thane 898–904, related to the royal family, headed the list of Aldermen 928–934

**Wulfstan** (939)

**Æþelwold** *940–946*: brother of Alderman Æþelstan of East Anglia, signed as thane from 931, area included Kent, Sussex, Surrey and possibly Essex

*under Eadric & Æþelsige of Central Wessex?*

**Ælfric** *957–958*: charter recipient 948–957

*under Ælfheah of Central Wessex & Ælfhere of Mercia?*

**Eadwine** *977*–982: area included Kent and Sussex, charter recipient 962–968

**Sigered** *1019–1023*

**Leofwine** *1057*–1066: killed at Hastings, brother of Harold II, area included Essex, Middlesex, Hertford, Kent and Surrey

**Oda** 1067–1082: Bishop of Bayeux, half–brother of Willelm I, co–regent of England in 1067

## Mercia

**Wulfgar** *926–927*: charter recipient as a thane 921

**Ealdred** 930–33

**Ealhelm** 940–*951*: signed as thane 930–940, father of Aldermen Ælfhere and Ælfheah

*under Æþelstan of East Anglia 951–56?*

**Ælfhere** 956–983: signed as thane in 956 (granted land in 951), brother of Alderman Ælfheah, headed the list of Aldermen 958–83, area included Worcester

**Ælfric** 983–985: exiled in 985, brother–in–law of Alderman Ælfhere

*under Æþelwine of East Anglia 985–90?*

**Leofwine** *994*–1023: granted land 985, area included Worcester, Warwick, Hereford, father of Alderman Leofric, subordinate to Eadric and Eglaf?

**Eadric** 1007–1017: executed 1017, joined Cnut against Æþelred and Eadmund 1015, son–in–law of Æþelred, headed the list of aldermen 1012–17, area included Chester, Shrewsbury, Stafford, Hereford, Gloucester, Worcester

**Eglaf** 1017–1024/1035: brother of Ulf, brother–in–law of Godwine, included Gloucester

**Leofric** 1023–1057: son of Alderman Leofwine, supported Harold I in 1035

**Ælfgar** *1057–1062*: transferred from East Anglia, exiled & reinstated 1058, son of Earl Leofric, father of Earls Eadwine and Morcere, area included Worcester, Warwick

**Eadwine** *1062–1069*: brother of Earl Morcere, area included Chester, Lincoln, Shrewsbury, Stafford, Worcester, senior Earl after the Battle of Hastings, killed 1071 in revolt against Willelm I.

## North-West Mercia

**Uhtred** 931–937

**Æþelmund** 940–*965*: signed charters as thane 928–940

## North-East Mercia

**Uhtred** *930–950*: granted land as thane in 926, area possibly included Derbyshire

## South-East Mercia

**Æþelferð** *883–916*: father of Aldermen Ælfstan, Æþelstan, Æþelwold, Eadric

**Ælfstan** *930–934*: son of Æþelferð

**Æþelstan** *940–949*

*under Æþelstan of East Anglia 949–55?*

**Æþelstan** (Rota) *955–970*: married *Æþelflæd*, widow of Eadmund I, headed the list of aldermen 956–57, area included Essex?

**Đurig** *1041–1044*: witnessed last charter 1044/51, area included Huntingdon, signed charter as thane 1038, addressed in writs 1040/42, 1043/49

### South-East Mercia (continued)

**Beorn** *1045*–1049: son of Ulf and *Estrið*, nephew of Godwine and Cnut, area included Hertford
**Siward** 1049–1055: Earl of York
**Tostig** 1055–1065: Earl of York, area included Northampton
**Walþeof** 1065–1075: son of Earl Siward of York, area included Huntingdon, supported Eadgar II 1069–70, Earl of Bamburgh 1072, executed 1076

### East Anglia

**Ælfred** *930*–931/32
**Æþelstan** 931/32–956: retired to Glastonbury, son of Alderman Æþelferð, father of Aldermen Æþelwold and Æþelwine, headed the list of Aldermen 943–956, area included Norfolk, Suffolk, Cambridge, Huntingdon, Holland, Northampton, known as the 'Half King'
**Æþelwold** 956–962: son of Alderman Æþelstan, married *Ælfþryð*, daughter of Ordgar 956
**Æþelwine** 962–992: brother of Æþelwold, headed the list of Aldermen 983–90, signed charter as thane 958, area included Holland and Cambridge
**Leofsige** *994*–1002: held with Essex, exiled 1002 for murdering a Sheriff
*Ulfcytel*: killed at Assandun 1016, signed charters as thane 1002–16, never Alderman but led the forces of East Anglia against the Danes
**Ðurcyll** 1017–1021: invaded England 1009, served Æþelred 1012
*Osgod (Clapa)*: exiled 1046, died 1054, signed charters as thane and Constable 1026–46, never Earl but a major landowner in East Anglia
**Harold** 1045–53: exiled 1051–52, transferred to Wessex 1053, son of Earl Godwine, area included Norfolk, Suffolk, Essex, Cambridge, Huntingdon
**Ælfgar** 1051–52, 1053–57: in exile 1055, transferred to Mercia 1057, son of Alderman Leofric, area included Holland
**Gyrð** *1057*–1066: brother of Earl Harold, killed at Hastings 1066, area included Norfolk, Suffolk, Oxford
**Raulf** 1067–1069: Constable of Eadward III
**Raulf** 1069–1075: son of Raulf, rebelled against Willelm I 1075 and fled abroad, area included Holland

### Essex

**Ælfgar** 944/46–*951*: father-in-law of Eadmund I and Brihtnoð
**Brihtferð** 953/55–956: area included Middlesex
**Æþelwold** 956: son of Alderman Æþelstan, transferred to East Anglia 956
**Brihtnoð** 956–991: killed at Maldon, area included Northampton and Huntingdon, possibly subordinate to East Anglia, son-in-law of Alderman Ælfgar
**Leofsige** *994*–1002: also East Anglia, area included Buckingham, Oxford

## York

*under Bamburgh?* 927–39, 944–47, 948–49, 954–66

**Oslac** 966–975: exiled 975, signed charter as Earl 963 but appointment recorded in 966

**Þored** 975/79–992/93: father in law of Æþelred

**Ælfhelm** 992/93–1006: murdered 1006, father of *Ælfgyfu* (wife of Cnut)

**Uhtred** 1006–1016: submitted to Cnut 1016, son of Walþeof, son–in–law of Æþelred, also Earl of Bamburgh

**Yric** 1016–1023/33: brother–in–law of Cnut, regent of Norway 1000–15

**Siward** 1022/33–1055: also Earl of Huntingdon, and of Bamburgh after 1041, father of Earl Walþeof

**Tostig** 1055–1065: expelled 1065 after a revolt against him, brother of Earl Harold, killed fighting for Harold of Norway at Stamford Bridge, area included Nottingham, also Earl of South-East Mercia

**Morcere** 1065–*1069*: brother of Earl Eadwine, rebelled against Willelm I 1071, imprisoned until 1087


## Bamburgh

**Ealdred** *913–946*

**Oswulf** *946–966*

**Eadwulf** *968–970*

**Walþeof** (994): father of Uhtred & Eadwulf

**Uhtred** 995–1016: son of Walþeof, father of Ealdred, Earl of York 1006

**Eadwulf** (Cudel) 1016–1019: brother of Uhtred

**Ealdred** 1019–1038: son of Uhtred

**Eadwulf** 1038–1041: brother of Ealdred

*to York* 1041–1065

**Oswulf** 1065–1067: son of Eadwulf

**Copsig** 1067: former associate of Tostig, killed by Oswulf

**Gospatric** 1067–1068: kinsman of Eadgar II, supported Eadgar against Willelm 1068

**Rodbert** (de Commines) 1068–1069: killed in English revolt 1069

**Gospatric** 1069–1072: restored, dismissed 1072 and fled to Scotland (ancestor of the Earls of Dunbar)

**Walþeof** 1072–1075: also Earl of Huntingdon (see South-East Mercia)


## Others

**Oswulf** *934–937*: perhaps the Alderman of Eadward I *901–09*

**Uhtred** *956–958:* of the family of the Earls of Bamburgh?

**Godric** *1014–1022*

### Others (continued)

**Hacun** *1019–*1030: regent of Norway 1028, son of Yric, nephew–in–law of Cnut, area included Worcester

**Hranig** *1018–1041*: area included Hereford

**Norðman** (994): somewhere in Northumbria

**Odda** 1052–1055: transferred from Western Wessex to Worcester, retired to become a monk, died 31st August 1056, signed as thane 1014–1050

**Raulf** *1050–*1057: nephew of Edward III, area included Hereford by 1055, Oxford 1053/57, came to England in 1041 with Eadward

**Swegn** *1043–*1047, 1050–1051: exiled 1047–50 and 1051, died 1052, son of Earl Godwine, area included Oxford, Gloucester, Hereford, Somerset, Berkshire

### Doubtful Aldermen and Earls

**Ælfwold** (946)

**Ælfsige** *956–58*: usually signed as thane, mistaken attribution as Earl

**Ælfwine** *1033–1035*: signed as thane usually, attribution as Earl probably a mistake

**Godwine** (1016): killed at Assandun 1016, signed only as thane 996–1016

**Norðman** (1017): died 1017, son of Alderman Leofwine, signed charters as thane only 996–1017

### Danish Earls Before 1016

After the Danelaw and York were brought into England, a number of Earls who had Danish names signed charters. In spite of their high status, they may have been the equivalents of Sheriffs elsewhere, being responsible for one district rather than groupings of shires. There were never more than seven at any one time and may have included the Five Boroughs (Derby, Leicester, Lincoln, Nottingham, and Stamford) along with shires in the southern Danelaw, and York. The Anglo–Saxon Chronicle refers to the Seven Boroughs within the Danelaw in 1015, although by then there were no longer Earls with Danish names covering the area.

**Guþrum** *928–935*

**Hawerd** *929*

**Gunner** *929*

**Fræna** *929–930*

**Grim** *929–930*

**Styrcær** *929–930*

**Rægnold** *930–932*

**Healfdene** *930–946* (Bedford or Hertford?)

**Urm** *930–958*

**Þurferð** *931–932* (Northampton?)

**Hadder** *931–934* (in East Anglia? )
**Scule** *931–949* (in East Anglia?)
**Inwær** *932–934*
**Hereric** 932/956 (Cambridge?)
**Grim** *946–949*
**Coll** *946–949*
**Morcere** *946–958*
**Gunner** *956–963* (in Durham?)
**Liot** *956–958*
**Anferð** *956–958*

## Norman Marcher Earls

After 1068, Willelm I seems to have avoided appointing new Earls on the old regional model. New appointments were confined to single shires on the Welsh border to break up English resistance in Mercia and reduce the potential threat from Earl Eadwine, whose family had traditional political ties with the Welsh Kings.

**Gerbod** 1068–1070: Chester
**Hugo** 1070–1101: Chester
**Roger** (de Montgomerie) 1068–1094: Shrewsbury
**Roger** 1071–1075: Hereford, son of Earl Willelm (FitzOsbern)

# Appendix 3

# BISHOPS

Establishing lists of Bishops is not easy for this period. Chronicles and charters provide some dates, as do later Bishops' lists preserved by 12th century historians. These are however, of varying reliability. Dates given as e.g. 930/31 are of appointment or death somewhere between those two dates. A date given in *italics* means appointment sometime before, or death sometime after that date. A single date in brackets is a date when the person was known to be Bishop with no other dates known for that person. Saints include locally venerated saints as well as those officially canonised. Only Bishops holding office under Kings of England are included. This excludes Bishops from outside Wessex before incorporation into England. The Archbishops collected the badge of their metropolitan authority from Rome and the date of this is noted where known. Lists of Abbots for this period can be found in Knowles, Brooke and London 1972.

## Archbishops of Canterbury

**Æþelred** 870–888: in dispute with Ælfred in 878

**Plegmund** 890–923: King's priest and scholar from Mercia, the last Archbishop to issue his own coinage, Saint

**Æþelhelm** 923–926: Bishop of Wells 909–23, uncle of Archbishop Dunstan, Saint

**Wulfhelm** 926–941: the first Archbishop to go to Rome for the pallium in 927, Bishop of Wells 923–26, influential in promulgating Æþelstan's laws

**Oda** 941–958: visited Rome 942, Danish father, uncle of Archbishop Oswold of York, made a monk at Fleury, Bishop of Ramsbury 923/27–41, in opposition to King Eadwig, Saint

**Ælfsige** 958–958: died on the way to Rome for the pallium, Bishop of Winchester 951–58

**Brihthelm** 959–959: monk of Glastonbury?, Bishop of London 953, then of Wells 956–73 and of Sherborne 958–63, removed from office by Eadgar I

**Dunstan** 959–988: received his pallium at Rome 21st September 960, Abbot of Glastonbury 940, Bishop of Worcester 957–61 & London 959–61, Saint

**Æþelgar** 988–990: Abbot of New Minster 964, Bishop of Selsey 980

**Sigeric** 990–994: Abbot of St Augustine's 975, Bishop of Ramsbury 985

**Ælfric** 995–1005: Abbot of St Alban's 970, Bishop of Ramsbury 990–1002, established a monastic Cathedral chapter, Saint

## Archbishops of Canterbury (continued)

**Ælfheah** 1006–1012: murdered by Danes (in captivity since September 1011), Abbot of Bath 963, Bishop of Winchester 984, Saint

**Lyfing** 1013–1020: went to Rome for the pallium 1017, Abbot of Chertsey 988/93, Bishop of Wells 998

**Æþelnoð** 1020–1038: received the pallium in Rome 7th October 1022, consecrated 13th November 1020, provost of Canterbury, son of Alderman Æþelmær, Saint, acted for by Eadsige as Bishop of St Martin's 1035–38

**Eadsige** 1038–1050: went to Rome for the pallium 1040, retired ill 1044 (acted for by Siward, Abbot of Abingdon as Bishop of St Martins 1044–48 and Godwine as Bishop of St Martins 1048–50), King's priest, Bishop of St Martin's 1035, Saint

**Rodbert** 1051–1052: went to Rome for the pallium 1051, consecrated 29th June 1051, fled England 1052, died possibly before 1058, Prior of St Ouen, Abbot of Jumieges 1037, Bishop of London 1044–51

**Stigand** 1052–1070: sent a pallium by Benedict X 1058, annulled January 1059, deposed 1070, died 1072, King's priest under Cnut by 1020, Bishop of Elmham 1043, of Winchester 1047–70

**Landfranc** 1070–1089: monk of Bec (Prior), Abbot of Caen 1063, Italian

## Archbishops of York

**Hroþward** 904/28–931

**Wulfstan** 931–956: supported Norse Kings at York against Eadmund and Eadred, imprisoned 951–53

**Oscytel** 956–971: received the pallium 958, Bishop of Dorchester 949–958, assistant Archbishop? 955

**Eadwold** 971: resigned

**Oswold** 971–992: Bishop of Worcester 961–992, nephew of Archbishop Oda of Canterbury, kinsman of Archbishop Oscytel, Saint

**Ealdwulf** 995–1002: Abbot of Peterborough *980*–992, Bishop of Worcester 992–1002

**Wulfstan** 1002–1023: monk, Bishop of London 996–1002, Bishop of Worcester 1002–1017, author and influential legal adviser of Æþelred and Cnut

**Ælfric** (Puttoc) 1023–1051: received the pallium in Rome 1026, Provost of Winchester, Bishop of Worcester 1040–41

**Cynesige** 1051–1060: King's priest

**Ealdred** 1061–1069: monk of Winchester, Abbot of Tavistock 1027–1046, Bishop of Worcester 1046–1062, ambassador to Germany 1054

**Thomas** 1070–1100: canon of Bayeux

## Bishops of Chester le Street and Durham

**Tilred** 915–928

**Wigred** 928–944

## Bishops of Chester le Street and Durham (continued)

**Uhtred** 944

**Seaxhelm** 944: expelled by the cathedral chapter

**Ealdred** 944–968

**Ælfsige** 968–990

**Ealdhun** 990–1018: transferred the see to Durham in 995

**Eadmund** 1020–1042: monk of Durham

**Eadred** 1042: provost of Durham

**Æþelric** 1042–1056: monk of Peterborough, retired 1056

**Æþelwine** 1056–1071: monk of Peterborough, brother of Æþelric, joined the revolt against Willelm in 1069, deposed 1071

**Walchere** 1071–1080: canon from Lotharingia, murdered 1080

## Bishops of Cornwall

**Censtec** *870–888*

**Asser** *893–909*: scholar and biographer of Ælfred, Welsh, Bishop of Sherborne 900-909

*part of Crediton 909–928?*

**Cunan** 928?–953/55: see established at St German's

**Daniel** 955/56–*959*: monk of Glastonbury

**Wulfsige** (Comoere) *963–981*

**Ealdred** *990–1002*: Abbot of Tavistock? 975/80–983, independent of Crediton from 994

**Æþelsige** *1009–1011*

**Burhwold** *1012–1019*

*merged with Crediton 1027*

## Bishops of Crediton and Exeter

**Eadwulf** 909–934

**Æþelgar** 934–953: his see included Cornwall

**Ælfwold** 953–972: monk of Glastonbury

**Sideman** 973–977: Abbot of Exeter, tutor to Eadward II

**Ælfric** 977–*986*: Abbot of Malmesbury *971*–977

**Ælfwold** *987*–?

**Ælfwold** ?–*1011*

**Eadnoð** *1015–1019*

**Lyfing** 1027–1046: Abbot of Tavistock *1009*–1027, Bishop of Worcester 1038–1046

**Leofric** 1046–1072: King's priest, see moved to Exeter 1050

**Osbeorn** 1072–1103: chaplain of Eadward III, Norman, brother of Earl Willelm FitzOsbern

## Bishops of Dorchester

**Ealheard** 874/88–893/96

**Wigmund** or **Wilferð**: both signed charters between 900 and 903 and were probably Bishops of Dorchester and Lichfield

**Cenwulf** (909): consecrated by Plegmund, possibly 909

**Wynsige** *925–934*

**Æþelwold** *939–945/49*

**Oscytel** *950–955?*: translated to York 955, kinsman of Archbishop Oswold

**Leofwine** (971): Bishop of Lindsey since *953*

**Ælfnoð** (975)

**Æscwig** *979–1002*: monk of Winchester, Abbot of Bath 959/63–975/79

**Ælfhelm** 1002–*1007*

**Eadnoð** *1009*–1016: monk of Worcester, Abbot of Ramsey 993/97–1008, killed at *Assandun*, Saint

**Æþelric** 1016–1034: monk of Ramsey

**Eadnoð** 1034–1049: monk of Ramsey

**Ulf** 1049–1052: King's priest, Norman, fled England 1052 at Earl Godwine's restoration

**Wulfwig** 1053–1067

**Remigius** 1067–1092: monk of Fecamp, Norman, moved the see to Lincoln

## Bishops of Durham

see Chester le Street

## Bishops of Elmham

**?Ælfred** *915–934*

*under Þeodred of London 934–951*

**Æþelwold** (951)

**Æþelwulf** *955–966*

**Ælfric** (970)

**Þeodred** (974)

**Þeodred** (995)

**Æþelstan** *997–1001*

**Ælfgar** 1001–?: monk of Ely, Provost of Canterbury, chaplain to Archbishop Dunstan, retired to Ely 1012 (assistant Bishop Ælfstan 1009/11)

**Ælfwine** *1019–1023*: monk of Ely

**Ælfric** (1038)

**Ælfric** *1039–1042*

**Stigand** 1043–1047: priest at *Assandun* 1020, deposed 1043–44 (see administered by Grimcytel of Selsey), translated to Winchester

## Bishops of Elmham (continued)

Æþelmær 1047–1070: brother of Stigand, married, deposed 1070
**Herfast** 1070–1085: chaplain of Willelm, Chancellor, married, moved the see to
  Thetford

## Bishops of Exeter

see Crediton

## Bishops of Hereford

**Deorlaf** 857/66–*884*
**Cynemund** (888): witnesses charter of 888 as Bishop elect
**Eadgar** *900*–930
**Tidhelm** *931–937*: had an assistant Bishop, Wulfhelm
**Ælfric** 940–*958*
**Æþelwulf** *971–1013*
**Æþelstan** *1016*–1056: became blind in 1043 (assistant Tremerin, Bishop of St
  David's)
**Leofgar** 1056: priest of Earl Harold, killed fighting the Welsh
*1056–60 held by Ealdred of Worcester*
**Walter** 1060–1079: Queen Eadgyð's priest, Lotharingian

## Bishops of Lichfield

**?Burgheard** (869)
**Wulfred** *883–89*
**Wilferð** or **Wigmund**: both signed charters between 900 and 903 and were
  probably Bishops of Lichfield and Dorchester
**Ælfwine** *915–935*
**Wulfgar** *941–946*
**Cynesige** *949–963*: under Bishop of Berkshire 926/28–942, kinsman of
  Archbishop Dunstan
**Wynsige** *964*–975
**Ælfheah** 975–*1002*
**Godwine** *1004–1017*: Abbot of Athelney? 997–1002
**Leofgar** (1026/27)
**Brihtmær** (1039)
**Wulfsige** 1039–1053
**Leofwine** 1053–1070: Abbot of Coventry *1043*–1053, married, resigned 1070
**Peter** 1072–1085: chaplain of Eadward III, Norman, moved the see to Chester

## Bishops of Lindsey (Within Dorchester Diocese)

**Eadberht** *869–875*
**Leofwine** *953*–955: Bishop of Dorchester by 971

## Bishops of Lindsey (continued)

**Sigeferð** *996–1004*
**Ælfstan** *1009–1011*

## Bishops of London

**Deorwulf** *860–867*
**Swiðwulf** (896)
**Heahstan** –897
**Wulfsige** *900–909*
**Æþelward** ?
**Leofstan** or **Ealhstan** ?
**Þeodred** *926–951*: also Bishop of Elmham
**Brihthelm** *953–957*
**Dunstan** *959–964*: Abbot of Glastonbury 940–956, exiled by Eadwig 956, recalled by Eadgar I 957, also Bishop of Worcester, translated to Canterbury 959
**Ælfstan** 964–*995*
**Wulfstan** *996–1002*: monk, translated to Worcester and York
**Ælfhun** *1004–1015*: Abbot of Milton 975–1002/04
**Ælfwig** *1018*–1035: consecrated 1014 while Ælfhun was in exile with Æþelred
**Ælfward** 1035–1044: monk of Ramsey, Abbot of Evesham 1014–1044, retired with leprosy, kinsman of Cnut
**Rodbert** 1044–1051: Prior of St Ouen, Abbot of Jumieges 1037, translated to Canterbury 1051, Norman
**Spearhafoc** 1051: Abbot of Abingdon 1047–51, Archbishop refused to consecrate him, deposed 1051
**Willelm** 1051–1075: King's priest, fled England 1052 but was recalled, Norman

## Bishops of Ramsbury

**Æþelstan** 909–?
**Oda** *927–941*: monk of Fleury, translated to Canterbury, kinsman of Archbishops Oswold and Oscytel, Viking father
**Ælfric** (949)
**Oswulf** 951–970
**Ælfstan** 970–981: monk of Abingdon, Abbot of Glastonbury 964–970, pupil of Bishop Æþelwold of Winchester, Saint
**Wulfgar** 981–*985*
**Sigeric** *986–990*: translated to Canterbury 990
**Ælfric** 991/93–1002: monk and Abbot of St Albans *970*–991/93, translated to Canterbury 995
**Brihtwold** *1005*–1045: monk of Glastonbury, Saint
**Hereman** 1045–1078: King's priest, from Flanders, resigned 1055–58 (see held by Ealdred of Worcester), held also Sherborne 1058–1078, transferred the joint see to Salisbury 1075

## Bishops of Rochester

**Cuðwulf** (868)
**Swiðwulf** *880–893/96*
**Ceolmund** *900–909*
**Cyneferð** *926–933*
**Burgric** *934–946*
**Brihtsige** *949–955*
**Ælfstan** *964*–995: monk of Winchester
**Godwine** 995–*1046*: possibly two people 995–*1013* & ?–1046.
*vacant?* 1046–1058
**Siward** 1058–1075: Abbot of Chertsey *1042*–1058

## Bishops of Selsey

**Guðhard** *845–860/63*
**Wighelm** *900–909*
**Beornheah** *925–930*
**Wulfhun** *931–940*
**Ælfred** *943–953*: also held Sherborne 934–*939*
*held by Wulfsige of Sherborne* 953
**Brihthelm** *956*–963: also Bishop of Sherborne 958–963 and of Winchester 959–963, kinsman of Eadgar I
**Eadhelm** 963–979
**Æþelgar** 980–988: monk of Glastonbury and Abingdon, Abbot of New Minster 964-988, translated to Canterbury, pupil of Archbishop Dunstan and follower of Bishop Æþelwold
**Ordbriht** *990*–1007/09: canon of Winchester, monk of Abingdon, Abbot of Chertsey 964–989, pupil of Bishop Æþelwold
**Ælfmær** *1011–1031*: monk of Glastonbury, Abbot of Tavistock *994*–1009
**Æþelric** 1032–1038: monk of Canterbury Cathedral
**Grimcytel** 1039–1047: monk of Canterbury Cathedral
**Heca** 1047–1057: King's priest
**Æþelric** 1058–1070: monk of Canterbury Cathedral, deposed 1070
**Stigand** 1070–1087: chaplain of Willelm, Norman, moved the see to Chichester

## Bishops of Sherborne

**Æþelheah** *871–879*
**Wulfsige** *889–892*

## Bishops of Sherborne (continued)

**Asser** *900*–909
**Æþelward** 909–909
**Wærstan** 909–918
**Æþelbald** ?
**Sigehelm** *925–932*
**Ælfred** *934–939*: also Bishop of Selsey *943–953*
**Wulfsige** *943*–958: also held Selsey 953–56/57
*held by Brihthelm of Selsey and Winchester* 958–963
**Ælfwold** 963/4–978: Abbot of Glastonbury 959–964
**Æþelsige** *979–991*: exiled by Æþelred
**Wulfsige** *993*–1002: Abbot of Westminster 958–993, established a monastic
  cathedral chapter, Saint
**Æþelric** 1002–*1011*: Abbot of Athelney *993*–1001/02
**Æþelsige** *1012–1014*
**Brihtwine** (1017)
**Ælfmær** 1017–1023: Abbot of St Augustine's 1006–23/27
**Brihtwine** 1023–1045: former Bishop, restored
**Ælfwold** 1045–1058: monk of Winchester, Saint, brother of Brihtwine
**Hereman** 1058–1078: also Bishop of Ramsbury

## Bishops of Wells

**Æþelhelm** 909–923
**Wulfhelm** *925*–926: translated to Canterbury 926
**Ælfheah** *928–937*
**Wulfhelm** *938*–956: assistant Bishop at Hereford since 931
**Brihthelm** 956–973: translated to Canterbury 959 by Eadwig but dismissed in
  favour of Dunstan
**Cyneward** *974*–975: monk of Glastonbury, Abbot of Milton 964–974, pupil of
  Archbishop Dunstan
**Sigegar** *979–996*: monk of Winchester, Abbot of Glastonbury *974*–975/79
**Ælfwine** *997–998*
**Lyfing** 999–1013: monk of Glastonbury, Abbot of Chertsey 989–998, translated
  to Canterbury, also known as Ælfstan
**Æþelwine** *1018*–?: see disputed with Brihtwig
**Brihtwig** *1024*–1033: Abbot of Glastonbury *1019*–24
**Duduc** 1033–1060: King's priest, Lotharingian
**Gisa** 1060–1088: King's priest, from Liege, see moved to Bath 1085

## Bishops of Winchester

**Ealhfrið** *862/67–871*
**Tunberht** *877–878*

**Denewulf** *879*–908
**Friðestan** 909–931: Saint, resigned, died 932
**Byrnstan** 931–934: Saint
**Ælfheah** 935–951: monk, kinsman of Archbishop Dunstan, Saint
**Ælfsige** 951–958: translated to Canterbury 958
*held by Brihthelm of Selsey and Sherborne 959–63*
**Æþelwold** 963–984: monk of Glastonbury, Abbot of Abingdon *953–963*,
   associate of Archbishop Dunstan, tutor of Eadgar I, established a monastic
   cathedral chapter, founded or reformed Ely, Peterborough, Thorney and
   Crowland, Saint
**Ælfheah** 984–1006: monk of Glastonbury, Abbot of Deerhurst 968–975/79,
   Abbot of Bath 975/79–984, translated to Canterbury 1006
**Cenwulf** 1006: Abbot of Peterborough 992-1006
**Æþelwold** *1007*–1012
**Ælfsige** *1013*–1032: Cnut tried but failed to have him replaced
**Ælfwine** 1032–1047: King's priest
**Stigand** 1047–1070: priest at *Assandun* 1020, Bishop of Elmham 1043–1047,
   translated to Canterbury 1052, deposed 1070, died 1072
**Walcelin** 1070–1098: canon of Rouen, Norman, chaplain of Willelm

## Bishops of Worcester

**Ealhun** 843/45–869/72
**Wærferð** 872–915: one of Ælfred's scholars, translated the *Pastoral Care* of
   Pope Gregory
**Æþelhun** 915–922
**Wilferð** 922–*928*
**Cenwold** *929–957*: monk, ambassador to Germany 929
**Dunstan** *958*–961: Abbot of Glastonbury 940–956, exiled by Eadwig 956,
   recalled by Eadgar I 957, also Bishop of London, translated to Canterbury 959
**Oswold** 961–992: monk of Fleury, translated to York 972, kinsman of
   Archbishops Oda and Oscytel
**Ealdwulf** 992–1002: Abbot of Peterborough *980*–992, translated to York 992, by
   later tradition a Chancellor of Eadgar I
**Wulfstan** 1002–1017: also Archbishop of York, Bishop of London 996–1002
**Leofsige** 1017–1033: assistant Bishop 1016
**Brihtheah** 1033–1038: nephew of Archbishop Wulfstan, Abbot of Pershore
**Lyfing** 1038–1040: also Bishop of Crediton
**Ælfric** 1040–1041: Archbishop of York
**Lyfing** 1041–1046: Bishop of Crediton restored
**Ealdred** 1046–1062; monk of Winchester, Abbot of Tavistock 1027–1046,
   translated to York 1061
**Wulfstan** 1062–1095: monk and provost of Worcester, Saint 1203

# Appendix 4

## SHERIFFS

Sheriffs were King's officials, appointed to every shire. Their duties were various. The earliest known Sheriff was Wulfsige of Kent 964/88. There are references earlier than this to King's reeves and it is probable that the Sheriff evolved out of reeves appointed to look after royal estates. Managing the estates and receiving their income on behalf of the King remained one of their duties. Collecting taxes and fines was an extension of this. Accounting for the King's finances involved a twice-yearly journey to the exchequer in the 12th century. Earlier arrangements are unknown but may have involved similar visits using wooden tallies rather than the exchequer counting table. Other tasks included supervising the judicial work of the hundreds and enforcing the decisions of the courts (what we might call police work). The Sheriff must also in practice have presided over the shire courts as their nominal heads, the Earl and Bishop, must often have been called away by other business. The final task of the Sheriff was to lead the military forces of the shire, either in its own defence or on campaigns elsewhere. In many of these functions, the Sheriff was subordinate to the Earl but he remained a royal official, appointed by, and responsible to, the King. It may be significant that early evidence for Sheriffs comes from the reign of Æþelred who may have been using them as a counterweight to the power of the Earls. The men appointed Sheriffs seem to have been lesser nobility, or even priests. Evidence from the Domesday survey shows some Sheriffs to have been in the upper rank of thanes but most were not. There is no evidence that Sheriffs had a fixed term of office at this date.

Much evidence for Sheriffs comes from writs sent by the King to the shire court where the Sheriff was addressed alongside the Earl and Bishop. Not all include the Sheriff's name and in some a name is given without the title of Sheriff (names given in italics below). Some of these may not be Sheriffs but other officials, although some are named as Sheriffs in the Domesday survey. Officials of the King's household, known as stallers, are sometimes addressed instead of the Sheriff. In Middlesex, the portreeves of London may have acted at times also as Sheriffs of Middlesex, marked (p) below. Sheriffs were also known as high reeves, and as shiremen, but the term Sheriff was more usual after the reign of Æþelred. The Latin terms used were praefectus or praepositus. Dates given below are notices of the person as Sheriff not when he assumed office. Some Anglo-Saxon Sheriffs are known from early post-conquest sources and *may have been* in office before 1066.

Sheriffs are listed below by shire. Dates are given according to the conventions used above in appendices 1–3. Sources are also given for the identification of the person as Sheriff with such biographical details as are known. The value of lands owned by the Sheriff in 1066 according to the Domesday survey is added in brackets.

## Bedford

| | | |
|---|---|---|
| **Ælfstan** | 1053/66 | *S1235* |

## Berkshire

| | | |
|---|---|---|
| **?Ælfgar** | 1007 | S915 |
| *Cyneward* | *1042–52* | *H3, S993, S999, S1020, S1023, S1025*, witnessed charters 1042–52 |
| **Godric** | 1053/66 | *DB*, killed at Hastings 1066, also Buckingham?, (£45) |

## Buckingham

| | | |
|---|---|---|
| **?Godric** | died 1066 | *DB*, also Berkshire |

## Cambridge

| | | |
|---|---|---|
| **?Blacwine** | (1066) | *DB* |
| **Ælfric** | after 1066 | *DB*, son of Godric, also Huntingdon |

## Chester

none known

## Cornwall

none known

## Devon

| | | |
|---|---|---|
| **Cola** | (1001) | *C*, high reeve |
| *Wada* | 1060/66 | *H120* |
| **Heca** | (1066) | *DB* |

## Derby

| | | |
|---|---|---|
| **Hearding** | 1066/86 | *RR223*, Butler in charters 1062/65, (£90) |

## Dorset

| | | |
|---|---|---|
| **Ælfred** | 1053/58 | *H1* |

## Essex

| | | |
|---|---|---|
| **Leofcild** | 1042/44 | *H73, H74, S1530*, witnessed charters 1042/44 |
| **?Ordgar** | (1066) | *DB* |

## Gloucester

| | | |
|---|---|---|
| ?**Ælfwig** | before 1086 | *DB* |
| ?**Brihtric** | (1067) | *RR9*, witnessed charters from 1059, (£560) |

## Hampshire

see Southampton

## Hereford

| | | |
|---|---|---|
| **Bruning** | 1016/35 | *S1462* |
| **Ulfcytel** | 1043/46 | *S1469* |
| **Ælfnoð** | –1056 | *C*, killed fighting the Welsh |
| ***Osbeorn*** | 1061/66 | *H50*, son of Ricard (Norman) |

## Hertford

| | | |
|---|---|---|
| **Eadmund** | (1067) | *RR16* |

## Huntingdon

| | | |
|---|---|---|
| ***Cynric*** | 1040/49 | *H57, H58* |
| **Ælfric** | 1050/66 | *H59, DB*, also Cambridge |

## Kent

| | | |
|---|---|---|
| **Wulfsige** | 964/88 | *S1458* |
| **Leofric** | 995/1006 | *S1456* |
| **Æþelwine** | 1016/20 | *S1461, H26*, witnessed charters 1022 & 1033 |
| ***Æþelric*** | (1035) | *H29, H30* |
| **Osward** | 1053/66 | *H35, H39, DB* |

## Leicester

none known

## Lincoln

| | | |
|---|---|---|
| **Mærleswegn** | 1055/60 –1068 | *RR8, DB, C, S1060*, witnessed charters 1055/60, rebelled against Willelm 1068, (£214) |

## Middlesex (London)

| | | |
|---|---|---|
| **Wulfgar** (p) | 1042/44 | *H51* |
| **Ulf** | | 1042/51 *H75, H77* |
| **Swetman** (p) | 1058/66 | *H43* |
| **Ælfgeat** | 1057/66 | *H86, H87*, witnessed charters 1061 |
| **Leofstan** (p) | *1054 –1065/66* | *H105, H106* |
| **Ælfsige** (p) | 1065/66 | *H105, H106* |

## Norfolk

| | | |
|---|---|---|
| **Æþelwig** | 1040/42 | *H56* |
| **?Tolig** | before 1066 | *H61, DB*, £75, also of Suffolk |
| **Æþelwig** | 1066 | *H56, DB* |

## Northampton

| | | |
|---|---|---|
| **Norðman** | 1053/66 | *H62, H94* |

## Northumberland

none known

## Nottingham

none known

## Oxford

| | | |
|---|---|---|
| **?Eadwine** | before 1086 | *DB* |
| **?Ælfwig** | before 1086 | *DB* |
| **Sæwold** | (1067) | *RR18* |

## Rutland

under Nottingham

## Shrewsbury

none known

## Somerset

| | | |
|---|---|---|
| **Godwine** | 1042/61 | *H64, H65, H66, H67, S1022*, witnessed charters 1033–49 |
| **Tofig** | 1061/67 | *H68, H69, H70, H71, DB, RR7, RR160* |

## Southampton

| | | |
|---|---|---|
| **?*Wulfmær*** | 984/1001 | *H107* |
| **?*Æþelward*** | 984/1001 | *H107, C*, killed at *Æþelingadene* 1001 |
| **Eadsige** | *1053–1066* | *S1476, DB* |

## Stafford

| | | |
|---|---|---|
| **?Æfic** | 1016/35 | *Hm* |
| **Þurcyll** | 1066/68 | *RR25* |

## Suffolk

| | | |
|---|---|---|
| **Leofstan** | 940/70 | *ME* |
| ***Ælfwine*** | 1043/44 | *H9* |
| **Tolig** | 1051/66 | *H10, H18, H20, H23, H24, H25, DB*, £75, also of Norfolk |

## Surrey

none known

## Sussex

none known

## Warwick

| ?Ælfwine | before 1066 | *DB* |
|---|---|---|
| ?Eadwine | (1066) | *DB* |

## Wilton

| Eadric | (1067) | *DB, RR9* |
|---|---|---|

## Worcester

| Æfic | 1016/35 | *Hm*, or Stafford |
|---|---|---|
| Leofric | 1010/30 | *H48, S1423, S1460* |
| ?Ricard | (1062) | *H116, H117*, housecarl, (Norman – Richard FitzScrob) |
| Cyneward | before 1069 | *Hm* |

## York

| Gamal | 1066/69 | son of Osbeorn |
|---|---|---|

## Unknown Shire

| Leofwine | −1001 | *C*, high reeve, killed at *Æþelingadene* |
|---|---|---|
| Æfic | −1002 | *C*, high reeve, killed by Alderman Leofwine |
| Æþelric | *1018–1042* | *S950, S993* |
| Ælfwine | (1022) | *S958* |
| Ælfric | (1022) | *S958* |
| Ælfward | *1022–1033* | *S958, S967* |
| Godric | *1022–1033* | *S958, S967*, witnessed charters 1035–45 |
| Ælfwig | *1022–1043* | *S958, S993, S999*, witnessed charters up to 1050 |
| Lyfing | (1032) | *S964*, witnessed charter 1032 |
| Osmund | (1033) | *S967*, witnessed charter 1033 |
| Ordgar | (1042) | *S993* |
| Wulfnoð | *1042–1043* | *S993, S999*, also witnessed charter 1044 |
| Æþelwine | 1042/44 | *S1044*, witnessed charter 1042/44 |
| Ælfwig | *1043–1050* | *S1020, S1022, S1025*, possibly Gloucester or Oxford |

## Early Borough Reeves

| Beornwulf | −893/96 | *C*, Winchester |
|---|---|---|
| Ælfred | −903 | *C*, Bath |

# Appendix 5

# THE UNIFICATION OF ENGLAND

The map shows the stages by which England was unified from 911 to 928. An important feature of this process was the use of fortresses. On the death of Æþelred of Mercia, Eadward I took over direct rule of London and Oxford. This allowed him to take action directly against the Vikings in the midlands by moving into Essex in 912. By 914, a chain of forward bases was set up in Wessex and Mercia from which a conquest of the Viking areas could proceed. These were Witham, Hertford, Buckingham, Warwick, Tamworth, Stafford and Eddisbury. Each was no more than 15 miles in a straight line from the next, a half day by fast rider and a day by a marching army. The taking of Bedford in 914 filled in the longest gap and pushed English forces north towards the Fens. Bedford had gained some land to the west from Eadward in 903. By concentrating on the area around Bedford for his advance, Eadward I was not only reversing that treaty but effectively dividing the Danes in two. Those to the north were harassed by *Æþelflæd* facing Derby and Leicester. East Anglia was tied down by building a fort at *Wigingamere* in 917 south-east of Cambridge. The decisive action took place at Tempsford, near Bedford, when a combined Danish force was defeated. By the end of 917 only Nottingham, Lincoln, Stamford and Leicester remained under Danish control and these were facing an assault on two fronts from Eadward I and *Æþelflæd*. They had surrendered by the end of 918 and Mercia was fully incorporated on the death of *Æþelflæd* that same year. Eadward's final advance was to occupy Manchester and the area south of the Ribble. This gave him a more secure border than the low-lying plain of the Mersey and allowed him to effectively control the Mersey estuary which was open to invasion from Dublin.

The threat from Dublin was a real one. Its Viking dynasty was busy establishing its power in York at the same time as Eadward was advancing northwards. Eadward secured his border by building a fort at Bakewell and securing the recognition of his power by the rulers to the north (which presumably involved his recognition of Dublin's rule at York). An attempt to neutralise this threat was made by Æþelstan marrying his sister to King Sihtric. Upon his death, Æþelstan took over York itself rather than rely on alliances of doubtful value. It was Æþelstan also who fixed the border with Wales in the south at the Wye and annexed the remaining part of Cornwall still under native rule. Charter evidence shows him at Lifton near the Tamar in 928 which may be the occasion of this final advance of England to the south-west.

It is important to understand that unification did not mean uniformity. The price of incorporating new areas under English rule was to accept their local customs. In the case of the Danelaw, this meant that the contribution of the Danes to England would be important and long lasting. The Danelaw kept its own legal system and organisation of local government. Viking landowners who submitted were allowed to keep their lands. Place-names, personal names and language in eastern and northern England still bear the traces of Viking settlement. In return, it was expected to show loyalty to its new Kings. There is little evidence that the Danelaw was dissatisfied with English rule. For a short while, the Norse King Anlaf won control of the Five Boroughs but there is little evidence for disaffection among the descendants of the Viking settlers in the Danelaw. Much of the Danelaw was placed under the family of Alderman Æþelstan who came from Wessex and were sure to be loyal to the King. The north was harder to keep. The Dublin Kings and a former King of Norway both succeeded in winning acceptance of their rule at York at various times between 940 and 954, but there is no evidence that separation from England remained an option after then. Cumbria was part of Anglo-Saxon Northumbria but fell to Strathclyde upon its dissolution. Its later history is poorly documented but it was under English rule for part of the 11$^{th}$ century and became finally part of England in 1157.

Within the Danelaw it was the northern parts and East Anglia which were most densely settled by the Vikings, whose legacy is left for us in the place-names of the area. Many modern maps show Watling Street as the border between English Mercia and the Danelaw. This was not the case. The treaty which Ælfred made with the Danes defined a boundary north of London up to Watling Street where it runs into Northamptonshire (*oð Wætlingastræt*) not along it. The Danish invasions during the reign of Æþelred are often said to have been made easier by ethnic sympathy from the Danelaw. This is unlikely. When Swegn invaded in 1013, the settlement of Vikings in the Danelaw had taken place 134 years before. It would be a thane's great-great-grandfather who settled the area in the 870s. An ethnic analogy would be expecting Britain to side with Germany in 1939 because George III had been Elector of Hanover in 1805. Some of the greatest resistance to the Danes came from Ulfcytel in East Anglia, a leading thane of the Danelaw and with a Danish name. Cnut's main supporter in England was the thoroughly English Alderman Eadric in west Mercia.

# Appendix 6

# THE DANISH CONQUEST OF ENGLAND

Map 5 presents a highly simplified representation of the conquest of England by Swegn and Cnut. The invasion led by Þorcyll from 1009 to 1012 had devastated most of south-eastern England, as shown. Both Swegn and Cnut avoided this area, apart from their attempts on London and Winchester, and both notably operated on its perimeter. Under Æþelred, London had become of key importance politically, but holding London by itself could not guarantee mastery of the rest of England, as both Æþelred in 1013 and Eadgar II in 1066 found out. One of the advantages the Danes had was sea power. Cnut was able to strike Dorset from the sea in 1015 and attack London in 1016 by bringing his army by ship from the Humber to the Thames. Cnut's other advantage was in being able to draw support from political factions opposed to Eadmund, in particular Alderman Eadric of Mercia. Eadric had been a favourite of Æþelred but found his position challenged by Eadmund who was Æþelred's heir. This explains Eadmund's attack on north-west Mercia. However, when Eadmund II successfully relieved London and drove Cnut back through Kent, Eadric changed sides and accepted Eadmund as King. Sources suggest that Eadric's lukewarm support for Eadmund was crucial in determining the outcome of the battle of *Assandun*. This factional strife was a feature of the reign of Æþelred. He had been unable to stand above faction and access to the King's favour had involved the mutilation, murder and execution of opponents. The Danish conquest can only be understood as an extension of this domestic politics. One of the people who submitted to Swegn in 1013 was Alderman Æþelmær who had seemingly retired from public life in protest at the rise of Eadric and his family. A further factor might have been Æþelred's policy of using Sheriffs and not appointing the sons of Aldermen as their successors to undermine the traditional elite.

The Battle of *Assandun* was a crushing defeat for Eadmund II. Until then, he had been gaining the upper hand. Cnut's forces in Wessex had been defeated by Eadmund at Penselwood and Sherston, and his own siege of London had been broken by Eadmund at Brentford. His English allies had begun to desert him and he was heading northwards where his follower Yric had been made Earl of Northumbria by him. Eadmund was presumably confident of finishing Cnut off at *Assandun*. In the event, the English were defeated, losing Aldermen Ælfric and Godwine, Ulfcytel of East Anglia, Bishop Eadnoð of Dorchester, Abbot Wulfsige of Ramsey and many others.

An important feature of the Danish conquest was the widespread devastation brought about between 1009 and 1016 leading up to the final battle at *Assandun*. The fact that Eadmund II and Cnut agreed to divide England by treaty after this battle suggests that neither was in a position to further carry on the war. Armies needed to be recruited, paid and fed. An exhausted land was making each of these difficult to achieve. There were plots against Cnut after 1016 but no active military resistance. Various members of the English ruling class were purged by Cnut. These included Prince Eadwig (Eadmund II's brother), Alderman Eadric, Alderman Æþelward, Alderman Leofwine's son Norþman, Alderman Æþelmær's son Æþelward, and the thane Brihtric.

The location of *Assandun* in Essex is disputed. An early identification was with Ashingdon but more recent scholarship has suggested Ashdon as more likely. It is the latter which is marked on this map. This would make strategic sense as Cnut may have been heading towards Ermine Street, the way north to where his follower Yric was probably attempting to bring Northumbria under control and which was the last part of England Cnut could rely on for help.

The Danish conquest is still less well understood than the Norman Conquest of 50 years later. Just two puzzling features may be highlighted. In 1013, Swegn had received the submission of Northumbria, Winchester and the south-west. Æþelred had sheltered in London but departed for Normandy leaving Swegn as *de facto* King over all England. Why did he then not go to London to secure his rule and block any hope of Æþelred's return? Instead, he returned north to his fleet at Gainsborough, the action of an invader still unsure of his position. Perhaps he was less of a *de facto* King than the chronicle stated. In 1016, after *Assandun*, Eadmund II retreated to Gloucestershire, an area not noted for being part of his power base. Why did he not go to London? The city was loyal and secure. It had resisted every Danish attack. It would have made strategic sense to concentrate on holding the London-Oxford-Winchester triangle. Perhaps the lower Severn offered the chance to rebuild an army based on the south-west and allies from Wales?

Marked on the map is the Battle of Carham in Northumbria. This was a decisive defeat of the English by Mælcolm of Scots in 1018, which led to the final cession of Lothian to Scotland. It may have been taken over by England after the defeat of Mælcolm at Durham in 1006.

# Appendix 7

# THE NORMAN CONQUEST OF ENGLAND

In contrast to the Danish conquest, most of the devastation involved in the Norman Conquest occurred after the key battle at Hastings. Harold II was facing three possible threats in 1066; from Swegn of Denmark, Harold of Norway and Willem of Normandy. That from Swegn did not materialise until 1069. The first military action was taken by Harold of Norway who attacked the north-east coast and defeated Earls Eadwine and Morcere at Fulford before taking York. Just five days later, the Norwegian army was shattered by Harold II at Stamford Bridge. Harold was in his turn broken at Hastings by Willem three weeks later. English resistance to Willem hinged on Eadgar II being able to hold on to London and assemble enough forces to oppose Willem's advance. Holding London was straightforward. However, gathering an army capable of fighting was not so easy. The core of the army had been destroyed at Hastings, along with the most experienced leaders, Harold II and his brothers. The forces of Eadwine and Morcere had been badly damaged at Fulford and Willem was able to bring over reinforcements from Normandy. A further factor in the English defeat might have been the shock of defeat at Hastings. Harold II was by far the most experienced and powerful layman in England and the army had just inflicted one of the most crushing military defeats of the age on the Norwegians. The effect of Hastings on English morale would have been shattering. Harold's extensive following would have been left leaderless. In the circumstances, the surrender of the 14-year-old Eadgar was understandable.

Opposition to Willem began in 1067. Dover received help from Eustatius of Bolougne in 1067 but this was easily quelled. Willem's nominee as Earl of Northumbria was killed by the incumbent Earl Oswulf, but he himself was killed later in the year. Hereford was the scene of unrest by Eadric. Much more serious was the possibility of revolt by Earls Eadwine and Morcere in 1068 in association with others. Whatever plot was afoot was forestalled by Willem placing garrisons in castles at Warwick, York, Nottingham, Lincoln, Huntingdon and Cambridge. New Earls were appointed to Chester and Shrewsbury, reducing Eadwine's power and influence, while Eadgar and his supporters fled to Scotland. There was also unrest in Exeter, which continued along with attacks in Somerset into 1069. Harold II's sons meanwhile attacked Somerset in 1068 and Devon in 1069, but had no support from the English there. Eadgar made a serious attempt to oust Willem in 1069–70 with Scottish and Danish allies in Northumbria. Some have seen this as an extension of northern resistance to southern rule, similar to that of the revolt of 1065 against Tostig. However, Tostig had been Earl for 10 years without problem and may have been toppled more by getting involved in northern feuds. The rebels had been happy to have a new Earl, Morcere, from south of the Humber. English resistance in Northumbria and western Mercia was ruthlessly put down, the devastation being recorded in the Domesday survey. The last flickers of revolt were quelled in the Fens around Ely in 1071. Eadgar remained a potential threat until he surrendered in 1074 and returned to live in England under Willelm.

Willelm's success was due to several factors. The core of Willelm's power in 1067 was in the south-east. This meant that resistance in the north and west would be on the edges of England and so difficult to co-ordinate. His use of castles to place garrisons in disaffected areas was a new feature that reduced the mobility of the rebels. His devastation of the north and west was particularly effective in removing the ability of rebels to draw on men and supplies. Resistance against Willelm was widespread and few English were trusted by Willelm with positions of power. Willelm appointed two native English Earls (and one naturalised English) and two English Abbots, as against five Norman Earls, two Norman Bishops and four Norman Abbots up to 1069. By 1074, the balance of power was decisively in Willelm's favour and against Eadgar. Of the Earls, Bishops and major Abbots there were 8 native English, 8 naturalised English against 20 Normans and other continental appointees of Willelm. If we include the lesser Abbots and known Sheriffs, there were still only 22 native English against 40 Norman officeholders. Eadgar was left with few options. There was no longer a significant party of English landowners or officials who could raise forces in his support and we can by no means assume that native English landowners would automatically look to Eadgar on ethnic grounds against Willelm. Furthermore, the Church showed no inclination to rebel against Willelm. He was a crowned King and as such, for good or ill, could not be overthrown. Archbishop Ealdred of York had been instrumental in bringing Eadgar's family back to England but he had also crowned Willelm and stayed loyal to the theology of Kingship. Eadgar's only foreign supporter, Mælcolm of Scotland had been neutralised by Willelm's invasion of Scotland in 1072. Other potential supporters like Philip of France were not prepared to invade England on Eadgar's behalf. England had passed into the hands of new masters and begun the second chapter of its history.

# Family Trees

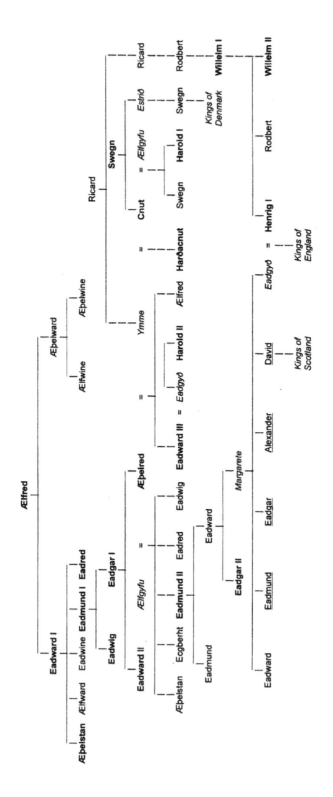

Simplified Family Tree of the Kings of England 871–1100 and Their Heirs
(Kings of England are in bold, Kings of Scotland are underlined)

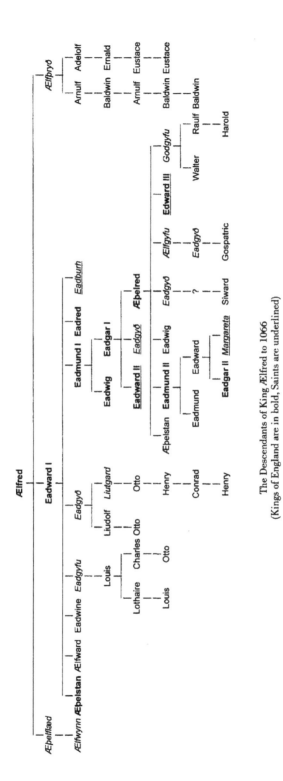

The Descendants of King Ælfred to 1066
(Kings of England are in bold, Saints are underlined)

157

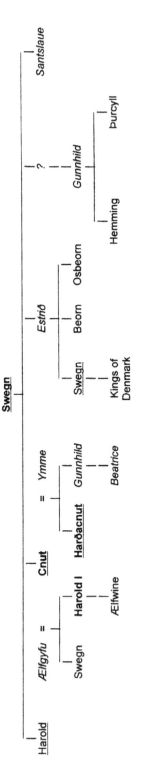

The Family of Swegn of Denmark

(Kings of England are in bold, Kings of Denmark are underlined)

# Maps

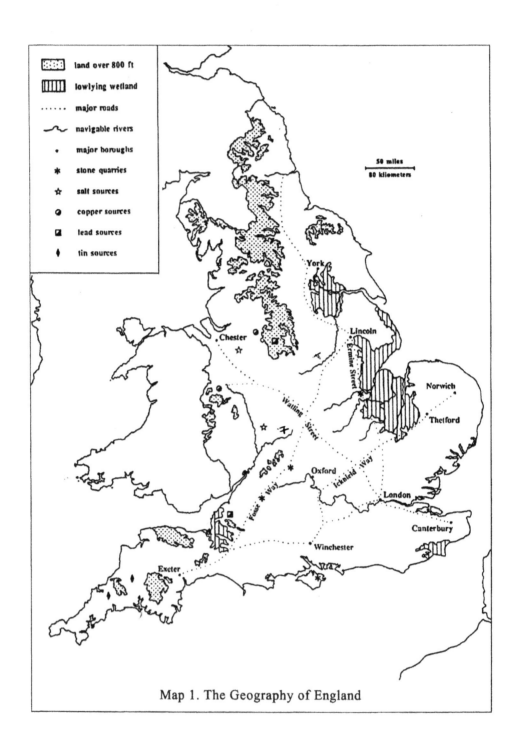

### Legend

- land over 800 ft
- lowlying wetland
- major roads
- navigable rivers
- major boroughs
- stone quarries
- salt sources
- copper sources
- lead sources
- tin sources

50 miles
80 kilometers

York

Chester

Lincoln

Ermine Street

Norwich

Thetford

Watling Street

Oxford

Icknield Way

London

Fosse Way

Winchester

Canterbury

Exeter

Map 1. The Geography of England

**Map 2. The Shires of England**

major boroughs
H  Huntingdon
M  Middlesex
R  Rutland

50 miles
80 kilometers

NORTHUMBERLAND

Amounderness
North Riding
YORK
East Riding
West Riding

Ribble Mersey
Lindsey
LINCOLN
CHESTER
DERBY
NOTTINGHAM
Kesteven
Holland
STAFFORD
SHREWSBURY
LEICESTER
R
NORFOLK
WORCESTER
WARWICK
NORTHAMPTON
H
CAMBRIDGE
SUFFOLK
HEREFORD
BEDFORD
GLOUCESTER
OXFORD
BUCKINGHAM
HERTFORD
ESSEX
BERKSHIRE
M
WILTON
SURREY
KENT
SOMERSET
SOUTHAMPTON
SUSSEX
DEVON
DORSET
CORNWALL

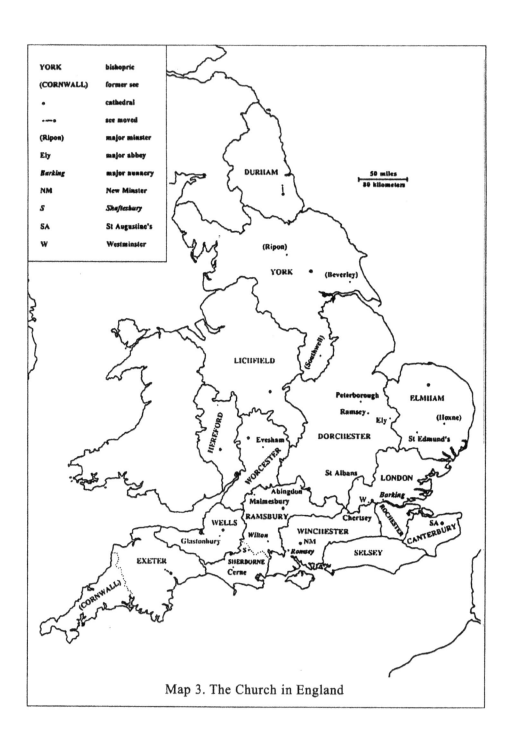

Map 3. The Church in England

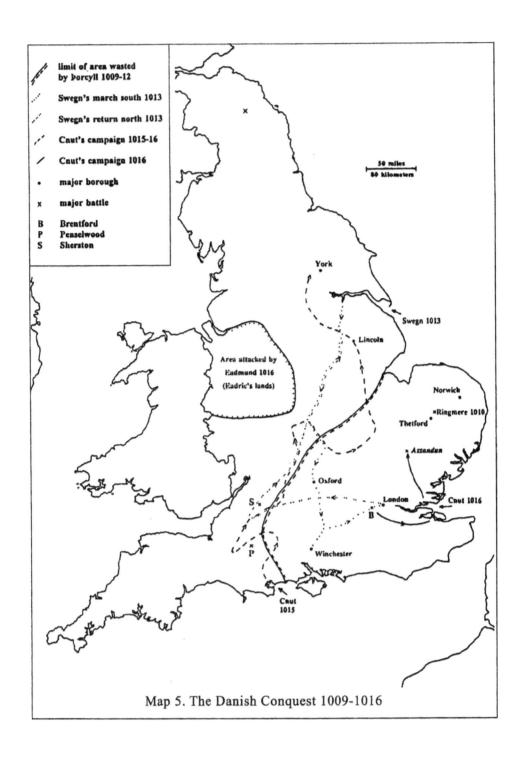

Map 5. The Danish Conquest 1009-1016

Legend:
- limit of area wasted by Þorcyll 1009-12
- Swegn's march south 1013
- Swegn's return north 1013
- Cnut's campaign 1015-16
- Cnut's campaign 1016
- • major borough
- x major battle
- B  Brentford
- P  Penselwood
- S  Sherston

Area attacked by Eadmund 1016 (Eadric's lands)

York
Lincoln
Swegn 1013
Norwich
×Ringmere 1010
Thetford
× Assandun
Oxford
London
Cnut 1016
S
B
P
Winchester
Cnut 1015

50 miles
80 kilometers

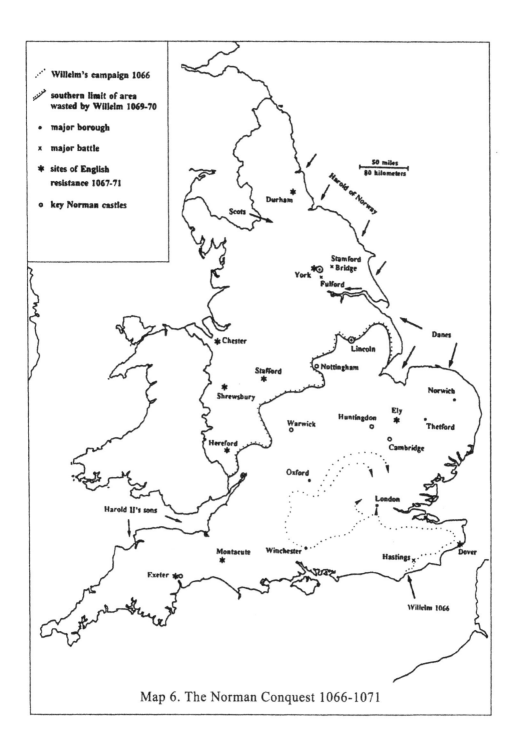

# Bibliography

# Primary Sources and Medieval Works

A    Asser – "Life of Ælfred"
     Whitelock, D  1959 (orig. ed. Stevenson, W H  1904)  *Asser's Life of King
          Alfred*
Ab   Abingdon Abbey
     Stevenson, J  1858  *Chronicon Monasterii de Abingdon* (Rolls Series)
Æ    Æþelward – "Latin Chronicle"
     Campbell, A  1962  *The Chronicle of Æthelweard*
Æs   Life of Æþelstan (preserved in William of Malmesbury)
     Stephenson, J  1854  *William of Malmesbury* (Church Historians of England)
     Stubbs, W. 1887–89  *Willelmi Malmesbiriensis Monachi de Gestis Regum
          Anglorum Libri Quinque*  (Rolls Series 90)  2 vols
Æw   Æþelwold – account of the monastic reformation
     Cockayne, T O  1864–66  *Leechdoms, Wortcunning and Starcraft of Early
          England* (Rolls Series) [Æþelwold on the revival of monasticism]
An   Anselm
     Mansi, J D  1759  *Sacrorum Conciliorum nova et amplissima Collectio* xix:
          742
AR   Ailred of Rievaulx
     Migne, J P  1844–64  "Ailred of Rievaulx: De Genealogiae Regum
          Anglorum", *Patrologia Latina* 195: 711–738
BT   Bayeux Tapestry
     Bernstein, D J  1986  *The Mystery of the Bayeux Tapestry*
     Grape, W  1994  *The Bayeux Tapestry*
C    Anglo-Saxon Chronicles
     Thorpe, B  1861  *The Anglo-Saxon Chronicle*, Rolls Series 23 (the only one
          to print all the versions in parallel)
     Plummer, C  1892–99  *Two of the Saxon Chronicles Parallel*
     Garmonsway, G N  1954  *The Anglo-Saxon Chronicle* (the main popular
          version)
     Whitelock, D  1961  *The Anglo-Saxon Chronicle*
     Taylor, S  1983  *The Anglo-Saxon Chronicle, Volume 4: Ms B*
     Bately, J  1986  *The Anglo-Saxon Chronicle, Volume 3: Ms A*
     Dumville, D  1995  *The Anglo-Saxon Chronicle, Volume 1: Ms F*
     Cubbing, G P  1996  *The Anglo-Saxon Chronicle, Volume 6: Ms D*
Cant. Canterbury obits
     Keynes, S  1980  *The Diplomas of King Æthelred "The Unready"*: 267,
          Cambridge
D    Life of St Dunstan – "Vita Dunstani" (B)
D    Stubbs, W  1874  *Memorials of St Dunstan, Archbishop of Canterbury*  (Rolls
          Series 21)

Dh    Durham – copy of the Chronicle
        Arnold, T 1882 *Symeonis Monachi Opera Omnia* (Rolls Series)

E      Eadmer
        Bosanquet, G 1964 *Eadmer's History of Recent Events in England*

Ed    Life of Eadgyð – "Vita Edithae"
        Wilmart, A 1938 "La legende de Ste Edith en prose et vers par le moine
          Goscelin", *Annalecta Bollandiana* 56

EE    Encomium Emmae
        Campbell, A 1949 *Encomium Emmae Reginae*

Ely   Ely obits
        Dickins, B 1937 "The day of Byrhtnoth's death and other obits from a
          twelfth century Ely Kalendar", *Leeds Studies in English and Kindred
          Languages* 6

Ev    Evesham Abbey
        *Chronicon Abbatiae de Evesham*, (Rolls Series 83)

Ey    Ely Abbey
        Blake, E O 1962 *Liber Eliensis* (Camden Soc. 3rd series 92)

F      Flodoard of Rheims
        Whitelock, D 1968 *English Historical Documents c500–1042*: 315–316

Fw    Folcwine of St Bertins
        Whitelock, D 1968 *English Historical Documents c500–1042*: 317–318

GA    Guy of Amiens – "Carmen de Hastingae Proelio"
        Morton, C & Muntz, H 1972 The Carmen de Hastingæ Proelio of Guy,
          Bishop of Amiens

Gm    Geoffrey Gaimar – French version of the Chronicle
        Bell, A 1960 *L'Estoire des Engleis* (Anglo-Norman Text Soc.)

H      Hyde Abbey – "Liber Vitae Hyda"
        Birch, W de G 1892 *Liber Vitae: Register and Martyrology of New Minster
          and Hyde Abbey Winchester*

Hm    Heming's Cartulary
        Hearne, T 1723 *Hemingi Chartularium Ecclesiae Wigorniensis*

Hr    Hrotsvit – "Gesta Ottonis"
        Poole 1911 "The Alpine son-in-law of Edward the Elder", *English
          Historical Review* 26: 310–317
        Homeyer, H 1970 *Hrotsvit Opera*

Hu    Henry of Huntingdon – Historia Anglorum
        Forester, T 1853 *The Chronicle of Henry of Huntingdon*
        Arnold, T 1879 *Henrici Archidiaconi Huntendunensis Historia Anglorum*
          (Rolls Series)

J      Jómsvíkingasaga
        Rafn, C C 1828 *Jómsvíkingasaga ok Knytlinga*
        Blake, N F 1962 *The Saga of the Jómsvíkings*

Kd    Knutsdrapa
       Ashdown, M  1930  *English and Norse Documents Relating to the Reign of*
         *Ethelred the Unready*

Ks    Knytlingasaga
       Petersons, C J F and Olson, E  1919  *Knytlinga Saga*

L     laws
       Attenborough, F L  1922  *The Laws of the Earliest English Kings*
       Robertson, A J  1925  *The Laws of the English Kings from Edmund to Henry I*

LE    Leges Edovardi Confessoris
       Wilkins, D  1721  *Leges Edovardi Confessoris*
       Riley, H.T  1853  *The Annals of Roger de Hoveden*
       Liebermann, F  1896–1912  *Die Gesetze der Angelsachsen*

LibE  Ely Abbey – "Liber Eliensis"
       Blake, E O  1962  *Liber Eliensis* (Camden Soc. 3$^{rd}$ series 92)

M    William of Malmesbury – Gesta Regum Anglorum
       Stephenson, J  1854  *William of Malmesbury* (Church Historians of England)
       Stubbs, W  1887–89  *Willelmi Malmesbiriensis Monachi de Gestis Regum*
        *Anglorum Libri Quinque* (Rolls Series 90)  2 vols

Me   Melrose Chronicle
       Anderson, A O & M O  1936  *The Chronicle of Melrose*

ME   St Edmund's Abbey
       Arnold, T  1890–96  *Memorials of St Edmund's Abbey* (Rolls Series)

O     Orderic Vitalis – Historia Ecclesiastica
       Chibnall, M  1969–80  *Orderic Vitalis: Historia Ecclesiastica Libri*
        *Tredecim*

OD   "De Obsessione Dunelmi" – the siege of Durham
       Hart, CR  1975  *The Early Charters of Northern England and the North*
        *Midlands*: 143–150

Pb   Peterborough Abbey
       Mellows, W T  1949  *The Chronicle of Hugh Candidus*

Pe   Pershore Abbey Annals
       Hearne, T  1715  *John Leland: Collectanea*

PE   "Passio Edwardi" – the martyrdom of Eadward II
       Fell, C E  1971  *Edward, King and Martyr*

R     Textus Roffensis
       Hearne, T  1720  *Textus Roffensis*

Ra   Ramsey Abbey
       Macray, W D  1886  *Chronicon Monasterii de Rameseia* (Rolls Series)

RD   Ralph Diceto
       Stubbs, W  1876  *The Historical Works of Master Ralph de Diceto, Dean of*
        *London* (Rolls Series)

RH   Roger of Howden – Chronicle
       Stubbs, W  1868–71  *Chronica Magistri Rogeri de Houdene* (Rolls Series)

RH   Riley, H T  1853  *The Annals of Roger de Hoveden*
Rk   Chronicon Roskildense
     Gertz, M C  1917–22  *Scriptores Minores Historiæ Danicæ Medii Ævii*
RR   writs after 1066 (with number)
     Davis, W H C  1913  *Regesta Regum Anglo-Normannorum* vol.1
RW   Roger of Wendover – Flores Historiarum
     Coxe, H O  1841–45  *Rogeri de Wendover Chronica sive Flores Historiarum*
       (Eng. Hist. Soc.)
S    charters (with number)
     Sawyer, P H  1968  *Anglo-Saxon Charters*, Royal Historical Society
       Handbook 8
SA   Lives of the Abbots of St Albans
     Riley, H T  1867–69  *Gesta Abbatum Monasterii de Sancti Albani* (Rolls
       Series)
SD   Simeon of Durham – Historia Regum
     Stephenson, J  1858  *The Works of Simeon of Durham*  (The Church
       Historians of England vol 3:2)
     Arnold, T  1882–85  *Symeonis Monachi Opera*  (Rolls Series 75)  2 vols
SE   St Edmund's Abbey
     Arnold, T  1890–96  *Memorials of St Edmund's Abbey* (Rolls Series)
SF   Saint Fois Abbey
     Stevenson, W H  1913  "An alleged son of King Harold Harefoot", *English
       Historical Review* 28: 112–117
Sn   Snorri Sturluson
     Laing, S  1930 (1844)  *Heimskringla: The Norse King Sagas*
     Aðalbjarnarson, B  1941–62  *Heimskringla*
Sx   Saxo Grammaticus
     Christiansen, E  1980–81  *Saxo Grammaticus: Danorum Regum Heroumque
       Historia*, BAR International Series 84 & 118
Th   Thietmar of Merseburg
     Holtzmann, R  1955  *Thietmar von Merseburg: Chronicon*
VÆ   Vita Ædwardi Regis
     Barlow, F  1962  *The Life of King Edward who Rests at Westminster*
VM   Vita Margareta
     Hinde, J H  1868  *Turgot: The Life of Margaret Queen of Scotland*, Surtees
       Society 51
     Anderson, A O  1922  *Early Sources for Scottish History AD 500–1286* II:
       59–88
VO   Vita Oswaldi
     Raine, J  1879–94  *Historians of the Church of York* (Rolls Series)
VW   Vita Wulfstani
     Darlington, R R  1928  *The Vita Wulfstani of William of Malmesbury*,
       Camden Soc. 3rd Ser. XL

W     Florence of Worcester – "Chronicon ex Chronicis" 1090–1117

       Thorpe, B 1848–49 *Florentii Wigorniensis Monachi Chronicon ex Chronicis* 2 vols

       Stephenson, J 1853 *Florence of Worcester: A History of the Kings of England*

Wd    Widukind of Corvy – "Res Gestae Saxonicae"

       Hirsch, P and Lohmann, H E 1935 *Die Sachsengeschichte des Widukind von Korvei*

We    Wells Cathedral

       Hunter, J 1840 *Ecclesiastical Documents* (Camden Soc.)

WH    writs before 1066 (with number)

       Harmer, F E 1989 *Anglo-Saxon Writs*

WJ    William of Jumieges – "Gesta Normannorum Ducum"

       van Houts, E M C 1992–95 *The Gesta Normannorum Ducum* 2vols.

WP    William of Poitiers – "Gesta Guillelmi Ducis"

       Foreville, R 1952 *Guillaume de Poitiers: Histoire de Guillaume le Conquerant*

       Douglas, D C & Greenaway, G.W 1981 *English Historical Documents II 1042–1189*

Wþ    Waltham Abbey

       Stubbs, W 1861 *The Foundation of Waltham Abbey*

Wu    Vita Wulfhilda

       Esposito, M "La vie de sainte Vulfhilde par Goscelin de Cantorbery", *Annalecta Bollandiana* 32

w     wills (Ælfred, Eadred)

       Harmer, F E 1914 *Select English Historical Documents of the Ninth and Tenth Centuries*, Cambridge

       (Æþelflæd, Ælfgyfu)

       Whitelock, D 1930 *Anglo-Saxon Wills*

# Modern Works

Listed below is a selection of books and articles. It is not a comprehensive list but covers the major works. More detailed bibliographies are available in many of the works cited. Bibliographies are given for every year since 1971 in the journal *Anglo-Saxon England*.

## Historical Sources

Allen Brown, R  1984  *The Normans* (Documents of Medieval History 5)

Ashdown, M  1930  *English and Norse Documents Relating to the Reign of Ethelred the Unready*

Cheney, C R  1981  *Handbook of Dates for Students of English History* (Royal Society Handbook 4)

Davies, H W C  1913  *Regesta Regum Anglo-Normannorum*

Douglas, D C and Greenaway, G W  1981  *English Historical Documents II 1042-1189*

Garmonsway, G N  1954  *The Anglo-Saxon Chronicle*

Gransden, A  1974  *Historical Writing in England c.550 to c.1307*

Harmer, F E  1914  *Select English Historical Documents of the Ninth and Tenth Centuries*

Harmer, F E  1989 (2nd Ed.)  *Anglo-Saxon Writs*

Harrison, K  1976  *The Framework for Anglo-Saxon History to AD 900*

Robertson, A J  1939  *Anglo-Saxon Charters*

Sawyer, P H  1968  *Anglo-Saxon Charters*, Royal Historical Society

Whitelock, D  1955  *English Historical Documents I c.500–1042*

## General History

Brooks, N  1984  *The Early History of the Church at Canterbury*

Campbell, J  1995  "The United Kingdom of England: the Anglo-Saxon achievement", in A Grant and K J Stringer *Uniting the Kingdom*

Dumville, D N  1992  *Wessex and England from Alfred to Edgar*

Fryde, E B, Greenway, D E, Porter, S and Roy, I  1986  *Handbook of British Chronology* (Royal Society Handbook 2, 3rd ed.)

Hart, C R  1992  *The Danelaw*

Higham, N J  1997  *The Death of Anglo-Saxon England*

John, E  1996  *Reassessing Anglo-Saxon England*

Loyn, H R  1991  *Anglo-Saxon England and the Norman Conquest*

Nelson, J L  1994  "England and the continent in the Anglo-Saxon period", in N Saul *England and Europe 1066–1453*

Stafford, P 1981 "The King's wife in Wessex, 800–1066", *Past and Present* 91
Stafford, P 1983 *Queens, Concubines and Dowagers: The King's Wife in the Early Middle Ages*
Stafford, P 1989 *Unification and Conquest*
Stenton, F M 1971 *Anglo-Saxon England*
Whitelock, D 1972 *The Beginnings of English Society*

## General Archaeology, Art and Architecture

Backhouse, J, Turner, D H and Webster, L 1984 *The Golden Age of Anglo-Saxon Art 966–1066*
Cameron, K 1977 *English Place-Names*
Campbell, J 1982 *The Anglo-Saxons*
Clarke, H and Ambrosiani, B 1991 *Towns in the Viking Age*
Fernie, E 1982 *The Architecture of the Anglo-Saxons*
Fisher, E A 1959 *An Introduction to Anglo-Saxon Architecture and Sculpture*
Graham-Campbell, J 1989 *The Viking World*
Haslam, J 1984 *Anglo-Saxon Towns in Southern England*
Hill, D 1981 *An Atlas of Anglo-Saxon England*
Hinton, D A 1990 *Archaeology, Economy and Society: England from the Fifth to the Fifteenth Century*
Hodges, R 1989 *The Anglo-Saxon Achievement*
Hooke, D and Burnell, S 1995 *Landscape and Settlement in Britain AD400–1066*
Laing, L & J 1996 *Art and Architecture in Anglo-Saxon England*
Nash, A 1988 "The population of southern England in 1086: a new look at the evidence of Domesday Book", *Southern History* 10: 1–28
North, J J 1980 *English Hammered Coinage I: Early Anglo-Saxon to Henry III c.600–1272*
Richards, J D 1991 *Viking Age England*
Roesdahl, E 1981 *The Vikings in England*
Taylor, H M and J 1965–78 (3 vols) *Anglo-Saxon Architecture*
Wilson, D M 1976 *The Archaeology of Anglo-Saxon England*
Wilson, D M 1981 *The Anglo-Saxons*

## Popular Histories

Best, N 1995 *The Kings and Queens of England*
Delderfield, E R 1995 *Kings and Queens of England and Great Britain*
Fraser, A 1975 *The Lives of the Kings and Queens of England*
Fry, P S 1990 *The Kings and Queens of England and Scotland*
Hibbert, C 1992 *The Story of England*
Horton, E 1995 *The Illustrated Kings and Queens of Great Britain*

## The Early Anglo-Saxons

Arnold, C J  1988  *An Archaeology of the Early Anglo-Saxon Kingdoms*
Bassett, S  1989  *The Origins of Anglo-Saxon Kingdoms*
Colgrave, B  1927  *The Life of Bishop Wilfrid by Eddius Stephanus*
Esmonde Cleary, A S  1989  *The Ending of Roman Britain*
Foot, S  1993  *The kingdom of Lindsey*, in A Vince *Pre-Viking Lindsey*
Gelling, M  1992  *The West Midlands in the Early Middle Ages*
Higham, N J  1992  *Rome, Britain and the Anglo-Saxons*
Higham, N J  1994  *The English Conquest: Gildas and Britain in the Fifth Century*
Higham, N J  1995  *An English Empire: Bede and the early Anglo-Saxon kings*
Hooke, D  1985  *The Anglo-Saxon Landscape: the Kingdom of the Hwicce*
Kirkby, D P  1991  *The Earliest English Kings*
Marsden, J  1992  *Northanhymbre Saga*
Morris, J  1973  *The Age of Arthur*
Stafford, P  1985  *The East Midlands in the Early Middle Ages*
Whittock, M J  1986  *The Origins of England 410–600*
Yorke, B  1990  *Kings and Kingdoms of Early Anglo-Saxon England*
Yorke, B  1995  *Wessex in the Early Middle Ages*

## The Rest of Britain (Medieval and Modern works)

Anderson, A O  1990 (1922)  *Early Sources of Scottish History AD 500 to 1286*
Barrow, G W S  1981  *Kingship and Unity: Scotland 1000–1306*
Crawford, B E  1987  *Scandinavian Scotland*
Davies, W  1982  *Wales in the Early Middle Ages*
Dark, K R  1994  *From Civitas to Kingdom: British Political Continuity 300–800*
Finberg, H P R  1964  "Sherborne, Glastonbury, and the expansion of Wessex",
    *Lucerna*: 95–115
Jones, T  1952  *Brut y Tywysogyon: Peniarth Ms20 Version*
Jones, T  1955  *Brut y Tywysogyon: Red Book of Hergest Version*
Jones, T  1971  *Brenhinedd y Saesson*
Smyth, A P  1977  *Scandinavian Kings in the British Isles 850–880*
Smyth, A P  1984  *Warlords and Holy Men: Scotland AD 80–1000*

## Government and Politics

Abels, P  1988  *Lordship and Military Obligation in Anglo-Saxon England*
Chadwick, H M  1905  *Studies on Anglo-Saxon Institutions*
Dumville, D N  1979  "The Aetheling: a study in Anglo-Saxon constitutional
    history", *Anglo-Saxon England* 8: 1–33
Green, J A  1990  *English Sheriffs to 1154*, HMSO (Public Record Office
    Handbook 24)

Hollister, W  1962  *Anglo-Saxon Military Institutions on the Eve of the Norman Conquest*

Keynes, S  1980  *The Diplomas of King Æthelred 'The Unready'*

Larson, L M  1904  *The King's Household in England before the Norman Conquest*

Loyn, H R  1984  *The Governance of Anglo-Saxon England 500–1087*

Mack, K  1986  "The stallers: administrative innovation in the reign of Edward the Confessor", *Journal of Medieval History* 12: 123–134

Nelson, J L  1986  *Politics and Ritual in Early Medieval Europe*

Olesen, T J  1955  *The Witenagemot in the Reign of Edward the Confessor*

Stafford, P  1981  "The king's wife in Wessex 800–1066", *Past and Present* 91:3–27

Williams, A  1978  "Some notes and considerations on problems connected with the English royal succession, 860–1066", *Proceedings of the Battle Abbey Conference (Anglo-Norman Studies* 1): 144–167

## Geography and Society

Darby, H C et al.  1952–67  *The Domesday Geography of England*, 5 vols.

Darby, H C  1977  *The Domesday Geography of England*

Fell, C  1984  *Women in Anglo-Saxon England*

Hallam, H E  1981  *Rural England 1066–1348*

Loyn, H R  1991  *Anglo-Saxon England and the Norman Conquest*

Maitland, F W  1897  *Domesday Book and Beyond*

Russell, J C  1969  *The Population of Europe 500–1500*

## The Church

Barlow, F  1963  *The English Church 1000–1066*

Barlow, F  1979  *The English Church 1066–1154*

Blair, J  1996  "Churches in the early English landscape: social and cultural contexts", in Blair, J & Pyrah, C *Church Archaeology: research directions for the future*  CBA Research Report 104: 6–18

Brooks, N  1984  *The Early History of the Church of Canterbury*

Butler, L & Morris, R (eds)  1986  *The Anglo-Saxon Church*, CBA Research Report 60

Deanesly, M  1961  *The Pre-Conquest Church in England*

Gem, R  1996  "Church buildings: cultural location and meaning", in Blair, J & Pyrah, C *Church Archaeology: research directions for the future*  CBA Research Report 104: 1–6

Godfrey, J  1962  *The Church in Anglo-Saxon England*

Harper-Bill, C  1992  *The Anglo-Norman Church*

Knowles, D, Brooke, C N L & London, V C M  1972  *The Heads of Religious Houses England and Wales 940–1216*

Knowles, D & Hadcock, R N  1953  *Medieval Religious Houses*

Morris, R  1983  *The Church in British Archaeology*, CBA Research Report 47

Morris, R 1989 *Churches in the Landscape*

O'Donovan, M A 1972 "An interim revision of episcopal dates for the province of Canterbury, 850–950: part I", *Anglo-Saxon England* 1: 23–44

O'Donovan, M A 1973 "An interim revision of episcopal dates for the province of Canterbury, 850–950: part II", *Anglo-Saxon England* 2: 91–114

Parsons, D 1975 *Tenth-Century Studies*

## Language, Literature and Culture

Bradley, S J 1982 *Anglo-Saxon Poetry*

Brown, M P 1991 *Anglo-Saxon Manuscripts*

Campbell, A 1959 *Old English Grammar*

Godden, M and Lapidge, M 1991 *The Cambridge Companion to Old English Literature*

Gordon, R K 1926 *Anglo-Saxon Poetry*

Greenfield, S B and Calder, D G 1986 *A New Critical History of Old English Literature*

Mitchell, B 1995 *An Invitation to Old English and Anglo-Saxon England*

Mitchell, B and Robinson, F C 1994 *A Guide to Old English*

Owen-Crocker, G R 1986 *Dress in Anglo-Saxon England*

Quirk, R and Wrenn, C L 1957 *An Old English Grammar*

Reaney, P H and Wilson, R M 1991 *A Dictionary of English Surnames*

Renwick, W L and Orton, H 1966 *The Beginnings of English Literature to Skelton 1509*

Swanton, M 1975 *Anglo-Saxon Prose*

Talbot Rice, D 1952 *English Art 871–1100*

Wilson, D M 1984 *Anglo-Saxon Art*

## Ælfred (see *A*)

Beaven, M L R 1917 "The regnal dates of Alfred, Edward the Elder, and Athelstan", *English Historical Review* 32: 517–531

Dumville, D N 1992 *Wessex and England from Alfred to Edgar*

Keynes, S & Lapidge, M 1983 *Alfred the Great*

Nelson, J 1986 "A king across the sea, Alfred in continental perspective", *Transactions Royal Historical Society* 5th series 36: 45–68

Peddie, J 1989 *Alfred the Good Soldier*

Smyth, A P 1995 *King Alfred the Great*

Sturdy, D 1995 *Alfred the Great*

Woodruff, D 1974 *The Life and Times of Alfred the Great*

# Eadward I

Angus, W S 1938 "The chronology of the reign of Edward the Elder", *English Historical Review* 53

Beaven, M L R 1917 "The regnal dates of Alfred, Edward the Elder, and Athelstan", *English Historical Review* 32: 517–531

Nelson, J L 1986 "The second English ordo", *Politics and Ritual in Early Medieval England*

Wainwright, F T 1952 "The submission to Edward the Elder", *History* New Series 27: 114–130

# Æþelflæd

Stansbury, D 1993 *The Lady Who Fought the Vikings*

Wainwright, F T 1959 "Æþelflæd, Lady of the Mercians", in Clemoes, P *The Anglo-Saxons*: 53–69

# Æþelstan (see *Æs*)

Beaven, M L R 1917 "The regnal dates of Alfred, Edward the Elder, and Athelstan", *English Historical Review* 32: 517–531

Dumville, D N 1992 "Between Alfred the Great and Edgar the Peaceable: Æthelstan, First Kings of England", in D N Dumville 1992 *Wessex and England from Alfred to Edgar*: 141–172

Poole, R L 1934 *Studies in Chronology and History*: 115–122 (foreign relations)

Robinson, J A 1923 *The Times of St Dunstan*: 51–80 (Æþelstan's piety)

Smyth, A P 1975–79 *Scandinavian York and Dublin*

Wood, M 1983 "The making of King Æthelstan's empire: an English Charlemagne?", in P Wormald *Ideal and Reality in Frankish and Anglo-Saxon Society*

# Eadgyfu

Hart, C 1977 "Two Queens of England", *Ampleforth Journal* 82

Meyer, M A 1977 "Women and the tenth-century English monastic reform", *Revue Benedictine* 87

# Eadmund I

Beaven, M L R 1918 "King Edmund I and the Danes of York", *English Historical Review* 33

Dumville, D N 1992 "Learning and the church in the England of King Edmund I", in D N Dumville 1992 *Wessex and England from Alfred to Edgar*: 173–184

Mawer, A 1926 "The redemption of the Five Boroughs", *English Historical Review* 38: 551–557

Smyth, A P 1975–79 *Scandinavian York and Dublin*

# Eadred

Campbell, A 1942 "The end of the kingdom of Northumbria", *English Historical Review* 57: 91–97

Smyth, A P 1975–79 *Scandinavian York and Dublin*

# Eadwig

Hart, C R 1975 *The Early Charters of Northern England and the North Midlands*: 319–323

Keynes, S 1980 *The Diplomas of King Æthelred "The Unready"*: 48–70

# Eadgar I

Banton, N 1982 "Monastic reform and the unification of tenth-century England", in S, Mews *Religion and National Identity*: 71–85

Ridyard, S J 1988 *The Royal Saints of Anglo-Saxon England* (St Eadgyð)

Stevenson, W H 1898 "The great commendation of King Edgar", in *English Historical Review* 13

# Ælfþryð

Hart, C 1977 "Two Queens of England", *Ampleforth Journal* 82

Meyer, M A 1977 "Women and the tenth-century English monastic reform", *Revue Benedictine* 87

# Eadward II

Fell, C E 1971 *Edward, King and Martyr*

# Æþelred

Hill, D (ed) 1978 *Ethelred the Unready* (British Archaeological Reports 59)

Keynes, S 1980 *The Diplomas of King Æthelred 'the Unready'*

# Ymme (see *EE*)

Barlow, F 1958 "Queen Emma's disgrace in 1043", *English Historical Review* 73: 651–655

Campbell, M W 1971 "Queen Emma and Ælfgyfu of Northampton: Canute the Great's women", *Medieval Scandinavia* 4: 66–79

Searle, E 1989 "Emma the Conqueror", in Harper-Bill, C, Holdsworth, C J & Nelson, J L *Studies in Medieval History*: 281–288

# Cnut and the Danish Conquest

Cooper, J 1993 *The Battle of Maldon: Fiction and Fact*

Fleming, R 1991 *Kings and Lords in Conquest England*: 1–104

Garmonsway, G N 1964 *Canute and His Empire*

Larson, L M 1912 *Canute the Great*

Lawson, M K  1993  *Cnut: the Danes in England in the Early Eleventh Century*
Mack, K  1984  "Changing thegns, Cnut's conquest and the English aristocracy",
  *Albion* 16: 375–387
Rumble, A R (ed)  1994  *The Reign of Cnut: King of England, Denmark and
  Norway*
Stafford, P  1981  "The laws of Cnut and the history of Anglo-Saxon royal
  promises", *Anglo-Saxon England* 10: 173–190

## Harold I

Stevenson, W H  1913  "An alleged son of King Harold Harefoot", *English
  Historical Review* 28: 112–117

## Godgyfu

Round, J H  1901  *Studies in Peerage and Family History*: 147–149

## Eadward III (see *VÆ*)

Barlow, F  1970  *Edward the Confessor*
Clarke, P A  1994  *The English Nobility under Edward the Confessor*
Freeman, E A  1869–75  *The History of the Norman Conquest of England* Vol. II
Keynes, S  1990  "The Æthelings in Normandy", *Anglo-Norman Studies* 13: 173–206
Oleson, T J  1955  *The Witenagemot in the Reign of Edward the Confessor*

## Eadgyð

Cutler, K E  1973  "Edith, Queen of England, 1045–1066", in *Medieval Studies* 35:
  222–231

## Harold II (see also Eadward III and the Norman Conquest)

Freeman, E A  1869–75  *The History of the Norman Conquest of England* Vol. III:
  1–522
Gravett, C  1992  *Hastings 1066: The Fall of Saxon England* (Campaign Series 13)
Loyn, H R  1966  *Harold, Son of Godwin*
Walker, I W  1997  *Harold: the Last Anglo-Saxon King*
Williams, A  1980  "Land and power in the eleventh century: the estates of Harold
  Godwineson", *Proceedings of the Battle Conference 1980*

## Eadgar II

Freeman, E A  1869–75  *The History of the Norman Conquest of England* Vol. III:
  523–562
Hooper, N  1985  "Edgar the Ætheling: Anglo-Saxon prince, rebel and crusader",
  *Anglo-Saxon England* 14: 197–214
Ronay, G  1989  *The Lost King of England*, Boydell (deals with Eadgar's father,
  Prince Eadward)

## Norman Conquest (see also Harold II)

Allen Brown, R 1984 *The Norman Conquest*
Barlow, F 1983 *The Norman Conquest and Beyond*
Brown, R A 1969 *The Normans and the Norman Conquest*
Douglas, D C 1964 *William the Conqueror*
Fleming, R 1991 *Kings and Lords in Conquest England*: 105–231
Freeman, E A 1869–75 *The History of the Norman Conquest of England*
Golding, B 1994 *Conquest and Colonisation: the Normans in Britain, 1066–1100*
Kapelle, W E 1979 *The Norman Conquest of the North*
Koerner, S 1964 *The Battle of Hastings, England and Europe*
Whitelock, D 1966 *The Norman Conquest: Its Setting and Impact*
Williams, A 1995 *The English and the Norman Conquest*
• the journal *Anglo-Norman Studies* has many important articles for this period

## Margaret

Wilson, A J 1993 *St Margaret: Queen of Scotland*

## Noble Families and Individuals

Campbell, A 1962 *The Chronicle of Æthelweard*
Finberg, H P R 1943 "The house of Ordgar and the family of Tavistock abbey", *English Historical Review* 58: 190–200
Harmer, F E 1989 *Anglo-Saxon Writs*
Hart, C R 1973 "Athelstan half-king and his family", *Anglo-Saxon England* 2:115–144
Hart, C R 1975 *The Early Charters of Northern England and the North Midlands*
Knowles, D, Brooke, C N L & London, V C M 1972 *The Heads of Religious Houses England and Wales 940–1216*
Maund, K L 1988 "The Welsh alliances of Earl Ælfgar of Mercia and his family in the mid-eleventh century", *Anglo-Norman Studies* 11: 181–190
O'Donovan, M A 1972 "An interim revision of episcopal dates for the province of Canterbury, 850–950: part I", *Anglo-Saxon England* 1: 23–44
O'Donovan, M A 1973 "An interim revision of episcopal dates for the province of Canterbury, 850–950: part II", *Anglo-Saxon England* 2: 91–114
Oleson, T J 1955 *The Witenagemot in the Reign of Edward the Confessor*
Raraty, D G J 1989 "Earl Godwine of Wessex: the origins of his power and political loyalties", *History* 74: 3–19
Robertson, A J 1939 *Anglo-Saxon Charters*
Sawyer, P H 1979 *Anglo-Saxon Charters II: Charters of Burton Abbey* 38–43 (Alderman Ælfhelm and family)
Williams, A 1981 "Princeps Merciorum gentis: the family, career and connections of Ælfhere, ealdorman of Mercia", *Anglo-Saxon England* 10: 143–172

Williams, A 1989 "The king's nephew: the family and career of Ralph, Earl of Hereford", in Harper-Bill, C, Holdsworth, C J & Nelson, J L *Studies in Medieval History*: 327–343

Yorke, B 1988 *Bishop Æthelwold, His Career and Influence*

# Index

# Index

People are listed below in alphabetical order (Æ appearing after A, and Þ appearing after T). Bynames and surnames are ignored. Names are given in their 11th century English form. The equivalent modern forms can be found by consulting the section on names on page 46. Where there is more than one page listed after a person's name, the main biographical reference is given in bold.

# A

*Agatha* (mother of Eadgar II), 95
Alan, Count of Brittany, 75
Alan, Steward, 120
Alexander, King of Scots, 112
Anferð, Earl (Danelaw), 131
Anglo-Saxon settlement in Britain, 12
Anlaf, King of Norway, 89, 91
Anlaf I, King of York, 77, 150
Anlaf II, King of York, 77, 79
Arncyll, thane, 114
Assandun, battle of, 58, 95, 96, 99, 125, 128, 130, 136, 141, 151, 152
Asser, Bishop of Cornwall & Sherborne, 63, 135, 140

# A

Æfic, Sheriff, 147
Æfic, Sheriff of Worcester or Stafford, 146, 147
Ælfgar, Alderman of Essex, 76
Ælfgar, Bishop of Elmham, 136
Ælfgar, Earl of Mercia, 16, 106, 108, 110, 127, 128
Ælfgar, Sheriff of Berkshire?, 144
Ælfgar, thane, 80, 90
*Ælfgyfu* (daughter of Æþelred), 87
*Ælfgyfu* (daughter of Eadward I), 69
*Ælfgyfu* (wife of Æþelred), 87
*Ælfgyfu* (wife of Cnut), 97
*Ælfgyfu* (wife of Eadmund I), 76
*Ælfgyfu* (wife of Eadwig), 80, 83
*Ælfgyfu* (wife of Harold I), 101
Ælfheah I, Bishop of Winchester, 141
Ælfheah, Alderman of Wessex, 76, 78, 80, 81, 83, 119, 125–27
Ælfheah, Archbishop of Canterbury, 92, 98, 99, 134, 141
Ælfheah, Bishop of Lichfield, 137
Ælfheah, Bishop of Wells, 140
Ælfhelm, Alderman of York, 90, 91, 95, 97, 129
Ælfhelm, Bishop of Dorchester, 136
Ælfhere, Alderman of Mercia, 80, 81, 83, 84, 86, 90, 105, 119, 125–27
Ælfhere, Alderman of Wessex, 125
Ælfhun, Bishop of London, 92, 138
*Ælflæd* (wife of Eadward I), 68
Ælfmær, Bishop of Selsey, 139

Ælfmær, Bishop of Sherborne, 140
Ælfnoð, Bishop of Dorchester, 136
Ælfnoð, Sheriff of Hereford, 145
Ælfred, Alderman in Mercia, 125
Ælfred, Alderman of Devon, 124
Ælfred, Alderman of East Anglia, 128
Ælfred, Alderman of Surrey, 124
Ælfred, Bishop of Elmham, 136
Ælfred, Bishop of Selsey & Sherborne, 139, 140
ÆLFRED, KING, 15, 17, 42, 63–67, 150
Ælfred, Portreeve of Bath, 147
Ælfred, Prince, 88, 92, 102, 103
Ælfred, Sheriff of Dorset, 144
**Ælfric (brother of Earl Odda)**, 105
Ælfric I, Bishop of Elmham, 136
Ælfric I, Bishop of Ramsbury, 138
Ælfric I, Chamberlain, 120
Ælfric II, Bishop of Elmham, 136
Ælfric II, Chamberlain, 120
Ælfric III, Bishop of Elmham, 136
Ælfric, Abbot of Eynsham, 42, 89, 126
Ælfric, Alderman of Eastern Wessex, 126
Ælfric, Alderman of Mercia, 90, 127
Ælfric, Alderman of Wessex, 90, 91, 95, 96, 125, 151
Ælfric, Archbishop of Canterbury, 121, 133, 138
Ælfric, Archbishop of York, 103, 134, 141
Ælfric, Bishop of Crediton, 135
Ælfric, Bishop of Hereford, 137
Ælfric, Sheriff, 147
Ælfric, Sheriff of Cambridge & Huntingdon, 144, 145
Ælfsige I, Steward, 119
Ælfsige II, Bishop of Winchester, 141
Ælfsige II, Steward, 119
Ælfsige, ?Alderman, 130
Ælfsige, Archbishop of Canterbury, 133, 141
Ælfsige, Bishop of Chester le Street, 135
Ælfsige, Portreeve of London, 145
Ælfsige, thane, 90
Ælfstan, Alderman of Kent, 124
Ælfstan, Alderman of South East Mercia, 73, 127
Ælfstan, Bishop of Lindsey, 138
Ælfstan, Bishop of London, 138
Ælfstan, Bishop of Ramsbury, 138
Ælfstan, Bishop of Rochester, 90, 139
Ælfstan, Constable, 120
Ælfstan, Sheriff of Bedford, 144

*Ælfswið* (wife of Alderman Ælfheah), 76, 80
*Ælfþryð* (daughter of Ælfred), 64
*Ælfþryð* (wife of Eadgar I), 30, 83, 86, 90
Ælfward, Bishop of London, 98, 138
Ælfward, Prince, 68, 73
Ælfward, Sheriff, 147
Ælfward, Steward, 120
Ælfwig, Bishop of London, 138
Ælfwig, Butler, 120
Ælfwig, Sheriff, 147
**Ælfwig, Sheriff of Gloucester?**, 145
**Ælfwig, Sheriff of Oxford**, 146
**Ælfwine (son of Æþelward)**, 63
Ælfwine, ?Earl, 130
Ælfwine, Bishop of Elmham, 136
Ælfwine, Bishop of Lichfield, 137
Ælfwine, Bishop of Wells, 140
Ælfwine, Bishop of Winchester, 141
Ælfwine, Prince, 101
Ælfwine, Sheriff, 147
Ælfwine, Sheriff of Suffolk, 146
**Ælfwine, Sheriff of Warwick?**, 147
Ælfwine, Steward, 119
Ælfwine, thane, 100
Ælfwold I, Bishop of Crediton, 135
Ælfwold I, Bishop of Sherborne, 140
Ælfwold II, Bishop of Crediton, 135
Ælfwold II, Bishop of Sherborne, 140
Ælfwold III, Bishop of Crediton, 135
Ælfwold, ?Alderman, 130
Ælfwold, Alderman in Mercia, 125
Ælfwold, Alderman of Devon, 124
Ælfwold, Alderman of Wessex, 125
*Ælfwynn* of Mercia, 63, 72
Æscberht, Alderman of Western Wessex, 126
Æscwig, Bishop of Dorchester, 136
Æþelbald, Bishop of Sherborne, 140
Æþelferð, Alderman in Mercia, 125
Æþelferð, Alderman of South East Mercia,
   127
*Æþelflæd* (wife of Eadgar I), 82
*Æþelflæd* (wife of Eadmund I), 76
*Æþelflæd* of Mercia, 15, 63, 71, 72, 73, 149
Æþelgar, Archbishop of Canterbury, 133, 139
Æþelgar, Bishop of Crediton, 135
*Æþelgyfu* (daughter of Ælfred), 63
Æþelheah, Bishop of Sherborne, 139
Æþelhelm, Alderman of Wiltshire, 68, 124
Æþelhelm, Archbishop of Canterbury, 133
Æþelhelm, Bishop of Wells, 140
Æþelhelm, Prince, 64

*Æþelhild* (daughter of Eadward I), 69
Æþelhun, Bishop of Worcester, 141
Æþelmær, Alderman of Wessex, 125
Æþelmær, Alderman of Western Wessex, 88,
   91, 92, 95, 120, 126, 134, 151
Æþelmær, Bishop of Elmham, 114, 137
Æþelmund, Alderman of North West Mercia,
   127
Æþelnoð, Alderman of Somerset, 124
Æþelnoð, Archbishop of Canterbury, 101, 134
Æþelred of Mercia, 63, 67, 71, 149
Æþelred, Alderman of Devon, 124
Æþelred, Archbishop of Canterbury, 133
ÆÞELRED, KING, 83, 86, 87–93, 150, 151
Æþelred, Prince of Scotland, 112
Æþelric I, Bishop of Selsey, 139
Æþelric II, Bishop of Selsey, 114, 139
Æþelric, Bishop of Dorchester, 136
Æþelric, Bishop of Durham, 114, 135
Æþelric, Bishop of Sherborne, 140
Æþelric, Sheriff, 147
Æþelric, Sheriff of Kent, 145
Æþelsige I, Bishop of Sherborne, 140
Æþelsige II, Bishop of Sherborne, 140
Æþelsige, Alderman of Wessex, 125
Æþelsige, Bishop of Cornwall, 135
Æþelsige, Butler, 120
Æþelsige, Chamberlain, 120
Æþelsige, thane, 90
Æþelstan (brother in law of Æþelred), 88, 92
Æþelstan I, Alderman of South East Mercia,
   127
Æþelstan II (Rota), Alderman of South East
   Mercia, 76, 127
Æþelstan, Alderman of Devon, 124
Æþelstan, Alderman of East Anglia, 73, 77,
   78, 81, 83, 128
Æþelstan, Bishop of Elmham, 136
Æþelstan, Bishop of Hereford, 109, 137
Æþelstan, Bishop of Ramsbury, 138
ÆÞELSTAN, KING, 15, 17, 68, 73–75, 149
Æþelstan, Prince, 87, 92
*Æþelswið* (sister of Ælfred), 64
Æþelward (son of Alderman Æþelmær), 99
Æþelward (son of Alderman Æþelwine), 96
Æþelward I, Alderman of Western Wessex,
   80, 83, 88–90, 126
Æþelward II, Alderman of Western Wessex,
   99, 126, 152
Æþelward, Bishop of London, 138
Æþelward, Bishop of Sherborne, 140

Æþelward, Prince, 63
Æþelward, Sheriff of Hampshire, 146
Æþelward, Steward, 120
Æþelwig I, Sheriff of Norfolk, 146
Æþelwig II, Sheriff of Norfolk, 146
**Æþelwine (son of Æþelward)**, 63
Æþelwine, Alderman of East Anglia, 83, 86, 128
Æþelwine, Bishop of Durham, 114, 135
Æþelwine, Bishop of Wells, 140
Æþelwine, Sheriff, 147
Æþelwine, Sheriff of Kent, 145
Æþelwold I, Bishop of Winchester, 34, 53, 84, 90, 141
Æþelwold II, Bishop of Winchester, 141
Æþelwold, Alderman, 83
Æþelwold, Alderman in Mercia, 125
Æþelwold, Alderman of East Anglia, 83, 86, 128
Æþelwold, Alderman of Kent, 124
Æþelwold, Bishop of Dorchester, 136
Æþelwold, Bishop of Elmham, 136
Æþelwold, Prince, 64, 69, 71
Æþelwulf, Alderman in Mercia, 125
Æþelwulf, Alderman of Dorset, 124
Æþelwulf, Bishop of Elmham, 136
Æþelwulf, Bishop of Hereford, 137
Æþelwulf, King of Wessex, 63
Ætsere, Steward, 120
*Agatha* (mother of Eadgar II), 95
Alan, Count of Brittany, 75
Alan, Steward, 120
Alexander, King of Scots, 112
Anferð, Earl (Danelaw), 131
**Anglo-Saxon settlement in Britain**, 12
Anlaf I, King of York, 77, 150
Anlaf II, King of York, 77, 79
Anlaf, King of Norway, 89, 90
Arncyll, thane, 114
Assandun, battle of, 58, 95, 96, 99, 125, 128, 130, 136, 141, 151, 152
Asser, Bishop of Cornwall & Sherborne, 63, 135, 140

**B**

Beocca, Alderman, 124
Beorn, Earl of South East Mercia, 107, 128
Beornheah, Bishop of Selsey, 139
Beornwulf, Portreeve of Winchester, 147
bishoprics, 33, 35

bishops, 34
**Blacwine, Sheriff of Cambridge?**, 144
Bondig, Constable, 121
boroughs, 4, 19, 20, 22–28, 31, 39, 41, 44, 49, 55, 65, 70, 74, 77, 92, 123, 130, 147, 150, 178
Brand, Abbot of Peterborough, 113
Brihtferð, Alderman of Essex, 128
Brihtferð, monk of Ramsey, 42, 89
Brihtferð, thane, 80
Brihtheah, Bishop of Worcester, 141
Brihthelm, Archbishop of Canterbury, 84, 133, 140
Brihthelm, Bishop of London, 138
Brihthelm, Bishop of Selsey, Sherborne & Winchester, 139, 140, 141
Brihthelm, Bishop of Winchester, 83
Brihtmær, Bishop of Lichfield, 137
Brihtnoð, Alderman in Mercia, 125
Brihtnoð, Alderman in Wessex, 124
Brihtnoð, Alderman of Essex, 86, 89, 90, 128
Brihtric (brother of Alderman Eadric), 99
**Brihtric, Sheriff of Gloucester**, 145
Brihtric, Steward, 119
Brihtsige, Bishop of Rochester, 139
Brihtwig, Bishop of Wells, 140
Brihtwine, Bishop of Sherborne, 140
Brihtwold (kinsman of Æþelred), 88
Brihtwold, Bishop of Ramsbury, 138
Brihtwulf, Alderman in Wessex, 124
Brihtwulf, Alderman of Essex, 124
Bruning, Sheriff of Hereford, 145
Burgheard, Bishop of Lichfield, 137
Burgric, Bishop of Rochester, 139
Burhred, King of Mercia, 64, 66
Burhwold, Bishop of Cornwall, 135
Byrnstan, Bishop of Winchester, 141

**C**

Cadwgaun, King of Glywysing, 79
Canterbury, 22, 26, 32–35, 37, 45, 50, 59, 65, 84, 89, 91, 92, 99, 106, 114, 121, 133, 134, 136, 138–41, 168, 173, 176, 177, 181
Censtec, Bishop of Cornwall, 135
Cenwold, Bishop of Worcester, 141
Cenwulf, Bishop of Dorchester, 136
Cenwulf, Bishop of Winchester, 141
Ceolmund, Alderman of Kent, 124
Ceolmund, Bishop of Rochester, 139
Ceolwulf, King of Mercia, 66

church finance, 33
CNUT, KING, 92, 94, 96–100, 150, 151
Cola, Sheriff of Devon, 144
Coll, Earl (Danelaw), 131
commoners, 40
Copsig, Earl of Bamburgh, 129
Cornwall, 14–16, 20, 22–24, 26, 36, 74, 90, 126, 135, 144, 149
Cradoc, King of Gwent, 109
craft and industry, 20
*Cristina* (sister of Eadgar II), 95
Cuðred, Alderman of Hampshire, 124
Cuðwulf, Bishop of Rochester, 139
Cunan, Bishop of Cornwall, 135
Cynað, King of Scots, 85
Cyneferð, Bishop of Rochester, 139
Cynemund, Bishop of Hereford, 137
Cynesige, Archbishop of York, 134
Cynesige, Bishop of Lichfield, 137
Cyneward, Bishop of Wells, 140
Cyneward, Sheriff of Berkshire, 144
Cyneward, Sheriff of Worcester, 147
Cynric, Sheriff of Huntingdon, 145

**D**

Danelaw, 23, 25, 27, 28, 31, 33, 54, 67, 70, 83, 92, 123, 130, 150
Danes, 45, 53, 61, 69–72, 88, 89–92, 96–100, 114, 128, 134, 149–52
Daniel, Bishop of Cornwall, 135
Dauid, King of Scots, 112
daylight hours, 21
Denewulf, Bishop of Winchester, 141
Deorlaf, Bishop of Hereford, 137
Deormod, Steward, 119
Deorwulf, Bishop of London, 138
Duduc, Bishop of Wells, 140
Dufenal, King of Strathclyde, 85
Dunecan, King of Scots, 103
Dunstan, Archbishop of Canterbury, 33, 34, 53, 77, 81, 84, 86, 90, 133, 136–41

**E**

Eadberht, Bishop of Lindsey, 137
*Eadburh* (daughter of Eadward I), 69
*Eadflæd* (daughter of Eadward I), 68
EADGAR I, KING, 16, 17, 42, 76, 78, 81–85
EADGAR II, KING, 95, 112–15, 151, 153
Eadgar, Bishop of Hereford, 137

Eadgar, King of Scots, 112, 113
Eadgar, Prince, 87
*Eadgyð* (daughter of Æþelred), 87
*Eadgyð* (daughter of Eadgar I), 82, 98
*Eadgyð* (daughter of Eadward I), 68, 69, 74
*Eadgyð* (wife of Eadward III), 30, 105, 107, 111
*Eadgyð* (wife of Harold II), 110
*Eadgyð*, Princess of Scots, 112
*Eadgyfu* (a) (daughter of Eadward I), 69
*Eadgyfu* (b) (daughter of Eadward I), 69
*Eadgyfu* (daughter of Eadmund I), 76
*Eadgyfu* (wife of Eadward I), 30, 69, 73, 77
Eadhelm, Bishop of Selsey, 139
*Eadhild* (daughter of Eadward I), 69, 74
Eadmund (son of Eadgar I), Prince, 83
Eadmund (son of Eadmund II), Prince, 95, 99, 107
Eadmund (son of Harold II), 110
EADMUND I, KING, 16, 69, 76–77
EADMUND II, KING, 73, 87, 92, 95–96, 151
Eadmund, Alderman of Western Wessex, 81, 126
Eadmund, Bishop of Durham, 135
Eadmund, King of East Anglia, 98
Eadmund, King of Scots, 112
Eadmund, Sheriff of Hertford, 145
Eadnoð I, Bishop of Dorchester, 96, 136, 151
Eadnoð II, Bishop of Dorchester, 136
Eadnoð, Bishop of Crediton, 135
Eadnoð, Constable, 121
Eadred, Bishop of Durham, 135
EADRED, KING, 69, 73, 77, 78–79
Eadred, Prince, 87
Eadric, Alderman of Mercia, 91–93, 95, 96, 99, 105, 127, 151
Eadric, Alderman of Wessex, 125
Eadric, Sheriff of Wiltshire, 147
Eadric, thane, 114, 153
Eadsige, Archbishop of Canterbury, 134
Eadsige, Sheriff of Hampshire, 146
EADWARD I, KING, 15, 17, 63, 68–72, 149
EADWARD II, KING, 82, 86, 90, 91, 98
EADWARD III, KING, 29, 88, 92, 102, 103, 105–9
Eadward, Prince, 95, 99, 107, 108
Eadward, Prince of Scotland, 112
EADWIG, KING, 76, 78, 80–81
Eadwig, Prince, 87, 99, 152
Eadwine, Alderman of Eastern Wessex, 126

Eadwine, Earl of Mercia, 109, 111, 113, 127, 153
Eadwine, Prince, 68, 73, 74
**Eadwine, Sheriff of Oxford?**, 146
**Eadwine, Sheriff of Warwick?**, 147
Eadwold, Alderman in Mercia, 125
Eadwold, Archbishop of York, 134
Eadwulf I, Alderman of Bamburgh, 129
Eadwulf II, Earl of Bamburgh, 99, 104, 129
Eadwulf III, Earl of Bamburgh, 129
Eadwulf, Alderman of Somerset, 124
Eadwulf, Bishop of Crediton, 135
*Ealdgyð* (wife of Eadmund II), 95
*Ealdgyð* (wife of Harold II), 110, 113
Ealdhun, Bishop of Chester le Street & Durham, 135
Ealdred of Bamburgh, 74, 129
Ealdred, Abbot of Abingdon, 114
Ealdred, Alderman of Mercia, 127
Ealdred, Archbishop of York, 107, 108, 109, 110, 113, 114, 134, 137, 141, 154
Ealdred, Bishop of Chester le Street, 135
Ealdred, Bishop of Cornwall, 135
Ealdred, Earl of Bamburgh, 129
Ealdred, Steward, 119
**Ealdred, thane**, 105
Ealdwulf, Archbishop of York, 121, 134, 141
Ealheard, Bishop of Dorchester, 136
Ealhelm, Alderman in Mercia, 125
Ealhelm, Alderman of Mercia, 81, 127
Ealhfrið, Bishop of Winchester, 140
Ealhstan?, Bishop of London, 138
*Ealhswið* (wife of Ælfred), 63
Ealhun, Bishop of Worcester, 141
Eanwulf, Steward, 119
**early Anglo-Saxon Kingdoms**, 13
East Anglia, 10, 12, 14, 15, 17, 20, 21–24, 27, 28, 35, 37, 59, 64, 65, 67, 71, 72, 92, 99, 107, 114, 126–28, 131, 149, 150
Ecgberht, Prince, 87
*Ecgwynn* (wife of Eadward I), 68
Eglaf, Earl of Mercia, 127
Elisedd, King of Gwynedd, 77
**England, creation of**, 15, 149
Eohric, King of East Anglia, 71
Eowils, King of York, 71
Esgar, Constable, 121
*Estrið* (sister of Cnut), 94
Eustatius, Count of Boulogne, 108

**F**

farming, geography of, 20
Five Boroughs, 22–25, 28, 77, 92, 130, 150, 178
Fræna, Earl (Danelaw), 130
Friðestan, Bishop of Winchester, 141

**G**

Gamal, Sheriff of York, 147
Garwulf, Alderman of Kent, 124
Gerbod, Earl of Chester, 131
Gisa, Bishop of Wells & Bath, 34, 140
Gloucester, 20, 23, 24, 28, 55, 63, 73, 130, 147
*Godgyfu* (daughter of Æþelred), 88, 105
Godric, Earl, 129
Godric, Sheriff, 147
Godric, Sheriff of Berkshire, 144
**Godwine (son of Harold II)**, 110
Godwine, ?Alderman, 96, 130, 151
Godwine, Bishop of Lichfield, 137
Godwine, Bishop of Rochester, 139
Godwine, Earl of Wessex, 29, 98–108, 125
Godwine, Sheriff of Somerset, 146
Gospatric, Earl of Bamburgh, 105, 112, 114, 129
Griffin, King of Deheubarth, 107, 108
Griffin, King of Gwynedd, 108
Grim I, Earl (Danelaw), 130
Grim II, Earl (Danelaw), 131
Grimcytel, Bishop of Selsey, 136, 139
Guðhard, Bishop of Selsey, 139
Gunner I, Earl (Danelaw), 130
Gunner II, Earl (Danelaw), 129
*Gunnhild* (daughter of Cnut), 98
*Gunnhild* (daughter of Harold II), 110
*Gunnhild (niece of Cnut)*, 107
*Gunnhild* (wife of Swegn), 94
Guþfrið, King of York, 74
Guþrum, Earl (Danelaw), 130
Guþrum, King of East Anglia, 64, 66, 67
*Gyða* (daughter of Harold II), 110
*Gyða* (sister of Cnut), 94
Gyrð, Earl of East Anglia, 108, 111, 128

**H**

Hacun (son of Earl Swegn), 111
Hacun, Earl, 100, 130

Hacun, King of Norway, 75
Hadder, Earl (Danelaw), 131
HARÐACNUT, KING, 98, 100, 101, 103–4
Harold (brother of Cnut), 94
HAROLD I, KING, 97, 101–3
HAROLD II, KING, 16, 106–8, 108, 110–11,
  120, 126, 128, 153
Harold III, King of Norway, 107, 111, 153
Harold, Prince, 110
Hastings, battle of, 21, 110–13, 126–28, 144,
  153
Hawerd, Earl (Danelaw), 130
Heahferð, Alderman of Somerset, 124
Heahstan, Bishop of London, 138
Healfdene, Earl (Danelaw), 130
Healfdene, King of York, 71
Hearding, Butler, 120
Hearding, Sheriff of Derby, 144
Heca, Bishop of Selsey, 139
Heca, Sheriff of Devon, 144
HENRIG I, KING, 113
Henrig III, Emperor, 107
Hereman, Bishop of Ramsbury & Sherborne,
  34, 108, 138, 140
Hereward, thane, 114
Herfast, Bishop of Elmham & Thetford, 137
Hloþwig, King of France, 75
Howel, King of Gwynedd, 85
Hranig, Earl of Hereford, 130
Hroþward, Archbishop of York, 134
Hugo, Chamberlain, 120
Hugo, Earl of Chester, 131
Hugo, thane, 108

## I

Iago, King of Gwynedd, 85
Idwal, King of Gwynedd, 77
Iehmarc, King of Man, 100
Inwær, Earl (Danelaw), 131

## K

King of England, 7, 9–12, 15, 51, 57, 59, 61,
  105, 133
King of the Anglo-Saxons, 15, 63, 68, 73, 76,
  80, 97, 105
King of the English, 15, 63, 68, 73, 76, 78, 80,
  82, 86, 87, 97, 103, 105, 110
King of the Saxons, 63, 68, 73, 80
King's household, 29, 30, 31, 119, 143
Kings and government, 29

## L

Landfranc, Archbishop of Canterbury, 134
landscape of England, 19
Leofcild, Sheriff of Essex, 144
Leofgar, Bishop of Hereford, 109, 137
Leofgar, Bishop of Lichfield, 137
Leofric, Abbot, 113
Leofric, Bishop of Crediton & Exeter, 121,
  135
Leofric, Chamberlain, 120
Leofric, Earl of Mercia, 98, 100, 101, 106,
  108, 109, 127
Leofric, Sheriff of Kent, 145
Leofsige, Alderman of East Anglia, 91, 128
Leofsige, Bishop of Worcester, 141
Leofstan, Portreeve of London, 145
Leofstan, Sheriff of Suffolk, 146
Leofstan?, Bishop of London, 138
Leofwine, Alderman of Mercia, 127, 152
Leofwine, Bishop of Lichfield, 114, 137
Leofwine, Bishop of Lindsey & Dorchester,
  136, 137
Leofwine, Earl of Eastern Wessex, 108, 111,
  126
Leofwine, Sheriff, 147
Lincoln, 22, 23, 25, 34, 35, 48, 55, 93, 113,
  127, 130, 136, 145, 149, 153
Liot, Earl (Danelaw), 131
local government, 31
London, 21–23, 25, 33–35, 42, 51, 55, 67, 71,
  74, 77, 78, 81, 87, 89, 90–93, 95–99, 101,
  106–8, 112, 113, 133, 134, 136, 138, 141,
  143, 145, 149–53
Lyfing, Archbishop of Canterbury, 134, 140
Lyfing, Bishop of Crediton & Worcester, 103,
  135, 141
Lyfing, Constable, 121
Lyfing, Sheriff, 147

## M

Macbeoþen, King of Scots, 100, 108
Mælcolm I, King of Scots, 77
Mælcolm II, King of Scots, 91, 99
Mælcolm II, King of Strathclyde, 85
Mælcolm III, King of Scots, 95, 108, 113,
  114, 154
Mærleswegn, Sheriff of Lincoln, 114, 145
Magnus (son of Harold II), 110
Magnus, King of Norway, 106–9

Magnus, King of the Isles, 85
*Margareta* (sister of Eadgar II), 17, 95, 112, 114
*Maria,* Princess of Scots, 112
Mercia, 13–17, 20, 22–25, 27, 28, 33, 35, 58, 59, 63–67, 70–73, 81, 82, 90, 91, 96, 97, 99, 101, 124, 125, 128, 131, 149, 150, 154, 181
monasteries, 36, 37
Morcere, Earl (Danelaw), 131
Morcere, Earl of York, 109, 111, 113, 129, 153
Morcere, thane, 92
Mucel, Alderman of Sussex, 124

### N

Norðman (son of Alderman Leofwine), 99
Norðman, ?Alderman (son of Leofwine), 130
Norðman, Alderman in Northumbria, 130
Norðman, Sheriff of Northampton, 146
Northumbria, 14–16, 23, 25, 28, 33, 50, 53, 54, 58, 59, 64, 66, 67, 71, 73, 74, 77–79, 81, 82, 84, 86, 89, 90, 92, 93, 97, 99, 101, 109, 150–54
Norwich, 25, 27, 34, 50, 91, 97

### O

Oda, Archbishop of Canterbury, 77, 81, 133, 138
Oda, Earl of Eastern Wessex & Bishop of Bayeux, 126
Odda of Germany, cousin of Æþelred, 90
Odda, Alderman of Devon, 124
Odda, Earl of Western Wessex, 105, 108, 126, 130
Odda, Emperor, 83, 88
Old English language, 28, 42–44, 51
Old English literature, 42
Ordbriht, Bishop of Selsey, 139
Ordgar, Alderman of Western Wessex, 126
Ordgar, Alderman of Wiltshire & Western Wessex, 124, 126
Ordgar, Sheriff, 147
**Ordgar, Sheriff of Essex?**, 144
Ordgar, thane, 83
Ordlaf, Alderman of Hampshire, 124
Ordmær, thane, 82
Ordulf, Steward, 90, 91
Ordwulf, Alderman of Berkshire, 124
Ordwulf, Steward, 120
Osbeorn, Bishop of Exeter, 135

Osbeorn, Sheriff of Hereford, 145
Osbeorn, thane, 108
*Osburh* (mother of Ælfred), 63
Oscytel, Archbishop of York, 134, 136
Osferð, Alderman of Kent and Eastern Wessex, 64, 69, 73, 124, 126
Osgod, Constable, 120, 128
Osgod, thane, 99, 107
Oslac, Alderman of York, 86, 129
Oslac, thane, 99
Osmund, Sheriff, 147
Osred, Alderman, 124
Osward, Sheriff of Kent, 145
Oswold, Archbishop of York, 34, 53, 84, 85, 86, 133, 134, 136, 141
Oswold, Prince, 64
Oswulf I, Alderman of Northumbria, 129
Oswulf II, Earl of Bamburgh, 129, 153
Oswulf of Bamburgh, 79
Oswulf, Alderman of Berkshire, 124, 129
Oswulf, Bishop of Ramsbury, 138
Oxford, 20, 23, 24, 25, 27, 38, 68, 71, 92, 98, 99, 101, 109, 128, 130, 146, 147, 149, 152

### P

Peter, Bishop of Lichfield & Chester, 137
Plegmund, Archbishop of Canterbury, 133
population, 23

### R

Rægnold I, King of York, 72
Rægnold II, King of York, 77
Rægnold, Earl (Danelaw), 130
Raulf I, Earl of East Anglia, 121, 128
Raulf II, Earl of East Anglia, 128
Raulf, Earl, 105, 108, 130
Regenbald, 'Chancellor', 121
regional divisions, 23
Remigius, Bishop of Dorchester & Lincoln, 136
Ricard, Count of Normandy, 88
Ricard, Sheriff of Worcester, 147
Rodbert, Archbishop of Canterbury, 106, 108, 134, 138
Rodbert, Constable, 105, 121
Rodbert, Duke of Normandy, 113
Rodbert, Earl of Bamburgh, 114, 129
Rodulf, Abbot of Abingdon, 105
Roger, Earl of Hereford, 131
Roger, Earl of Shrewsbury, 131

## S

Sæwold, Sheriff of Oxford, 146
*Santslaue* (sister of Cnut), 94
Scule, Earl (Danelaw), 131
Seaxhelm, Bishop of Chester le Street, 135
shires, 22–25, 25, 29, 31, 34, 37, 39, 40, 50, 52, 70, 83, 89, 92, 123–25, 130, 131, 143, 147
Sideman, Bishop of Crediton, 135
Sigeferð, Bishop of Lindsey, 138
Sigeferð, thane, 92, 95
Sigegar, Bishop of Wells, 140
Sigehelm, Alderman of Kent, 69, 124
Sigehelm, Bishop of Sherborne, 140
Sigered, Earl of Eastern Wessex, 126
Sigeric, Archbishop of Canterbury, 133, 138
Sigewulf, Alderman of Kent, 124
Sigewulf, Butler, 120
*Sigrið* (wife of Swegn), 94
Sihtric, Earl of Western Wessex, 126
Sihtric, King of York, 72, 74
Siward Barn, thane, 114
Siward of Maldon, thane, 114
Siward, Bishop of Rochester, 139
Siward, Earl of Northumbria, 100, 108, 128, 129
Siward, thane, 105, 114
slaves, 40
Spearhafoc, Bishop of London, 108, 138
Stigand, Archbishop of Canterbury, 106, 107, 108, 113, 114, 134, 136, 141
Stigand, Bishop of Selsey & Chichester, 139
Styrcær, Earl (Danelaw), 130
succession to the throne, 29
**Swegn (son of Rodbert)**, 105
Swegn II, King of Denmark, 106, 107, 114, 153
Swegn, Earl, 107, 130
SWEGN, KING, 88, 90, 92, 94, 150, 151
Swegn, King of Norway (son of Cnut), 97, 100
Swetman, Portreeve of London, 145
Swiðwulf, Bishop of London, 138
Swiðwulf, Bishop of Rochester, 139

## T

taxation, 32
thanes, 39

## Þ

Þeodred I, Bishop of Elmham, 136
Þeodred II, Bishop of Elmham, 136
Þeodred, Bishop of London, 138

## T

Thetford, 25, 27, 34, 55, 79, 91, 92, 137
Thomas, Archbishop of York, 134

## Þ

Þored, Alderman of York, 84, 87, 129
Þored, Constable, 120
Þored, thane, 99
Þurcyll, Earl of East Anglia, 91, 92, 98, 99, 128
Þurcyll, Sheriff of Stafford, 146
Þurcyll, thane, 114
Þurcytel, Earl of Bedford, 71
Þurferð, Earl (Danelaw), 130
Þurig, Earl of South East Mercia, 127

## T

Tidhelm, Bishop of Hereford, 137
Tilred, Bishop of Chester le Street, 134
Titstan, Chamberlain, 120
Tofig, Constable, 120
Tofig, Sheriff of Somerset, 146
Tofig, thane, 99
**Tolig, Sheriff of Norfolk & Suffolk**, 146
Tostig, Earl of Northumbria, 108, 109, 111, 128, 129
travel, 21
Tunberht, Bishop of Winchester, 140

## U

Uhtred, Alderman of North East Mercia, 127
Uhtred, Alderman of North West Mercia, 127
Uhtred, Alderman of Northumbria, 91, 92, 93, 105, 129
Uhtred, Alderman under Eadgar I, 129
Uhtred, Bishop of Chester le Street, 135
Ulf (son of Harold II), 110
Ulf, Bishop of Dorchester, 108, 136
Ulf, Sheriff of Middlesex, 145
Ulfcytel of East Anglia, 91, 92, 95, 96, 128, 150, 151
Ulfcytel, Sheriff of Hereford, 145
Urm, Earl (Danelaw), 130

## V

Vikings, 7, 9, 10, 14, 15, 17, 21, 22, 28, 32, 33, 35, 36, 38, 45, 54, 59, 64, 65, 66, 67, 70, 71, 75, 77, 88, 90, 91, 107, 125, 138, 149, 150
Vikings, 15

## W

Wada, Sheriff of Devon, 144
Wærferð, Bishop of Worcester, 141
Wærstan, Bishop of Sherborne, 140
Walcelin, Bishop of Winchester, 141
Walchere, Bishop of Durham, 135
Walter, Bishop of Hereford, 113, 137
Walþeof I, Alderman of Bamburgh, 129
Walþeof II, Earl of Bamburgh, 113, 128, 129
Wessex, 9, 12–16, 20, 22–28, 32, 33, 37, 58, 59, 63–67, 70–72, 81, 90–92, 96, 99, 101, 103, 110, 114, 119, 120, 124–28, 130, 133, 149–51
Wighelm, Bishop of Selsey, 139
Wigmund, Bishop of Dorchester or Lichfield, 136, 137
Wigod, Butler, 120
Wigod, thane, 105
Wigred, Bishop of Chester le Street, 134
Wilferð II, Bishop of Worcester, 141
Wilferð, Bishop of Lichfield or Dorchester, 136, 137
Willelm II, Duke of Normandy, 108, 109, 111, 113, 153
Willelm, Bishop of London, 108, 138
Willelm, Earl of Wessex, 126
Winchester, 7, 21, 23, 25, 26, 34–37, 42, 45, 50, 55, 59, 60, 63, 68–71, 78, 80, 83, 84, 85, 89, 90, 92, 97, 98, 101, 103, 105, 113, 133, 134, 136, 138–41, 141, 151, 152
women, position of, 41
Wulfgar I, Steward, 119
Wulfgar II, Steward, 119
Wulfgar, Alderman of Mercia, 127
Wulfgar, Alderman of Western Wessex, 126
Wulfgar, Bishop of Lichfield, 137
Wulfgar, Bishop of Ramsbury, 138
Wulfgar, Butler, 120
Wulfgar, Portreeve of London, 145
Wulfhelm II, Bishop of Wells, 140
Wulfhelm, Archbishop of Canterbury, 133, 140

Wulfhelm, Steward, 119
Wulfhere, Alderman of Wiltshire, 124
*Wulfhild* (?daughter of Æþelred), 87
Wulfhun, Bishop of Selsey, 139
Wulfmær, Sheriff of Hampshire?, 146
Wulfnoð (brother of Harold II), 111
Wulfnoð (father of Earl Godwine), 91
Wulfnoð, Sheriff, 147
Wulfred, Alderman of Hampshire, 124
Wulfred, Bishop of Lichfield, 137
Wulfric, Abbot of Ely, 105
Wulfsige I, Bishop of Sherborne, 139
Wulfsige II, Bishop of Sherborne & Selsey, 139, 140
Wulfsige III, Bishop of Sherborne, 140
Wulfsige, Abbot, 96
Wulfsige, Alderman, 124
Wulfsige, Bishop of Cornwall, 135
Wulfsige, Bishop of Lichfield, 137
Wulfsige, Bishop of London, 138
Wulfsige, Sheriff of Kent, 145
Wulfstan I, Archbishop of York, 77, 79, 134
Wulfstan II, Archbishop of York, 34, 42, 89, 98, 99, 134, 138, 141
Wulfstan II, Bishop of Worcester, 113, 141
Wulfstan, Alderman of eastern Wessex?, 126
Wulfstan, Steward, 120
*Wulfþryð* (wife of Eadgar I), 82
Wulfwig, Bishop of Dorchester, 121, 136
Wullaf, Alderman, 124
Wynsige, Bishop of Dorchester, 136
Wynsige, Bishop of Lichfield, 137
Wynsige, Chamberlain, 120
Wynstan, Chamberlain, 120

## Y

*Ymme* (wife of Æþelred & Cnut), 30, 88, 91, 92, 97, 99, 101, 103, 107
York, 10, 17, 21–25, 28, 32–34, 36, 50, 55, 59, 64, 66, 68, 70, 72, 74, 77–79, 84, 85, 89, 93, 94, 110, 111, 113, 114, 121, 128–30, 133, 134, 136, 141, 147, 149, 150, 153, 154
Yric, Earl of York, 99, 129, 151
Yric, King of York, 78

# Some of our other title

Please see www.asbooks.co.uk for up to date availability and prices

## The English Warrior from earliest times till 1066

**Stephen Pollington**

This is not intended to be a bald listing of the battles and campaigns from the Anglo-Saxon Chronicle and other sources, but rather it is an attempt to get below the surface of Anglo-Saxon warriorhood and to investigate the rites, social attitudes, mentality and mythology of the warfare of those times.

> "An under-the-skin study of the role, rights, duties, psyche and rituals of the Anglo-Saxon warrior. The author combines original translations from Norse and Old English primary sources with archaeological and linguistic evidence for an in-depth look at the warrior, his weapons, tactics and logistics.
>
> A very refreshing, innovative and well-written piece of scholarship that illuminates a neglected period of English history"
>
> *Time Team Booklists* - Channel 4 Television

**Revised Edition**

An already highly acclaimed book has been made even better by the inclusion of additional information and illustrations.

£16.95   hardback   304 pages

## The Mead Hall   The feasting tradition in Anglo-Saxon England

**Stephen Pollington**

This new study takes a broad look at the subject of halls and feasting in Anglo-Saxon England. The idea of the communal meal was very important among nobles and yeomen, warriors, farmers churchmen and laity. One of the aims of the book is to show that there was not just one 'feast' but two main types: the informal social occasion *gebeorscipe* and the formal, ritual gathering *symbel*.

Using the evidence of Old English texts - mainly the epic *Beowulf* and the *Anglo-Saxon Chronicles*, Stephen Pollington shows that the idea of feasting remained central to early English social traditions long after the physical reality had declined in importance.

The words of the poets and saga-writers are supported by a wealth of archaeological data dealing with halls, settlement layouts and magnificent feasting gear found in many early Anglo-Saxon graves.

Three appendices cover:
- Hall-themes in Old English verse;
- Old English and translated texts;
- The structure and origins of the warband.

£18.95   24 illustrations   296 pages

## Anglo-Saxon Food & Drink
### Production, Processing, Distribution, and Consumption
#### Ann Hagen

Food production for home consumption was the basis of economic activity throughout the Anglo-Saxon period. Used as payment and a medium of trade, food was the basis of the Anglo-Saxons' system of finance and administration.

Information from various sources has been brought together in order to build up a picture of how food was grown, conserved, distributed, prepared and eaten during the period from the beginning of the 5th century to the 11th century. Many people will find it fascinating for the views it gives of an important aspect of Anglo-Saxon life and culture. In addition to Anglo-Saxon England the Celtic west of Britain is also covered.

This edition combines earlier titles – *A Handbook of Anglo-Saxon Food* and *A Second Handbook of Anglo-Saxon Food & Drink*.

Extensive index.

£25   512 pages

## First Steps in Old English
### An easy to follow language course for the beginner
#### Stephen Pollington

A complete and easy to use Old English language course that contains all the exercises and texts needed to learn Old English. This course has been designed to be of help to a wide range of students, from those who are teaching themselves at home, to undergraduates who are learning Old English as part of their English degree course. The author has adopted a step-by-step approach that enables students of differing abilities to advance at their own pace. The course includes practice and translation exercises, a glossary of the words used in the course, and many Old English texts, including the *Battle of Brunanburh* and *Battle of Maldon*.

£16-95   272 pages

## Old English Poems, Prose & Lessons        2 CDs
### read by Stephen Pollington

These CDs contain lessons and texts from *First Steps in Old English*.

Tracks include: 1. Deor. 2. Beowulf – The Funeral of Scyld Scefing. 3. Engla Tocyme (The Arrival of the English). 4. Ines Domas. Two Extracts from the Laws of King Ine. 5. Deniga Hergung (The Danes' Harrying) Anglo-Saxon Chronicle Entry AD997. 6. Durham 7. The Ordeal (Be ðon ðe ordales weddigaþ) 8. Wið Dweorh (Against a Dwarf) 9. Wið Wennum (Against Wens) 10. Wið Wæterælfadle (Against Waterelf Sickness) 11. The Nine Herbs Charm 12. Læcedomas (Leechdoms) 13. Beowulf's Greeting 14. The Battle of Brunanburh 15. A Guide to Pronunciation.
And more than 30 other lessons and extracts of Old English verse and prose.

£15   2 CDs - Free Old English transcript from www.asbooks.co.uk.

## Learn Old English with Leofwin
**Matt Love**

This is a new approach to learning old English – as a *living language*. Leofwin and his family are your guides through six lively, entertaining, topic-based units. New vocabulary and grammar are presented in context, step by step, so that younger readers and non-language specialists can feel engaged rather than intimidated. The author has complemented the text with a wealth of illustrations. There are listening, speaking, reading and writing exercises throughout. Free soundtracks available on the Anglo-Saxon Books website.

£16.95  160 pages

## Wordcraft: Concise English/Old English Dictionary and Thesaurus
**Stephen Pollington**

This book provides Old English equivalents to the commoner modern words in both dictionary and thesaurus formats. The Thesaurus presents vocabulary relevant to a wide range of individual topics in alphabetical lists, thus making it easily accessible to those with specific areas of interest. Each thematic listing is encoded for cross-reference from the Dictionary. The two sections will be of invaluable assistance to students of the language, as well as to those with either a general or a specific interest in the Anglo-Saxon period.

£9.95  256 pages

## An Introduction to the Old English Language and its Literature
**Stephen Pollington**

The purpose of this general introduction to Old English is not to deal with the teaching of Old English but to dispel some misconceptions about the language and to give an outline of its structure and its literature. Some basic knowledge of these is essential to an understanding of the early period of English history and the present form of the language.

£5.95  48 pages

## Monasteriales Indicia
### The Anglo-Saxon Monastic Sign Language
**Edited with notes and translation by Debby Banham**

The *Monasteriales Indicia* is one of very few texts which let us see how evryday life was lived in monasteries in the early Middle Ages. Written in Old English and preserved in a manuscript of the mid-eleventh century, it consists of 127 signs used by Anglo-Saxon monks during the times when the Benedictine Rule forbade them to speak. These indicate the foods the monks ate, the clothes they wore, and the books they used in church and chapter, as well as the tools they used in their daily life, and persons they might meet both in the monastery and outside. The text is printed here with a parallel translation. The introduction gives a summary of the background, both historical and textual, as well as a brief look at the later evidence for monastic sign language in England.

£5.95  96 pages

## English Heroic Legends

### Kathleen Herbert

The author has taken the skeletons of ancient Germanic legends about great kings, queens and heroes, and put flesh on them. Kathleen Herbert's extensive knowledge of the period is reflected in the wealth of detail she brings to these tales of adventure, passion, bloodshed and magic.

The book is in two parts. First are the stories that originate deep in the past, yet because they have not been hackneyed, they are still strange and enchanting. After that there is a selection of the source material, with information about where it can be found and some discussion about how it can be used.

£9·95  268 pages

## Peace-Weavers and Shield-Maidens: Women in Early English Society

### Kathleen Herbert

The recorded history of the English people did not start in 1066 as popularly believed but one-thousand years earlier. The Roman historian Cornelius Tacitus noted in *Germania*, published in the year 98, that the English (Latin *Anglii*), who lived in the southern part of the Jutland peninsula, were members of an alliance of Goddess-worshippers. The author has taken that as an appropriate opening to an account of the earliest Englishwomen, the part they played in the making of England, what they did in peace and war, the impressions they left in Britain and on the continent, how they were recorded in the chronicles, how they come alive in heroic verse and riddles.

£5.95  64 pages

## Anglo-Saxon Runes

### John. M. Kemble

Kemble's essay *On Anglo-Saxon Runes* first appeared in the journal *Archaeologia* for 1840; it draws on the work of Wilhelm Grimm, but breaks new ground for Anglo-Saxon studies in his survey of the Ruthwell Cross and the Cynewulf poems. It is an expression both of his own indomitable spirit and of the fascination and mystery of the Runes themselves, making one of the most attractive introductions to the topic. For this edition new notes have been supplied, which include translations of Latin and Old English material quoted in the text, to make this key work in the study of runes more accessible to the general reader.

£5.95  80 pages

## Looking for the Lost Gods of England

### Kathleen Herbert

Kathleen Herbert sifts through the royal genealogies, charms, verse and other sources to find clues to the names and attributes of the Gods and Goddesses of the early English. The earliest account of English heathen practices reveals that they worshipped the Earth Mother and called her Nerthus. The tales, beliefs and traditions of that time are still with us in, for example, Sand able to stir our minds and imaginations.

£5.95  64 pages

## Rudiments of Runelore

### Stephen Pollington

This book provides both a comprehensive introduction for those coming to the subject for the first time, and a handy and inexpensive reference work for those with some knowledge of the subject. The *Abecedarium Nordmannicum* and the English, Norwegian and Icelandic rune poems are included in their original and translated form. Also included is work on the three Brandon runic inscriptions and the Norfolk 'Tiw' runes.

£5.95   88 pages

## Anglo-Saxon FAQs

### Stephen Pollington

125 questions and answers on a wide range of topics.

Are there any Anglo-Saxon jokes?  Who was the Venerable Bede?  Did the women wear make-up? What musical instruments did they have?  How was food preserved? Did they have shops?  Did their ships have sails?  Why was Ethelred called 'Unready'?  Did they have clocks?  Did they celebrate Christmas?  What are runes? What weapons and tactics did they use?  Were there female warriors?  What was the Synod of Whitby?

£9.95   128pages

## Tastes of Anglo-Saxon England

### Mary Savelli

These easy to follow recipes will enable you to enjoy a mix of ingredients and flavours that were widely known in Anglo-Saxon England but are rarely experienced today. In addition to the 46 recipes, there is background information about households and cooking techniques.

£5.95   80 pages

## Dark Age Naval Power

### A Reassessment of Frankish and Anglo-Saxon Seafaring Activity

### John Haywood

In the first edition of this work, published in 1991, John Haywood argued that the capabilities of the pre-Viking Germanic seafarers had been greatly underestimated. Since that time, his reassessment of Frankish and Anglo-Saxon shipbuilding and seafaring has been widely praised and accepted.

In this second edition, some sections of the book have been revised and updated to include information gained from excavations and sea trials with sailing replicas of early ships. The new evidence supports the author's argument that early Germanic shipbuilding and seafaring skills were far more advanced than previously thought. It also supports the view that Viking ships and seaborne activities were not as revolutionary as is commonly believed.

> 'The book remains a historical study of the first order. It is required reading for our seminar on medieval seafaring at Texas A & M University and is essential reading for anyone interested in the subject.'

F. H. Van Doorninck, *The American Neptune*

£18.95  hardback  224 pages

# Organisations

## Centingas

Centingas is a living history group devoted to the Anglo-Saxon way-of-life. The core of our membership is in the South East of England but it is constantly expanding. We have set ourselves the task of gaining expertise in the widest possible range of period crafts and skills. Our specialist areas include textiles, language and weapons.

We provide displays and information for schools and museums, and take part in re-enactment events around England.

For latest details and information visit  www.centingas.co.uk

## Þa Engliscan Gesiðas (The English Companions)

Þa Engliscan Gesiðas is a historical and cultural society exclusively devoted to Anglo-Saxon history. The Fellowship publishes a quarterly journal, *Wiðowinde,* and has a website with regularly updated information and discussions. Local groups arrange their own meetings and attend lectures, exhibitions and events. Members are able to share their interest with like-minded people and learn more about the origins and growth of English culture, including language, literature, archaeology, anthropology, architecture, art, religion, mythology, folklore and material culture.

For further details see www.tha-engliscan-gesithas.org.uk or write to:

  Membership Secretary,  The English Companions, PO Box 62790, London, SW12 2BH

## Regia Anglorum

Regia Anglorum is an active group of enthusiasts who attempt to portray as accurately as possible the life and times of the people who lived in the British Isles around a thousand years ago. We investigate a wide range of crafts and have a Living  History Exhibit that frequently erects some thirty tented period structures.

We have  a thriving membership and 40 branches in the  British Isles and United States - so there might be one near you. We especially welcome families with children.

www.regia.org    *General information* eolder@regia.org    *Membership* join@regia.org

## The Sutton Hoo Society

Our aims and objectives focus on promoting research and education relating to the Anglo Saxon Royal cemetery at Sutton Hoo, Suffolk in the UK. The Society publishes a newsletter SAXON twice a year, which keeps members up to date with society activities, carries resumes of lectures and visits, and reports progress on research and publication associated with the site. If you would like to join the Society please see website: www.suttonhoo.org

## Wuffing Education

Wuffing Education provides those interested in the history, archaeology, literature and culture of the Anglo-Saxons with the chance to meet experts and fellow enthusiasts for a whole day of in-depth seminars and discussions. Day Schools take place at the historic Tranmer House overlooking the burial mounds of Sutton Hoo in Suffolk.

For details of programme of events contact:-
Wuffing Education, 4 Hilly Fields, Woodbridge, Suffolk IP12 4DX
email education@wuffings.co.uk  website www.wuffings.co.uk
Tel. 01394 383908 or 01728 688749

## Places to visit

### Bede's World at Jarrow

Bede's world tells the remarkable story of the life and times of the Venerable Bede, 673–735 AD. Visitors can explore the origins of early medieval Northumbria and Bede's life and achievements through his own writings and the excavations of the monasteries at Jarrow and other sites.

Location – 10 miles from Newcastle upon Tyne, off the A19 near the southern entrance to the River Tyne tunnel. Bus services 526 & 527

Bede's World, Church Bank, Jarrow, Tyne and Wear, NE32 3DY

Tel. 0191 489 2106; Fax: 0191 428 2361; website: www.bedesworld.co.uk

### Sutton Hoo near Woodbridge, Suffolk

Sutton Hoo is a group of low burial mounds overlooking the River Deben in south-east Suffolk. Excavations in 1939 brought to light the richest burial ever discovered in Britain – an Anglo-Saxon ship containing a magnificent treasure which has become one of the principal attractions of the British Museum. The mound from which the treasure was dug is thought to be the grave of Rædwald, an early English king who died in 624/5 AD.

This National Trust site has an excellent visitor centre, which includes a reconstruction of the burial chamber and its grave goods. Some original objects as well as replicas of the treasure are on display.

2 miles east of Woodbridge on B1083     Tel. 01394 389700

### West Stow Anglo-Saxon Village

An early Anglo-Saxon Settlement reconstructed on the site where it was excavated consisting of timber and thatch hall, houses and workshop. There is also a museum containing objects found during the excavation of the site. Open all year 10am (except Christmas) Last entrance summer 4pm; winter 3-30pm. Special provision for school parties. A teachers' resource pack is available. Costumed events are held on some weekends, especially Easter Sunday and August Bank Holiday Monday. Craft courses are organised.

For further details see www.weststow.org or contact:

The Visitor Centre, West Stow Country Park, Icklingham Road, West Stow, Bury St Edmunds, Suffolk IP28 6HG   Tel. 01284 728718

Lightning Source UK Ltd.
Milton Keynes UK
UKOW05f0951300516

275212UK00001B/6/P